Divine Communion

A EUCHARISTIC THEOLOGY
OF SEXUAL INTIMACY

JAY EMERSON JOHNSON

Seabury Books
NEW YORK

Unless otherwise noted, the Scripture quotations contained herein are from the New Revised Standard Version Bible, copyright © 1989 by the Division of Christian Education of the National Council of Churches of Christ in the U.S.A. Used by permission. All rights reserved.

Cover design by Laurie Klein Westhafer
Typeset by Rose Design

Library of Congress Cataloging-in-Publication Data

Johnson, Jay Emerson.
 Divine communion : a eucharistic theology of sexual intimacy / Jay Emerson Johnson.
    pages cm
 Includes bibliographical references.
 ISBN 978-1-59627-252-1 (pbk.)—ISBN 978-1-59627-253-8 (ebook) 1. Sex—Religious aspects—Christianity. 2. Sex—Religious aspects—Episcopal Church. 3. Lord's Supper. 4. Lord's Supper—Episcopal Church. I. Title.
 BT708.J64 2013
 241'.664—dc23
                          2013022306

Seabury Books
19 East 34th Street
New York, New York 10016

www.churchpublishing.org

An imprint of Church Publishing Incorporated

Printed in the United States of America

CONTENTS

*Arise, my love, my fair one,
and come away. . . .
let me see your face,
let me hear your voice;
for your voice is sweet,
and your face is lovely.*

—SONG OF SOLOMON, 2:13B, 14B

And here we offer and present unto thee,
O Lord, ourselves, our souls and bodies,
to be a reasonable, holy, and living sacrifice unto thee . . .

—"EUCHARISTIC PRAYER 1"
THE BOOK OF COMMON PRAYER

What do Christians want to say theologically about sexual intimacy? I do not mean to ask about whatever we might want properly to say and to do about sexual *ethics*, or the behavioral rules and institutional regulations that so many assume "ethics" to entail. I mean, rather, from a Christian perspective what is the *theological* and *spiritual* significance of sex? Would Christians offer the same response if asked about the theological significance of marriage? Questions like these generate a host of others. Do sex and marriage belong to a private realm of affectional intimacy only or do they also bear theologically on the Church's witness to the Gospel in the world? Does theological reflection on sex apply only to intimate personal encounters or does it carry implications for a Christian engagement with the wider social spheres of race, ethnicity, economics, class, and politics? Could theological reflection on sex contribute meaningfully to the planetary crisis of decimated ecosystems and global climate change? In more traditional language, these questions evoke an ancient quandary concerning the relationship between souls (the purely spiritual) and bodies (the resolutely physical).

Souls imply the celestial timelessness of heavenly harps and angelic choirs. Speaking the word "soul" can shift the cadence of a conversation toward the indestructible and the essential, the unseen and ethereal, the spiritual equivalent of stainless steel residing at the core of human life, pure and clean. Bodies by contrast are fragile and fierce. Bodies grow and decay as they exhibit a wide range of physical urges, from the desire for food and shelter to the longing for sexual pleasure and intimacy. Bodies vibrate with energies and yearnings that can frighten as well as amuse. Bodies exalt with delight and become unbearably messy. Then they die.

Christians present not just one of these but both at the Eucharistic Table. In some liturgical traditions Christians not only present both body and soul at the Table, but also offer them there as a "living sacrifice." Offering our whole selves to the Eucharistic celebration prompts another ancient quandary concerning change and permanence. If only the soul endures beyond the body's loss, what precisely about our bodily exaltations and fragilities do we wish to present with gratitude at the Table, where the Church memorializes the torture, suffering, and death of the body of Jesus? Do Christians prefer instead to reflect on bodily realities when proclaiming the promise of resurrection at that same Table? Which parts of our embodied lives do we leave behind in that Table's foretaste of the heavenly life to come? Do we bring our racial differences with us? Do we notice the scars and wrinkles on outstretched hands? Do we carry with us our bodily entanglements with non-human animals, the ones we keep as companions as well as the ones we eat? If the citizens of heaven no longer practice marriage (Matthew 22:30), do they engage in sexual intimacy there, and if so, why? If not, then what purpose does sexual intimacy serve here, in this life of transient and often messy mortality?

This book offers a series of extended reflections on God. This book also and *therefore* offers a series of extended reflections on sex, or more precisely, on sexual intimacy. Reflecting on one leads organically to reflecting on the other. God and sex are closely intertwined and always have been, not least because the struggle to discern the meaning of human life has rarely strayed very far from the mysterious meaning of divine life. How God and sex interrelate has varied widely over many centuries, at times with rites of exuberant embrace and at others with exhortations to abstinence. Religious traditions may try to repress sexual desire or treat it with suspicion, but even then the bond between God and sex remains, though clearly troubled and contested.

As the contestations over sexuality in Christian churches continue to roil and vex, the intertwining of God and sex today reduces almost entirely to ethical debates over "homosexuality."[1] Rather than lamenting that reduction, I believe those debates offer an unprecedented opportunity to reflect on God and sex and what one has to do with the other. I want to invite Christian communities to engage in that kind of reflection for the sake of refreshing and reenergizing their witness to the good news of the Gospel—the good news for *both* soul *and* body.

This book began to gestate some years ago as I reflected on how the professional and personal aspects of my life intersect. Professionally, as an Episcopal priest, presiding at celebrations of the Holy Eucharist has been the most visible mark of my religious vocation for nearly twenty-five years. Over time I have come to recognize the erotic energy percolating in those celebrations, which the stylized gestures of the liturgy tend to obscure. Whatever else Christians want to say about the Eucharist, we consistently refer to that ritual act of worship as an act of *communion*.

Personally, as a human being, sexual desire ripples throughout my bodily life and relational encounters. I also identify as a gay man, which carries its own socio-religious consequences in a number of ways. Like many others, regardless of sexual orientation and gender identity, I have come to recognize over time the spiritual significance of erotic desire, which the follies and foibles of romance only occasionally reflect. Whatever else sexual intimacy signifies, it springs from a desire for *communion*.

Noticing "communion" as a common term bridging the professional and personal aspects of my life occurred mostly by addressing the protracted controversy over lesbian and gay people in Christian churches. Sorting through the biblical, ethical, and theological arguments in that controversy leads eventually to sex itself as the proverbial elephant in Christianity's living room. What do Christians want to say, if anything, about the theological and spiritual significance of sexual intimacy? I believe only sustained reflection and conversation on that question will break the stalemate so many Christian communities have reached today in their debates over "homosexuality."

---

1. The word "homosexuality" will appear in quotation marks in this book for several reasons, not least to indicate its relatively recent origins (late nineteenth-century Germany) and its absence from the original Hebrew and Greek texts of the Bible.

My purpose here, however, extends beyond discerning the moral and ecclesial status of lesbian and gay persons. Those arguments have been made already. Before debating institutional regulations or policy decisions any further, I want to invite Christian communities to reflect theologically and spiritually on the desire for God and the desire for sexual intimacy as the same fundamental desire for *communion*.

Clearly, both "God" and "sex" do not always rise to the level of abstraction for which "communion" works as an apt description. We can sometimes and even regularly participate in religious ritual as a matter of rote obligation, scarcely reflecting at all on desire. We can likewise sometimes engage in acts of sexual intimacy that respond to a range of needs and wants that may seem rather far removed from "communion" (whether financial gain, power, control, or even violence). I do believe, however, that all human beings share a fundamental desire for encounter, intimacy, and union—a desire that the ancient Greeks tried to describe with the word *Eros*. Both God and sex can respond to that desire, and especially when they blend together in human experience, relationship, and worship.

Christian communities approach this mysterious confluence of body and soul every time we gather around the Eucharistic Table to share a simple meal of bread and wine. The erotic character of that shared worship, however, tends to retreat behind multiple layers of cultural and religious anxiety. Reflecting more deliberately on the eroticism of that rite—and its many theological and spiritual as well as ethical implications—may well mark the defining challenge for Christians today. The fundamental human desire for communion, as well as its disruptions and disappointments, echo throughout the overlapping spheres of political and social policy, economic systems, racial and ethnic cultural discourse, and the dismaying tenor of our ecological crises. In short, the vitality and even the relevance of twenty-first century Christian witness to the Gospel depends on exploring the depths of desire itself in the hope for divine communion—a hope both embodied and soulful.

I invite these reflections as an Episcopal priest and an academic theologian. For me, theological scholarship matters most when it informs and animates the liturgical patterns of Christian faith communities and the daily lives of Christians. While considerable academic work has been done in theology and ethics concerning human sexuality over the last fifty years, relatively little of this work has shifted the communal rhythms of Christian prayer, let alone how we live, vote, care for the planet, and engage in acts of social transformation both small and large. That gap appears vividly and ironically in liturgical celebrations of the Eucharist, precisely where the most obvious potential for prayerful reflection on sexual intimacy resides and where in turn it most often disappears behind a veil of institutional policy and regulation. Gathered around the Eucharistic Table, I want to invite Christians to reflect on the deep desire for communion that brought them there and what it might mean to embrace a "Eucharistic sexuality" at the heart of Christian faith and practice.

As I extend this invitation to Christian communities in particular, I certainly do not imagine theological reflection on sexual intimacy as an exclusively Christian endeavor. Indeed, Christians have much to learn and to offer in a broader, interreligious conversation about the deep longing for communion. Both ancient and contemporary Jewish approaches to bodily desire in relation to God, for example, can shed considerable light on what Christians mean by "incarnation." The alluring beauty of God in Islamic traditions could likewise enrich Christian reflection on desire itself. Those are only two among many nodes of intersecting religious conversations to which Christians could in turn offer our own Eucharistic perspectives on divine intimacy. The fruitfulness of that offering, however, will depend on the depth of our engagement with the rich peculiarities of our own tradition. Christians can do that theological and spiritual work best while gathered to share a simple meal of bread and wine.

My own process of theological and spiritual reflection on God and sex has been greatly enriched by the intellectual and social communion I have enjoyed with a number of friends and colleagues. Trying to name them all would inevitably omit some. Here I can only offer gratitude for the many communities in which I have had the privilege to preside at the Eucharistic Table and marvel at the hope of divine communion displayed in those gatherings. To all of them I owe a profound debt of gratitude, not only for honing the theological ideas offered here, but also, and more significantly, for providing a glimpse of that communion for which human beings continually yearn.

More specifically, from 2009 to 2012 I had the distinct privilege of working with the Standing Commission on Liturgy and Music of the Episcopal Church as they prepared materials for what came to be called "The Blessings Project." Known officially as *I Will Bless You and You Will Be a Blessing*, this project emerged in response to the 2009 General Convention of the Episcopal Church that called for the collection and development of theological and liturgical resources for blessing same-gender unions. I was invited to chair the task group charged with developing theological resources for this project, and I continue to be grateful for how much I learned from that work. I brought with me to that task many years of reflecting on my own sexual identity as well as nearly twenty years of academic work at the intersections of sexuality and Christian theology. The Blessings Project reflects some of those personal efforts; this book retrieves a good deal more.[2]

That project revealed in new ways the significant hunger in the Episcopal Church—and in many other Christian communions as well—for materials and resources to explore *theologically* and not only *ethically* the significance of sexual intimacy, including covenantal unions. We discovered in our work that we could not deal theologically with same-gender unions without also dealing with the diverse theological and liturgical history of marriage. We discovered further that theological resources for reflecting on marriage were all but absent from the lived experiences of "people in the pew," let alone the wider society. What then do Christians really want to say about the theological and spiritual significance of sexual intimacy? I offer this book as one response to that profound question.

Jay Emerson Johnson
Feast of the Presentation, 2013

---

2. For the theological, liturgical, and pastoral resources of this project, including the approved rite of blessing, see The Standing Commission on Liturgy and Music, *I Will Bless You and You Will Be a Blessing* (New York: Church Publishing, 2013).

The One Story

In the fullness of time bring us,
with all your saints,
from every tribe and language and
*   people and nation,*
to feast at the banquet prepared
from the foundation of the world.

—*"Eucharistic Prayer 2"*
Enriching Our Worship

*C*hristians make audacious claims; we always have. Some of these claims offend with exclusionary crudeness, whether by summarily consigning whole populations to perdition or justifying their annihilation in "holy" crusades. Other claims astonish with a vision for which it seems just too good to hope. To suppose, for example, that the incomprehensible arc of the universe from the big bang to the end of time leads eventually to a banquet certainly qualifies as astonishing. Even more, this banquet, prepared long before primordial dust and gas formed into stars and planets, includes "every tribe and language and people and nation."[1]

That excerpt from a Eucharistic prayer artfully combines theological notions of creation ("the foundation of the world") with eschatology ("the fullness of time") to claim a singular purpose and intent for the Creator: a *banquet*. That claim by extension renders the universe itself with a single story. The one story of the unfathomable reaches of the universe culminates not in cosmic fire or isolating

---

1. The Standing Liturgical Commission, *Enriching Our Worship* (New York: Church Publishing, 1998), 62.

frigidity, but instead and quite remarkably a *feast*. This claim, however, falls just short of the audacity it could have seized from the biblical and theological traditions from which it draws. Biblical writers, from ancient Hebrew prophets to early Christian evangelists, imagined not just any kind of banquet as the world's consummation, but quite particularly a *wedding* banquet.[2]

The stylized gestures and ritual patterns of both ancient and contemporary weddings tend to veil what every participant in those rites knows and which could have made that Eucharistic imagery truly audacious: a wedding feast celebrates sexual intimacy and bodily union. Could the deep desire and abiding hope of intimate union with another, so often inspired by witnessing a wedding, tell the one story of the universe? Prior to the modern period, many Christians told that very story. Omitting that story's overt eroticism from contemporary Christian texts and practices not only snips an important thread to historical traditions; it also misses a rich opportunity for revitalizing the Church's witness to the Gospel. That opportunity matters quite particularly in an era when so many believe that sexual intimacy has little if anything to do with the meaning and practice of Christian faith.

These images of a "banquet" and the "foundation of the world" come from a collection of alternative rites and liturgical texts approved by the Episcopal Church in 1997 to supplement the materials of the 1979 Book of Common Prayer. None of the three alternative Eucharistic texts mentions marriage explicitly or even alludes to nuptial union, let alone sexual intimacy. This omission distills in microcosm how modern Christianity more generally has relegated matters of human sexuality to regulatory policies rather than addressing them theologically or liturgically. To be sure, the 1979 Book of Common Prayer gestures toward sexual intimacy when it offers— as an option—to include the possible procreation of children in the Prayers of the People during the Celebration and Blessing of a Wedding.[3] Previous versions of the prayer book mostly omitted sexual

---

2. See, for example, Matthew 9:14–15, 22:1–14, 25:1–13; Luke 12:35–38; and Revelation 19:9.

3. The Book of Common Prayer (New York: Seabury Press, 1979), 429.

intimacy entirely. The one beautiful exception appears in the 1662 version of the wedding rite that includes this arresting phrase as part of the marital vows: "with my body I thee worship." Sadly, that tender embodiment disappears in later versions.

The reluctance to incorporate overtly erotic images in worship mirrors historical hesitations as well as contemporary cultural anxieties. This reluctance ought to puzzle more than it usually does given the rich though often troubled history of erotic language in Christian theological traditions. Puzzling but also lamentable for still another, though more cultural reason. These liturgical texts approved in 1997 emerged from a society deeply embroiled in the HIV/AIDS crisis, when the exchange of bodily fluids carried the risk of deadly infection and when newly created anti-retroviral drugs had only recently stemmed the rising tide of precipitous deaths. Erasing any explicit trace of weddings and their attendant sexual intimacy in these alternative liturgical rites, especially Eucharistic ones, suggests a brand of ecclesial detachment from the bodily existential angst defining the era that produced them.[4] Even more, this erasure mutes one of the more profound nodes of engagement with the Eucharist—a bodily sense of shared vulnerability. Surely there, in the simultaneous resilience and fragility of human life, Christians could make an audacious and hopeful claim about the incarnation of the divine Word.

The hesitancy of modern Western churches to address embodied sexual relations explicitly highlights a critical gap between today's Christian communities and historical traditions that I aim to bridge with this book. I aim to do so with renewed attention to the theological, liturgical, and spiritual significance of sexual intimacy and bodily eroticism. As I attempt that bridge-building, I imagine both biblical writers and Christian theologians over the centuries teetering on the brink of making the truly audacious claim they longed to make but could not quite bring themselves to do: erotic energy sits at the heart of Christian faith and practice.

---

4. Andrea Bieler and Luise Schottroff by contrast recount a liturgical moment when a Eucharistic minister pointed simultaneously to the bread on the Table and to himself and said, "This is the body of Christ; the body of Christ has AIDS" (*The Eucharist: Bodies, Bread, and Resurrection* [Minneapolis: Fortress Press, 2007], 134–35).

Christian history does present a treasure-trove of images to animate the erotic character of Christian faith, whether by referring to
the hoped-for union of the believer with God or the passionate ecstasies of mystical encounter or the oft-cited metaphor of the Church as
the "Bride of Christ." Explicitly embodied images for such eroticism,
however, languish in much of this provocative history. Retreating
from that bodily insight seems at least ironic given the fundamental
Christian claim that the Word of God became human flesh. Indeed,
the fleshliness of Christianity's origins more often stands in opposition to its later theological claims, pastoral exhortations, and institutional policies, especially in the realm of human sexual relations.
We can explain that opposition, at least in part, by recalling the ever-
shifting meanings of sexual intimacy over the centuries ("intimacy"
mattered less than the role sex played to mark social dominance in
the ancient Mediterranean world), as well as the complex evolutions
of the institution of marriage, which could just as easily seal an economic or political alliance as satisfy the longing for romantic companionship. Indeed, marrying for the sake of romantic love stands as
a remarkable modern innovation.[5] These multivalent meanings for
sexual relations clearly imbued the development of Christian theological ideas with some justified suspicion of bodily desire; but this
remains only a partial explanation of that reluctance to embrace a
fully embodied faith.

   I am persuaded, for reasons both historical and contemporary,
that Christians have generally resisted the fully embodied implications of the Gospel for fear of sounding *too* audacious and especially
scandalous in our theological claims—not to mention our spiritual
practices. No less historically than today, sexual intimacy presents
a host of ambiguities and vulnerabilities as well as their attendant
joys and exultations. Intimacy of any kind requires both courage
and trust because it comes with no guarantee whatsoever of recip-
rocation. As Rowan Williams so aptly describes it, sexual intimacy
invites the risk of letting one's body be recreated by another person.
Sex is "above all the area of our lives where we can be rejected in

---

5. See Stephanie Coontz, *Marriage, A History: How Love Conquered Marriage* (New York:
Penguin Books, 2006), esp. chapter 5, 145–60.

our bodily entirety, where we can find ourselves looking foolish or even repellent. . . ."[6] Bodily intimacy likewise implicates intimate partners in the inevitably messy realities of bodily life that we only temporarily soothe with the comfort of companionship or the fleeting surges of sexual pleasure. All of this sheds further light on why one might hesitate before tying divine reality to the transient, untidy, and sometimes repellent realities of carnal existence. Precisely there, however, the Gospel finds its most galvanizing traction, which Christians proclaim in every celebration of the Eucharist.

The ritual performance of Eucharist, and the communal memory on which it rests, in large measure generated the profound theological insights that unfolded in the first few centuries of Christian traditions. Early Christian worship orbited around a remarkable insight: God makes God's own self vulnerable to the ecstasies and foibles of bodily human intimacy. "Take, eat," Jesus says; "this is my body given for you" (Matthew 26:26). He says this with no guarantee whatsoever that this offering will be received well if at all. Notably, *God* initiates this moment of self-giving, and not in response to any request from God's creatures but instead from God's own desire for intimacy and union with us and indeed the rest of God's creation.

The audacity of Christian faith shimmers most vividly there, in a liturgical act routinely performed weekly by the vast majority of worldwide Christians and sometimes daily. Perhaps the rite's repetition has blunted our collective awareness of the extravagance of that ostensibly simple act. Gathering to share a meal of bread and wine offers a profound declaration at the core of Christian faith: the meaning of human life and of the whole creation derives from the hope for communion. This is first and foremost God's desire, which is only then the hope of God's creatures. More audaciously still, this desire and this hope for communion constitutes the *one story* of the cosmos, of God's own creation, to which Christian faith bears witness and in which Christians participate every time we celebrate the Eucharist. One further step remains to bring this theological audacity more fully into view: we can refresh our Christian witness to this

---

6. Rowan Williams, "The Body's Grace," in *Our Selves, Our Souls and Bodies: Sexuality and the Household of God*, ed. Charles Hefling (Cambridge, MA: Cowley Publications, 1996), 62.

profound story by turning to human sexual intimacy as a poignant instance of divine desire. Christians might readily imagine turning there when we experience such intimacy as ecstatically fulfilling; but we can also reflect on sexual intimacy, and perhaps especially so, when it leaves residual disappointment or even trauma in its wake. In all its delicate rhythms and relational frustrations, this bodily sign-post in spiritual practice can stimulate Christian witness to the One Story—the deep desire and abiding hope for divine communion.[7]

The audacity of that claim demands defense, but not merely for the sake of the academic coherence and integrity of Christian theology. That claim deserves defense for the sake of so many Christian communities torn asunder by debates over sexual ethics, which have tended for decades to focus more on the institutional and the procedural rather than the theological and the spiritual. Voting in legislative assemblies on the ecclesial status of divorced and remarried clergy, or whether lesbian and gay relationships may be acknowledged and celebrated, barely touches on the questions most people would prefer to ask about God and their own relational intimacies. The audacity of the One Story animating Christian faith thus deserves not only defense but also compassionate articulation in an era of increasing isolation and alienation, of domestic violence and international war, of systemic racism and poverty, and of unprecedented ecological anxieties. To suppose that the One Story can reach into that wide range of concerns is itself rather audacious.[8] I aim toward that audacity in the chapters that follow, not only to defend it but more importantly to extend it as a hopeful invitation.

The biblical First Letter of Peter includes this exhortation: "Always be ready to make your defense to anyone who demands from you an accounting for the hope that is in you" (1 Peter 3:15). This writer assumes, of course, that his readers actually live with hope. Defending the audacity of Christian claims begins there, with reasons for hope. Accounting for those reasons here begins by taking

---

7. "One Story" will appear throughout this book capitalized as such to indicate the centrality I believe it deserves in Gospel proclamation and Christian theological reflection.

8. L. William Countryman makes a similarly extensive claim about passionate love in *Love Human and Divine: Reflections on Love, Sexuality, and Friendship* (Harrisburg, PA: Morehouse Publishing, 2005).

seriously the current cultural climate of Western societies in which the words "God" and "sex" alike stand as curious (and sometimes irrelevant) questions rather than markers of hopefulness. We also need to consider how the One Story can invite insightful reading of biblical texts in Christian faith communities, especially given the confusions over what eroticism actually entails, not only in the many cultures represented by biblical texts but also the many cultures populating the planet today. The role played by the One Story in the history of Christian theological ideas likewise deserves sustained attention, as contemporary proclamations of the Gospel tend to reduce Christian faith to a brand of disembodied spiritual practice, setting soul against body once again. Some initial observations about each of these will begin to sketch the pattern of the One Story in this book, a pattern I am eager to extend as an invitation for personal, relational, and indeed planetary renewal.

THE ONE STORY IN WESTERN CULTURE

I enjoy cooking and eating, especially with good friends who help me in the kitchen and join me around the table. My Australian Shepherd dog, Tyler, usually enjoys these occasions as well, for the possibility of fallen scraps from the kitchen counter if not for the expanded social circle of human friends. I also enjoy a romantic evening with someone special, whether we see a movie or stroll along a beach gazing at the stars in a night sky. These activities with friends and a romantic partner draw equally from the erotic energy at the very heart of God's creation, the energy that creates all the conditions that make these activities both possible and desirable.

Many readers will likely find some surprises and unexamined assumptions in what I have just described. Few people today would use "erotic energy" to describe the companionship of good friends cooking food together and sharing a meal. If they do, they might assume that these friends were paired off as romantic couples. More than a few would certainly find it perplexing that "erotic energy" has anything to do with my canine companion. Many more would assume that the eroticism percolating in a romantic stroll on a beach eventually involves genital contact, even without mentioning it explicitly. If God and religion play any role in these surprises and assumptions, they usually serve as regulatory markers of what each situation would allow and permit for bodily interaction. I further imagine relatively few Christians today relating any of this analysis to the inherently erotic character of God and God's creative work.

Locating the One Story in modern Western culture might reasonably begin with those multiple layers of unexamined assumptions and their accompanying perplexities. The words "love," "erotic," "sex," and "sexuality" all stand in rather precarious relation to each other, occasionally as interchangeable terms and sometimes neatly cordoned off from the others in linguistic isolation. I am particularly worried that these confusions and conflations have flattened the richness of *Eros*. We might notice how every major urban center in the United States, and in many rural ones as well, carves out designated zones for nightclubs that advertise "exotic" and "erotic" dancers, as if those terms were mutually informing. We might browse library catalogues and notice how certain types of literature fall rather indignantly into the category "erotica" if they portray passionate desires leading to or at least implying bodily intimacy, genital or not. In ways similar to pornography (the definition of which can vary widely), all things "erotic" have languished in those bodily venues of whatever Western culture has deemed a bit naughty, vulgar, or illicit (and which are, therefore, for some, enticing and enthralling).

Academic Christian theology contributed to this cultural trajectory in a variety of ways, not least with the mid-twentieth-century work of Anders Nygren, who insisted on strictly separating the Greek word *agape* from *eros* in Christian faith.[9] This academic work achieved wider popular attention in the schema offered by C. S. Lewis of four distinct "loves" on the human menu of relational encounters. On the Christian version of that menu, *agape* (self-sacrificial love and affection) rises above all the others and *eros* (the lust for carnal pleasure) resides at the bottom of the list as virtually unworthy of spiritual consideration.[10] This degradation of *Eros* would certainly strike

---

9. Anders Nygen, *Agape and Eros: A Study of the Christian Idea of Love* (London: SPCK, 1953). For a nuanced and helpful analysis of Nygren's contributions, see Werner G. Jeanrond, *A Theology of Love* (London: T&T Clark, 2010), 113–20.

10. C. S. Lewis, *The Four Loves* (San Diego: Harcourt, Brace, Jovanovich, 1960).

ancient Mediterranean societies as at least odd if not confounding. The various Greek words for "love" did not neatly separate into the kind suitable for Christian relationships (*agape*) and the kind associated with mere physical lust (*eros*). The ancient Greeks generally perceived various types of love as intersecting and overlapping; they also tended to view erotic desire as the fountainhead of love's many diverse expressions, from friendship to romance and family. More broadly still, the ancient Greeks appeared to honor erotic energy for its capacity to reunite previously separated beings, a display of the deep desire for wholeness in the midst of fragmentation.[11] *Eros* thus enjoyed the status of a god.

Modern Western cultural anxieties about *Eros* seem strangely out of place when compared to ancient Greek sensibilities but also many others as well. Sexuality and religion have always tightly intertwined with each other. The character of those entanglements has evolved in dizzying complexities, from ancient fertility cults and temple prostitution to systems of ritual purity, monastic celibacy, mystical ecstasies, and ceremonial marriage. A short list of religion's imprint on our collective sexual imagination would stretch at least from ancient King David's dalliance with Bathsheba (2 Samuel 11:3–5) to the friar who tried to help star-crossed lovers in Shakespeare's *Romeo and Juliet*, as well as Pope Clement VII's refusal to grant a divorce for the English King Henry VIII and on into the twentieth-century confession made by then United States President Jimmy Carter that he occasionally harbored lust in his heart—a confession made by quoting from Matthew's gospel (5:28).

Notably, and easily overlooked, similar religious preoccupations attach to food. The dietary restrictions in the biblical book of Leviticus and the "scandalous" meals Jesus shared with his society's misfits are just some of the most familiar accents in the regulatory language that so many Christians have internalized. Christian history also includes accounts of saints living only on Eucharistic bread, sometimes for years, whether Catherine of Siena, Catherine of Genoa, or Joseph of Cupertino. Jayne Steel extends that historical trajectory

---

11. Jeanrond, *A Theology of Love*, 14–15. See also Virginia Ramey Mollenkott's passionate insistence on interweaving all these various forms of love in *Sensuous Spirituality: Out from Fundamentalism*, revised ed. (Cleveland, OH: The Pilgrim Press, 2007), 110.

into the present and argues that food continues to play "a vital role in our sense of spiritual self," and not coincidentally, therefore, also in our perceptions of the sexual self.[12]

Digesting these historical complexities, this much seems clear: genital sexual activity and eating meals have been the most frequently regulated aspects of human life in nearly every human society, and religion has most often been the means to regulate them. Given the role both food and sex play in the survival and in the thriving of the human species, it would be surprising if religion had nothing to do with either one. Elaborate rituals, intricate ceremonies, cultural artifacts, visual art, and music have all accompanied both food and sex for nearly as long as humans have chronicled our history. Traces of this dual preoccupation persist today in the tenor of Christian debates over "homosexuality," as well as divorce and remarriage. Beneath the many layers of those institutional machinations lies a primal baseline: sexual propriety serves as the qualifying condition for presiding at the community's Eucharistic Table, where food beckons our participation in a tantalizing spiritual feast.

Both food and sex clearly matter, especially in relation to things divine. How they matter in contemporary Western societies, however, sets our own era apart as oddly unique. Modern Western culture has taken the role sex has played in the multivalent ideas, forms, and practices of religion and systematically reduced it almost entirely to ethics, or more precisely to the regulatory policies of religious institutions. Rather than prompting spiritual insight, the relationship between God and sex today more closely resembles legislative debate over commerce; some argue for deregulation while others insist on ever more stringent and direct control, usually through institutional policies. Perhaps even more peculiar, relatively few religious communities question the notion of regulation itself as God's primary role in sexual intimacy. That role recurs frequently in popular culture, whether on film or television, where official representatives

---

12. Jayne Steel, "Chocolate and Bread: Gendering Sacred and Profane Foods in Contemporary Cultural Representations," *Theology and Sexuality* 14:3 (2008): 322. For more on these connections, see *The Journal of the American Academy of Religion*, which published a thematic issue on religion and food in 1995. The concluding essay by Gillian Feeley-Harnik offers a helpful overview of how extensively religion and food intertwine, historically and today ("Religion and Food: An Anthropological Perspective" 63:3 [1995], 565–82).

of Christianity usually portray a prudish disciplinarian in a society enamored with having sex. They might also appear as figures tormented by sexual desires they feel compelled to overcome in order to be effective or even valid representatives of Christian traditions.[13] Modern Western Christianity has travelled quite far indeed from the ancient praises of *Eros*.

Minority reports from this mainstream trend have proliferated in recent years, providing resources for a more holistic retrieval of eroticism's cultural and spiritual significance. Laurie A. Jungling, for example, has helpfully defined erotic energy as "the divine call into life as embodied relationality" or the "force that gives life the relational essence that fills and empowers all of creation."[14] James D. and Evelyn Eaton Whitehead embrace that expansive description by imagining *Eros* as "fueling every passionate engagement with life," the energy of divine vitality that animates our impulse to help, to heal, to live generously, and extravagantly with compassion.[15] Veronica Goodchild expands these definitions even further by supposing that "the God, *Eros*, lurks in the compelling desire of matter and spirit for each other to recover a lost wholeness."[16] An oft-cited essay from African-American poet Audre Lorde adds still more texture to this retrieval as she describes the erotic "providing the power which comes from sharing deeply any pursuit with another person. The sharing of joy, whether physical, emotional, psychic, or intellectual, forms a bridge between the sharers which can be the basis for understanding much of what is not shared between them, and lessens the threat of their difference."[17] In all these retrievals and reconstructions, erotic energy may in some sense relate to the common notion

---

13. Examples here include: Glenn Jordan, dir. *Mass Appeal* (Hollywood: Universal Pictures, 1984); Antonia Bird, dir. *Priest* (Los Angeles: Miramax, 1995); and almost any film produced by Merchant Ivory.

14. Laurie A. Jungling, "Creation as God's Call into Erotic Embodied Relationality," in Margaret D. Kamitsuka, ed., *The Embrace of Eros: Bodies, Desires, and Sexuality in Christianity* (Minneapolis: Fortress Press, 2010), 217.

15. James D. Whitehead and Evelyn Eaton Whitehead, *Holy Eros: Pathways to a Passionate God* (New York: Orbis Books, 2009), 9–10.

16. Quoted in Diarmuid O'Murchu, *The Transformation of Desire: How Desire Became Corrupted—and How We can Reclaim it* (Maryknoll, NY: Orbis Books, 2007), 66.

17. Audre Lorde, *Sister Outsider: Essays and Speeches by Audre Lorde* (Berkeley, CA: Crossing Press, 1984), 56.

of the "pornographic," but only as the idea of food might similarly relate to a solitary saltine cracker.

I find these expansions of the erotic illuminating and useful, but I also worry about their shyness when it comes to genital sexual intimacy; some of these sources omit such intimacy entirely from their constructive retrievals of eroticism. I worry about this in an age of increasingly casual approaches to sex, facilitated in new ways by online social media and the ever-diminishing credibility of religious institutions (whether because of financial mismanagement or clergy sexual abuse). My concern here, however, has less to do with morality than with meaning, or rather with the perceived irrelevance of religious ethical ideals for the process of making spiritual sense from our intimate human encounters—including whether such encounters have any such "spiritual" meaning at all. Werner Jeanrond frames this cultural dilemma succinctly: "[B]etween the secular prophets of total sexual liberation, on the one hand, and the clerical administrators of total sexual control, on the other hand, a vacuum has emerged in which many young adults often feel very lost."[18] Christian churches perpetuate that gap between moral guidance and meaningful intimacies even further by marginalizing theological reflection on bodily desires, and particularly on the hope those desires can waken. Deliberate attention to the erotic character of Eucharistic spiritual practice can bridge that gap, not only for Christians but also for how the Church bears witness to the Gospel more widely.

Christian churches today face the same challenge as Christians have always faced in the midst of complex cultural sensibilities. The question of how and even whether we embrace the audacity of an incarnational faith that finds bodily desires and intimacies spiritually insightful has hovered around Christian proclamation for centuries. In the chapters that follow I want to invite Christian communities to explore our audacious faith by plumbing the depths of *love* at the heart of the Gospel. I do not mean the sanitized or sentimental versions of love that proliferate in greeting cards. I mean, rather, exploring the many forms love can take, all of which exhibit an *erotic* character, the hope for encounter and intimacy. Christians can

---

18. Jeanrond, *A Theology of Love*, 250.

claim even further that this deep desire for love originates with God, whose longing for intimacy not only shines forth from biblical texts and theological traditions but also in every elegant, fumbling, joyous, and disappointing or even traumatic encounter we have with sex and sexual intimacy. Divine eroticism shines forth from all these moments precisely because God created their physical and material conditions. God has done something else as well. By making human bodies, with their complex physiology and all their various parts and organs, God has planted in each of us a carnal pathway for encountering divine love.

Given all these theological and cultural complexities of love, "sexual intimacy" in this book refers to a wide range of bodily relations and encounters, whether or not genitalia play any role at all. The breadth of that range may seem odd in contemporary Western culture, which tends to operate with various and sometimes conflicting definitions of sex. In the midst of these contestations and quandaries, we do not cease being bodily or even sexual when engaged in otherwise "intellectual" work or when having an intense conversation with a good friend. Werner Jeanrond agrees and encourages a view of sexuality beyond genital activity alone since sexuality "concerns our whole personality, our intimate as well as our public relationality in this universe."[19] Diarmuid O'Murchu echoes that expansive view by describing our "desire to relate" as "primordially a sexual endowment, always imbued with cosmic yearnings."[20]

These expansions of sexual intimacy invite an equally wide range of moments that qualify as "spiritual" experiences. Imagine, for example, those moments when the confluence of released hormones, rising blood pressure, engorged organs, rapid breathing, and the tingling sensations of physical pleasure accompany an instance of sexual intimacy. Now consider how that description of human physiology during genital activity and intercourse can apply just as well to the consumption and digestion of a fine meal. It may seem merely coincidental that eating food and having sex share many of the same bodily responses, but for Christians that confluence belongs to the

19. Jeanrond, *A Theology of Love*, 250.
20. O'Murchu, *The Transformation of Desire*, 106.

audacity of an incarnational faith. Indeed, these bodily moments of desire, ecstasy, pleasure, and fulfillment properly belong in a vibrant Christian witness to the erotic handiwork of the Creator.

Western society today eagerly awaits sustained theological and spiritual attention to the erotic, the sexual, and to love itself. The future of human and planetary thriving may well depend on it. In a world of deep polarization and hostility, from the personal and the political to the widely social and international, human beings yearn for reasons to renew their hope in the possibility of communion. Responding to that yearning, however, presents significant challenges in a society that obsesses over food and sex and finds both so perplexing. The latest obesity rates in the United States can alarm public health officials even as bookstore shelves overflow with cookbooks and the Iron Chef makes enticing meals on cable television with ingredients that keep cardiologists in business. Meanwhile, advertising firms use sex and sexuality in the guise of rail-thin women and muscular men to sell just about anything, from car parts to dog kibble, while online pornography continues to rank as the most promising investment for Internet entrepreneurs.

These apparently intractable confusions about food and sex in contemporary Western culture present a rich opportunity to tell the One Story in new and compelling ways. Christians tell that story every time we gather to share a simple meal of bread and wine. Refreshing our witness to that story and its hope begins and returns often to the vexing contestations over the Bible in Christian churches as well as the wider society.

THE ONE STORY IN THE BIBLE

What kind of story does the Bible tell? Surveys of even small Christian congregations would yield multiple answers to that ostensibly simple question. Some would focus on ethics and treat the Bible as a moral compass. Others would choose to stress humanity's sinfulness and the need for salvation. Still others might seek a hidden secret to the meaning of human existence, or solutions to troubled relationships, or even a recipe for material prosperity. In the Evangelical Christianity of my youth, I simply assumed that the Bible tells one continuous, coherent story with a clearly defined beginning, middle, and end. I believed that for theological reasons, but mostly for story-telling reasons. Human beings want to tell inviting and compelling stories for reasons similar to wanting to share food with friends and sexual intimacy with a partner—the desire for communion.

The Bible itself, however, refuses to tell us what kind of story it tells, let alone a single story. More pointedly, as Dale Martin reminds us, texts do not actually "speak." Asking what the Bible "says" or what it can "tell" us mistakes an inanimate object for a subject with agency and will. A better question to ask, as Martin suggests, is to wonder what people want to say with the texts of the Bible.[21] What kind of story do *we* want to tell with those texts? In addition to our own perspectives and commitments, the Bible's complex and often convoluted history belongs to any story we want to tell with it. What did the Church want to say by including some texts and omitting others in the canon of Scripture?

The one book commonly called the Bible contains many books and various types of literature representing diverse communities stretching over many centuries. Some of these books read like histories or biographies while others are mostly poetry or distilled bits of practical wisdom. Some of these "books" are actually letters written to particular communities of faith and some defy any precise categorization, like the type of literature Christians came to call "gospel" or the densely metaphorical writings of apocalyptic prophets. Why then did these particular texts and not others find their way into one official collection? Did the Church have a single story it wanted to tell by herding these diverse "books" into a single compendium of sacred writings?

For modern readers of the Bible, a possible and rather curious answer to that question appears in the history of both Jewish and Christian commentaries on the Song of Songs, sometimes called the Song of Solomon. This ancient Hebrew text is a short love poem, tucked away in Christian versions of the Bible between Ecclesiastes and Isaiah. It rarely gets mentioned in public discourse about

---

21. Dale B. Martin, *Sex and the Single Savior: Gender and Sexuality in Biblical Interpretation* (Louisville, KY: Westminster John Knox Press, 2006), 1–2.

the Bible, preachers mostly ignore it, and it appears nowhere in the three-year lectionary cycle for Sunday worship in the Book of Common Prayer.[22] Most Christians today are likely puzzled by the inclusion of this obscure and often passionately erotic text in the Bible, yet it was anything but obscure for most of Christian history.

One of the founders of rabbinic Judaism, Rabbi Akiba, acknowledged the holiness of all the biblical writings but then apparently designated the Song of Songs as the "holy of holies," a description that seized the Christian imagination as well. The Song of Songs has been the one text most often copied, the one text most often chosen for commentaries, and the one text most often selected by preachers (prior to the modern period). More Latin manuscripts of this short text exist than any other biblical book. More medieval sermons were preached on it than any other and it took its place among the four gospel accounts as among the most important for many centuries; at times the Song of Songs was read more often than any of the gospel texts except John.[23]

The peculiar prominence of erotic poetry in historical Christianity and its subsequent demotion to obscurity in modern churches sheds considerable light on the One Story in the Bible. When considering the many reasons informing the Church's long and arduous process of selecting texts for the canon of Scripture, we might suppose that the hope for divine communion played a vital role, a hope to which the Song of Songs bears eloquent witness. Douglas Burton-Christie supports that supposition by reading medieval spirituality through the lens of that ancient love poem. Only erotic language can capture the passionate urgings that animated those so-called "dark ages," the deep longing for God and indeed God's own longing for us.[24] Those frequently labeled as "mystics" in Christian traditions resorted to erotic imagery at nearly every turn, whether Teresa of Avila or John of the Cross or Matilde of Machtenburg, who

---

22. A short portion of the Song of Songs was included in the Revised Common Lectionary shared by a number of Christian communions, including the Episcopal Church, but only as an alternative reading on one Sunday, for Proper 17 in Year B.

23. David M. Carr, *The Erotic Word: Sexuality, Spirituality, and the Bible* (Oxford: Oxford University Press, 2003), 3–4.

24. Douglas Burton-Christie, "Into the Body of Another: *Eros*, Embodiment and Intimacy with the Natural World," *Anglican Theological Review* 81:1 (1999), 20–21.

wrote passionately concerning her marriage to Jesus, who replaced her earthly husband. Much earlier than these medieval encounters, Origen in the second century favored the Song of Songs as the interpretive key for Christian faith and spiritual practice.[25]

Each of these historical moments draws on rich veins of biblical material, including the oft-employed image of marriage and adultery in the Hebrew Bible to describe the relationship between God and the people of Israel (see Jeremiah 3:8–9 and Hosea 3:1, for example). Early Christian writers retrieved that image to describe the relationship between Christ and his "bride," the Church (Ephesians 5:25–27 and Revelation 21:2, 9). Isaiah leaves little doubt about the spiritual significance of this metaphor:

> You [Israel] shall no more be termed Forsaken,
>   and your land shall no more be termed Desolate;
> but you shall be called My Delight Is in Her,
>   and your land Married;
> for the Lord delights in you,
>   and your land shall be married.
> For as a young man marries a young woman,
>   so shall your builder marry you,
> and as the bridegroom rejoices over the bride,
>   so shall your God rejoice over you. (Isaiah 62:4–5)

Gerard Loughlin encourages Christian readers to take these texts more seriously still by noting how strange early Christian readings of the Bible appear to modern sensibilities. The story of Jesus turning water into wine at a wedding offers a classic case in point (John 2:1–12). Loughlin's retrieval of early Christian interpretations of that story deftly overturns the bulk of pre-marital counseling materials available to Christian clergy today, materials that portray Jesus blessing marital union merely by attending a wedding. Loughlin invites this reorientation by reminding us that the gospel stories, and especially the ones in John, relied on spiritual metaphor. Many early

---

25. For both a survey and more in-depth analysis of these erotic mystical readings, see Peter S. Hawkins and Lesleigh Cushing Stahlberg, eds., *Scrolls of Love: Ruth and the Song of Songs* (New York: Fordham University Press, 2006).

Christians, as Loughlin describes it, interpreted the Cana story in John as that moment when Jesus *marries his disciples*.[26] While most modern Western Christians would find such a reading perplexing if not absurd, that Johannine text belongs in the same interpretive bin as the many parables Jesus told about weddings. That "bin" is the One Story of God's desire for communion.

These traditional hallmarks of an erotic Christian faith make the precipitous decline of the popularity of the Song of Songs in the modern period seem quite strange indeed. Nineteenth-century biblical scholarship helps to explain that decline, at least in part. Historical-critical scrutiny of the Song of Songs made explicit what previous readers surely knew but to which they assigned virtually no importance: that short biblical text nowhere makes any mention of God. Modern biblical scholarship, in other words, effectively evacuated the spiritual significance of the Song of Songs by making it "merely" sexual.[27]

The modern construal of the Song of Songs as simply carnal erotica mirrors the equally peculiar approach among medieval commentators—making that biblical text "merely" spiritual. These two approaches, actually flip sides of the same coin, reveal something still more insightful. Nearly all ancient, medieval, and modern readings of that biblical elegy to erotic love omit any union of the sexual and the spiritual, or body and soul, to which a genuinely incarnational faith presumably wishes to point. While one era exalts in the spiritual at the expense of the physical, another dismisses the sexual to languish in the regulatory regimes of bodily relations. In *both* cases bodily desire has been syphoned off from the abiding hope for divine communion.

Human bodily life, however, remains stubbornly resistant to its erasure by religious fiat. Religious institutions may rather ironically strive to subdue sexual passions by repeatedly citing a biblical text steeped in erotic desire, but doctrine proves a poor substitute for bodily passion and intimacy. Keith Jones is convinced that the Song of Songs retained its place of privilege among the ancients and

---

26. Gerard Loughlin, ed., *Queer Theology: Rethinking the Western Body* (Oxford: Blackwell Publishing, 2007), 1–3.

27. Carr, *The Erotic Word*, 4.

in medieval culture precisely because it excited the very hope that made Christian faith compelling in the first place. "By identifying the unnamed lover in the Song as Christ," Jones notes, "readers discerned that there is a genuine analogy between what we want in our love from other human beings and what God wants to give us."[28]

Twenty-first-century Western culture thus lives with a confounding legacy. The ascendancy of rationalism in the wake of the European Enlightenment, the rise of scientific method, shifts in familial patterns prompted by the industrial revolution, and the stress on ethics as the essence of religion—all this accompanied an equally galvanizing diminution of reading Christian faith mystically and erotically. Sexuality slowly but ineluctably migrated from the realm of theological metaphor and spiritual practice and began to reside almost exclusively in the regulatory mechanisms of biblical ethics. The One Story could still be retrieved in modern Western readings of biblical texts, but its lively entanglement with sexual intimacy faded nearly entirely from view.

If biblical texts cannot tell us what kind of story they tell, then Christians today, like every generation before us, must discern prayerfully and deliberately what kind of story God would have us tell with the Bible. Dale Martin refers to that discernment as the process of "making Scripture" from biblical texts.[29] Today's cultural confusions and obsessions with both food and sex present a rich opportunity for that "Scripture-making" work, for telling spiritually erotic stories and making biblical texts rhyme with our bodily hope for communion. David M. Carr invites precisely this approach to the Bible as "a call to a life of erotic passion: passion for others, passion for God, passion for the earth." As Carr urges, "read as a whole, [the Bible] can bring many aspects of our erotic life together."[30]

Whenever Christians gather to celebrate the Eucharist, we draw from this deep well of historical Scripture-making stretching over many generations. That rich legacy of biblical eroticism preserved the truly audacious vision of the "banquet prepared from the foundation

---

28. Keith Jones, *Adam's Dream: Human Longings and the Love of God* (London: Continuum, 2007), 70.

29. Martin, *Sex and the Single Savior*, 8–10.

30. Carr, *The Erotic Word*, 3.

of the world" as the culmination of God's own passionate desire. That desire moved the writer of Genesis to place the Tree of Life at the heart of God's harmonious garden (Genesis 2:9) just as it inspired the writer of the Revelation to John to describe the One Tree at the heart of the heavenly Jerusalem, whose leaves are for the healing of the nations (Revelation 22:2). The Church placed the former text at the beginning and the latter text at the end of its canonical collection of sacred writings. The Church chose two bookends for the story it wanted to tell, and which we can tell anew today—the One Story of the deep desire and abiding hope for divine communion.

THE ONE STORY IN CHRISTIAN THEOLOGY

Why would Christian ideas matter in an era of waning interest in religion? Has Christianity suffered an irredeemable tainting from its centuries-long association with American patriotism and a Puritan-like hedging of sex? What finally is Christian faith all about? Could deliberate and sustained theological reflection contribute to a compelling story in answer to that question? As a theologian I am persuaded of the importance of theological ideas, not first as a matter of doctrinal acuity but as the distillation into speech of a tantalizing, life-changing invitation. What if Christian theological ideas charted a spiritual path to follow marked by bodily desire? Christians can affirm that path by bearing witness to the One Story, to the profound hope for communion, which would dissolve the isolation and hostility that mars human life and diminishes avenues for the flourishing of planetary intimacy. This might actually change the world.

I imagine sparking such world-changing moments by saying the word "church" on a street corner and asking passers-by what comes to mind when they hear it. While responses will vary, I imagine many would include the prominence of sin and judgment and eventually (if not quickly) sex and sexuality as well. What Christianity now means for large segments of the world's populace frequently reduces to moralistic aphorisms or institutional regulation about with whom and when to have sex. "Church" could elicit something far more compelling by attending carefully to Christianity's own theologically erotic history rather than relying so often on the regulatory regime of institutional sexual propriety. Christians do have a compelling theological story to tell that could craft a response to those passers-by on a street corner with something a bit more audacious: "Church" bears witness to the erotic energy that animates the whole of God's creation with the desire for communion. That claim might provoke curiosity and intrigue, but few people today would find it recognizably *Christian*.

If Christian theology offers a single story at all, most people would not expect erotic desire to play any significant role. The history of Christian theology exacerbates that challenge by exhibiting no less diversity than the texts of the Bible; the diversity of Christian traditions actually multiplies with each passing century. Even theologians historically grouped together as "orthodox" (rather than "heretical") offered theological insights that seem difficult, if not impossible, to harmonize. While the diversity of historical Christian theology defies nearly every attempt to create a coherent narrative from it, Christian traditions do share this much in common from one generation to the next: *food* and *sex*.

Food plays a remarkably central role in biblical texts, from the fabled "apple" that tempted the first humans in Eden to the dietary restrictions of ancient Israel and the many meals Jesus shared with "unworthy" dinner-party guests. Christian theologians have for centuries woven this biblical thread into their own musings on the "heavenly food" of the Eucharist, including who may or may not properly receive it and preside over its consecration. Those guidelines and restrictions most often turned, both historically and today, on one's sexual behavior or even reputation. Early Christians tended to eschew the cultural practice of marriage as a distraction from their spiritual quest, which led eventually to celibate monastic vocations as the pinnacle of spiritual piety in the medieval church; only in the sixteenth-century Protestant reformation did the primacy of monasticism give way to particularly Christian affirmations of marriage. Modern Western Christianity reflects this historical arc with its struggles over divorce and remarriage for both lay and ordained as well as the divisive debates over lesbian and gay relationships. All of these historical and contemporary moments bind sexual behavior to the sharing of a communal meal.

Food and sex matter, especially when they coalesce in religious ideas and practices. That entanglement suggests, in turn, that bodily desire itself—either its exuberant embrace or anxious refusal—provides a galvanizing lens through which to read the multivalent layers of Christian theological history. Consider some of the earliest articulations of Christian theology. Those often halting articulations of divine presence exhibit a pattern of God's creating, saving, and sustaining work, eventually crystallizing into the complexities of Trinitarian doctrine with all its attendant philosophical arguments, ecclesial denunciations, and circuitous reasoning. While these speculative ideas can seem rather far removed from quotidian engagements with bodily life, much more than a desire to craft accurate doctrinal formulations led to these complexities. Paul thought so as well, especially given the "groaning of anticipation," as he put it, that prompted such theological systems in the first place. At its best, Christian theological speech seeks above all to entice, lure, and invite us ever deeper into the mystery of God's own inherently social (Trinitarian) life. More simply, Christian theology seeks to give voice to creation's "groaning" for communion (Romans 8:18–23).[31]

The first few centuries of Christian thinkers and writers took that challenge to heart and set in motion a theological posture toward biblical texts that would shape every generation to follow. Nearly without exception, particular approaches to early Christian theology depended on how a given theologian read the first three chapters of Genesis.[32] Those opening, iconic chapters of the Bible depict what has been replicated ever since in countless texts, works of art, and patterns of community formation: an act of creation marred by tragedy and the hope of recovery. Indeed, for many centuries Christian theologians turned to the third chapter of Genesis to explain what

---

31. See Christopher Southgate's compelling analysis of the urgency to include the whole of God's creation—including its pain and suffering—in Christian theological reflection in *The Groaning of Creation: God, Evolution, and the Problem of Evil* (Louisville, KY: Westminster John Knox Press, 2008).

32. For the reliance on Genesis in these formative centuries, see Peter Brown, *The Body and Society: Men, Women, and Sexual Renunciation in Early Christianity* (New York: Columbia University Press, 1988), 93; for a helpful overview of how early theologians read these texts, see Peter C. Bouteneff, *Beginnings: Ancient Christian Readings of the Biblical Creation Narratives* (Grand Rapids, MI: Baker Academic, 2008).

had gone so terribly wrong in God's plan for creation and how the Christian Gospel provides a solution.[33] Some have tried, both historically and today, to reorient that focus on humanity's "original sin" toward humanity's "original blessing" instead.[34] Rather than highlighting the third chapter of Genesis, this alternate reading stresses the first two chapters where the near-constant refrain "and God saw that it was good" repeats like a mantra.

How then do Christians today want to reflect theologically on the story that Christian faith presents? Do we emphasize the *problem* of humanity's sinfulness or the *blessing* of being created in God's image? How does each of these approaches invite us deeper into divine mystery and our participation in the triune life of God? The way in which Christians read those opening chapters of the Bible will inevitably inform what we expect from our encounters with God, whether we seek forgiveness or acceptance, mercy or embrace, tolerance or intimacy. Just as important, the history of Christian theological ideas actually resists nearly every attempt at choosing just one of those options. Reading that history in the shimmering light of the One Story suggests instead that all of these poignant markers of human existence belong together in a compelling invitation—to follow one's bodily desires toward the hope for divine communion, and with the assurance that such striving is not in vain.

The familiar story from the opening chapters of Genesis can indeed elicit that kind of invitation and still more than most readers imagine. The sense of familiarity that often attends those chapters usually stems from what people have been told about the story rather than what they have gleaned from actually reading it themselves. For me, those chapters continually bring to mind images of "home." I do not mean images of housework or domestic arguments or mortgage payments. I mean communities or places or relationships that help me reside comfortably in my own skin, relax into conversations, and give thanks for a life of meaning and purpose. Images of that kind refresh my readings of Genesis with a fundamental question: How

---

33. Carr, *The Erotic Word*, 40.

34. See Matthew Fox, *Original Blessing: A Primer in Creation Spirituality in Four Paths, Twenty-Six Themes, and Two Questions* (New York: Jeremy P. Tarcher/Putnam, 2000).

can I feel at home in the world—in my own body, among others, and with God? To feel truly at home in all three at the same time would be the experience of what God intended from the beginning: divine communion.

The hoped-for experience of communion remains, of course, a hope, and for many barely a glimmer on the horizon. Brief glimpses of that hope nonetheless offer a way to weave the first three chapters of Genesis together as something like a decoding device for interpreting the complexities of Christian theology. Such a device could help us notice how early Christian theologians read Genesis as an affirmation of *both* the unconditional goodness of what God creates *and* the tragic results of rejecting that goodness. This assessment has far less to do with causal arguments about human origins than a way to describe how human beings experience our mortal life, how the writers of those ancient texts lived then, and how we live now. The storyteller in Genesis, for example, describes rather powerfully the results of denying our God-given goodness. Like ripples in a pond, those results expand outward in ever-widening circles of alienation and isolation, of division, hostility, and violence. Surely this describes twenty-first-century human societies as much as ancient Mediterranean cultures.

Theologians over the ages have taken this insightful story from Genesis in many different directions; some of these may prove helpful to people today while others will not. No one person or community needs to embrace all of the options historical Christian theology presents, whether as the need for a welcoming embrace or the reassuring word of forgiveness or the continuing journey into wholeness. Regardless of the particular path they chart, each of these moments reverberates with the One Story, the deep desire and abiding hope for divine communion.

The paucity of honest and positive approaches to bodily sexual intimacy in the theological recounting of Christian hope may help to explain the animosity so many harbor when they hear the word "church." Theologians only exacerbate that animus by answering questions that most people have not thought to ask. As a theologian and Christian educator, I need constantly to remember that the most pressing concerns and moments of existential angst that Christians seek to address only occasionally intersect with the proper parsing of theological doctrines. I do not mean that theology is irrelevant. I mean that too many theologians have neglected their own bodily relations in the ideas they both craft and promulgate. Here the origins of Christian faith prove illuminating. Christianity emerged first as a hopeful bodily practice and only later as a theological system to organize and communicate the insights of that practice. That original practice of the earliest Christians evolved from table fellowship, or what came to be called "Eucharist." These early Christian rituals preserved something of the evocative character of the meals Jesus shared with a wide array of people and then soon expanded. Beyond localized questions of who may participate in these ritual meals, a broader horizon for these moments came into view—the abiding hope for communion, the analogy for which turned often to marriage.[35]

What then does table fellowship have to do with sexual intimacy? That question resides at the heart of this book. Responding to that question begins by reflecting on our relational intimacies, both the joys and the sorrows they bring, in light of the erotic desire at the very heart of the universe itself. Bringing those reflections with us to the Eucharistic Table not only carries the potential to enrich the relationships of sexually intimate couples; it would also ignite fresh approaches to Gospel witness in a world that so desperately needs it.

Whenever passers-by on a street corner perceive "church" to stand primarily as a regulatory regime, Christians have deep theological reasons to suggest an alternative. Christians might do so with theological words and concepts, but that alone will not suffice. As most novelists and essayists insist, persuasion happens by "showing" and not just "telling." Only when Christians live the communal Eucharistic practice of divine eroticism will the wider world take notice. This will mean taking far more seriously the theological implications of bodily sexual intimacy as a lens for analyzing racial discrimination, economic stratification, and environmental degradations. All of these display bodily signposts of the Creator's intent to draw "every tribe and language and people and nation" into a

---

35. See John D. Zizioulas, *The Eucharistic Communion and the World*, ed. Luke Ben Tallon (London: T&T Clark, 2011), 14–19.

heavenly banquet of divine communion. Our variegated engagements with sexual intimacy belong inextricably to that One Story. God calls the Church today to bear renewed witness to that story, and it would in every respect change the world.

THE ONE STORY IN THIS BOOK

Erotic energy animates the entire cosmos with the deep desire and abiding hope for divine communion. This desire originates with God and only then as hope among God's creatures, through Christ and in the alluring power of the Holy Spirit. This is the One Story of Christian faith and practice. Christians bear witness to that story in every celebration of Eucharist and in every moment of sexual intimacy, whether fumbling, elegant, tragic, or ecstatic.

In the following chapters the audacity of the One Story will rise up from a fairly standard pattern of Christian theology organized around the broad themes of creation, fall, and salvation. This may at first seem odd and even disconcerting for those who have found the One Story in their lives muted or even oppressed by that standard approach. For too many people—whether lesbian, gay, bisexual, and transgender people or the victims of sexual abuse and domestic violence, as well as the intentionally celibate or asexual and the unmarried mother, to name but a few—the standard pattern of Christian theology has too often denied the goodness of their humanity, or repressed their desire for sexual intimacy, or inhibited their search for a violence-free life of flourishing. These effects, however, betray the substance of Christian faith to which the One Story can once again bear renewed witness in the sexually intimate lives of Christians.

If we begin reflecting on human sexuality, not first with regulatory restrictions but with theology and spirituality, where it most properly belongs, Christian faith can shine as a surprising beacon of hope. It will shine surprisingly but also audaciously when it appears in the familiar arc of Christian theological ideas, precisely where so many would least expect to find it. Not only in Christian ideas, of course, but also in Christian worship and Christian ministry. To that end, each of the following chapters offers approaches to biblical texts and theological traditions that invite sexual intimacy into the very substance of Christian theological reflection. This theological work in turn invites a renewal of Eucharistic spirituality as the essence of Christian living.

Each chapter extends that invitation, but in slightly different though interrelated ways. Each will turn to the significance of the first three chapters of Genesis for Christian theology and frequently to the Gospel according to John. The pairing of those ancient texts can create a bridge from Eden to the bodily hope of incarnation. Walking that bridge together, we yearn with the whole creation, as Paul put it, for the "redemption of our bodies" (Romans 8:23). Embodying that hope in our intimacies and at the Eucharistic Table will mean turning not only to sensual desire, but also to shame, to carnal wisdom as well as folly, to bodily glory in the midst of violence. Each chapter invites a theological mapping of these bodily exultations and ecstasies, as well as the faults and foibles of sexual intimacy.

Overall, I hope that Christians will find fresh and invigorating ways to talk with each other about their own experiences with erotic desire and their longing for union with God. That conjunction describes the One Story of Christian faith and its kernel of good news for all those who ponder sexual ethics and who seek to live in a world of reconciliation and wholeness, with each other and with this planet of God's creation. Christian communities enact and proclaim this startling story every time we gather around a ritual table to share a simple meal of bread and wine—a remarkably erotic and hopeful performance of Divine Communion.

1

Creation

SENSUOUS DESIRE AND BODILY SHAME

In your infinite love
you made us for yourself . . .

—*"EUCHARISTIC PRAYER A"*
THE BOOK OF COMMON PRAYER

ood, sex, and, religion—these make human history possible to tell and to write, and not only because the human species would disappear without nourishing food and procreative sex. Human history has always dealt with more than merely surviving; human beings insist on making meaning from our existence. Religion in all its multivalent forms has been the primary way for humanity to hew meaning from both the triumphant glories and hard-scrabble conditions of human life. A failed crop, a successful pregnancy, abundant harvests, declining rates of childbirth—each of these has populated the explanatory and intercessory mechanisms of religion in various ways for millennia.

Some of the earliest religious rites in human history orbited around fertility and its twin expressions—the procreation of children and fruitful crops. Why religions have so often turned to progeny and food, or sexual intimacy and bodily sustenance, seems nearly self-evident when the conditions for the survival of a community hang in the balance. Food, sex, and religion all belong together naturally and even organically in societies with no guarantee of flourishing for their offspring. Those societies may or may not develop religious traditions that involve a Creator God, but they will undoubtedly generate rites that highlight the sensuality of human existence—tilling soil, planting seeds, eating food, bodily desire, sexual intimacy, giving birth, and, of course, dying.

The Book of Common Prayer retains traces of these ancient cycles of humanity's symbiotic relationship with Earth, with the wideness and depth of God's creation. Those roots stretch back to a European agrarian past and even farther back to ritual celebrations of agricultural fertility and sexual fecundity. Rural faith communities may appreciate that history more readily than today's urban or even suburban churches. Litanies and rites for "rogation days," for example, began in fifth-century France following a series of natural disasters, and evolved into liturgical occasions devoted to asking God for a healthy harvest from both land and sea ("rogation" comes from the Latin *rogare*, "to ask"). The 1979 Prayer Book expanded this "asking" to include those engaged in "commerce and industry" and more broadly still for all to renew our commitment to a proper "stewardship of creation."[1] These relatively minor liturgical traces of humanity's reliance on earth, rain, and crops will certainly take on newfound significance in an era of global climate change. Addressing effectively our growing ecological crises will demand more from us, however, than expanding the scope of rogation day prayers. Healing the breach between humans and our planetary home can begin by bringing the sensuous and bodily rhythms of sexual intimacy with us to the Eucharistic Table, where we offer tokens of Earth's bounty—bread and wine.

Christian communities have always worshipped the Creator God, yet modern Western culture has made the earthy and bodily roots of religious rites seem rather quaint, if not irrelevant. A host of factors contributed to this liturgical ambivalence toward the sensual rhythms of planetary life, including greater efficiencies in food production, the European Enlightenment (with its stress on rationality at the expense of embodied affectivity), the industrial revolution that obviated the need for many children to staff the family farm, and, of course, rapid technological advances that continue to widen the gulf ever further between human habitations and "this fragile earth, our island home."[2]

---

1. BCP, 258–59.
2. BCP, 370.

The seismic shifts in Western society over the last two centuries do mark a significant breach, not only with planetary rhythms but also and therefore with our sacred texts. The explosive growth of metropolitan centers far removed from the tilled soil that provides urban dwellers with food, for example, has distanced Christians from the earthy roots of the Bible. Few readers of Genesis today can imagine the intricate harmony portrayed in that ancient text between the first humans and a sensuous, paradisical garden. "Among the awakenings of our time," Diarmuid O'Murchu believes, "is the growing realization that we live far from where beauty first originates for us, namely in the earth itself." Alienation from that primal source of desire for "living beautifully" short-circuits our capacities for intimacy, not only with other humans but also other creatures and this planet that we all share.[3] The "awakenings" O'Murchu imagines would surely include the proliferation of urban farmers' markets that feature regionally grown produce and the many websites devoted to rooftop gardens for city-dwellers. Michael Pollan would include the "slow food" movement on that list, with its emphasis on sharing both cooking and eating fresh food in the relaxed sensuality of delectable scents, tastes, textures, and human communion.[4]

I started thinking liturgically about these bodily connections to Earth when the lure of sensuous worship prompted a curious mini-migration of Midwestern Evangelicals to the Episcopal Church in the late 1970s and early 1980s.[5] Curious, because the words "sensuality" and "worship" did not often appear together in the spirituality of Evangelical Christians. My own Evangelical childhood, in the Midwestern college town where much of this religious migration was centered, promoted a subtle association between sensuality and the exotic, if not the more titillating aspects of the sexual. Sensuality teetered on the brink of too much bodily excess for a tradition and a

---

3. O'Murchu, *The Transformation of Desire*, 65.

4. Michael Pollan, *In Defense of Food: An Eater's Manifesto* (New York: The Penguin Press, 2008), 194–96.

5. See Robert E. Webber, *Evangelicals on the Canterbury Trail: Why Evangelicals Are Attracted to the Liturgical Church* (Waco, TX: Jarrell, 1985). Webber was my undergraduate advisor at Wheaton College in Illinois, and my father, James L. Johnson, wrote an essay for this anthology; he was at that time a member of the faculty in Wheaton's graduate school.

community that preferred to consider the "spiritual" as superior to the merely "physical."

More than just curious, this mini-migration also proved illuminating. The "sensuality" of the worship to which so many were drawn consisted of liturgical colors for the seasons, candles on the altar, the sweet scent of incense, and the various bodily positions adopted during the course of a single liturgy (this included the moment of exchanging a "sign of peace" with others by actually touching them, either with a handshake or an embrace).[6] These may seem rather modest markers of the "sensuous," yet they went a long way toward making sense, quite literally, of bodily human life. Bringing our senses into our worship of the One who creates us as bodily creatures and who also saves us with an act of incarnation made liturgical worship tangible and physical. But did this worship also bring bodily *desires* along with our senses? That question haunted me for years.

I was introduced to the Episcopal Church in the small Anglo-Catholic parish where many of those migrating Evangelicals congregated. My first Easter Vigil liturgy in that parish made a deep impression. I stood transfixed as I watched the presiding priest chant the Eucharistic prayer and invite us to join the "chorus of angels and archangels and all the company of heaven." That moment was accompanied by timpani and trumpets, not to mention a transformed human at the altar. The priest's face was flushed, a condition accentuated by the candlelight when he stretched out his arms and gazed slightly upward. I expected at any moment that tears would flow down his cheeks. I felt myself lifted up as I watched and sang, lifted to the tips of my toes, as if gravity had given way to the celestial insistence on God's victory of life over death.

I felt something else as well: discomfort. That moment disoriented my spiritual compass toward something that felt far too bodily to be genuinely spiritual even though I yearned to give myself over, body and soul, to the heavenly chorus. I had trouble gazing at that priest who appeared so clearly caught up in bodily ecstasy, especially

---

6. My father found the otherwise simple exchange of peace startling and illuminating as a physical act of communion (Webber, *Evangelicals on the Canterbury Trail*, 106).

when I started to wonder whether this visage resembled the throes of sexual passion. I quickly chastened myself and dismissed that idea as utterly impious; it felt vaguely shameful.

I no longer consider that thought impious at all, let alone shameful. To the contrary, musing on the sensuality of embodied desire can spark a profound spiritual insight: bodily ecstasy properly accompanies humanity's hope for divine communion just as much as timpani and trumpets. The fruitfulness of that insight, moreover, tends to wither on the vine in the presence of shame. Renewing our witness to the Gospel could begin just there, by noting whatever prevents us from embracing a deceptively simple affirmation—out of infinite love God made us for God's self.[7] Recognizing ourselves and all others as made from the depths of unimaginable love sets a revolutionary agenda, not only for sensuous worship but also, and by extension, for Christian ministry and service.

Fully embodied, sensuous worship has not always seemed quite so extraordinary. In early Christian traditions, adult converts to Christian faith were baptized in the nude prior to receiving the Eucharist for the first time at the Great Vigil of Easter. After undergoing a rigorous course of catechetical instruction, these candidates for baptism stood in the midst of their newly adopted community, often on the bank of a river or on the lip of a pond, and stripped away their clothes. Upon rising from the baptismal waters, these newly minted Christians were anointed with oil from head to toe. I can scarcely imagine a more sensuous liturgical act; most Christians today would more likely associate it with a "spa day" than with worship.[8]

Needless to say, Christians today attend worship services fully clothed, and for good reasons. Bodily protection and communal hygiene demand at least minimal clothing when gathering with other people in public spaces. Western cultural standards of bodily propriety would also render naked bodies far too distracting for traditional forms of liturgical worship. I suspect however that such distraction would have less to do with sexual titillation than with contemporary

---

7. BCP, 362.

8. Peter Brown offers a helpful analysis and some caveats about this naked sacrament, including the presumption that nakedness indicated a return to childhood and thus a renunciation of sexuality and its inherent shamefulness (*The Body and Society*, 96–97).

cultural obsessions over youthful, muscle-toned bodies. Even when fully clothed, most people today worry about whether their own bodies meet current standards of attractiveness; stripping away the veils of clothing would only redouble that anxiety. More than all of this, nearly everyone in a liturgical gathering of naked people would likely experience a residual sense of shame over being naked—shame, that is, over standing in the very condition in which their Creator made them.

Both cultural expectations and typical forms of modern religious instruction instill a deep sense of discomfort around unclothed bodies. Most Euro-American children are taught from an early age to keep their bodies covered, even in their own homes. "Wardrobe malfunctions" that briefly reveal a celebrity's breast sufficiently scandalize to make headline news.[9] This posture toward the human body creates the suspicion that a naked human being, by definition, ought to trouble or disturb us—or perhaps excite with too much desire. The history of Christian art and iconography perpetuates that assumption by depicting Jesus as naked on only two, perhaps three, occasions: at the beginning of his life, as an infant in his mother's arms, and at the end, while dying on a cross. Some iconographers suggest nakedness at his baptism by John but rarely confirm it.[10]

What might we learn about ourselves, about the world, and about God by addressing residual bodily shame in our Eucharistic liturgies? Could the Eucharist inspire renewed gratitude for the sensuality of human life? How might that gratitude reshape the implications of our personal intimacies for wider social interactions and more broadly still with our currently troubled relationship with Earth, with God's astonishing creation? Exploring such questions can begin with the kind of theological reflection that frequently escapes the gaze of

9. The halftime show of the 2004 Super Bowl included a performance by Janet Jackson, whose right breast was briefly exposed during that performance. After more than seven years of court cases and millions of dollars in legal fees, CBS Television was released from its obligation to pay an "indecency" fine levied by the Federal Communications Commission of more than $500,000.

10. Most icons of the Crucifixion include a loincloth on the suffering or dead Jesus, yet that Roman practice of execution nearly always ensured that the one executed was completely naked—to add shame to the physical torture. See Mark D. Jordan's insightful analysis of the effects of that loincloth both historically and today (*Telling Truths in Church: Scandal, Flesh, and Christian Speech* [Boston: Beacon Press, 2003], 84–88).

Christian liturgical piety in at least two respects: the effects of bodily shame in human relationships and the image of an erotic Creator. Interrelated observations about both will suggest some vital retrievals of the Eucharist as fundamentally an erotic rite. After all, that rite invites Christians to commune with another's body—an invitation that shimmers with sensuous desire.

SHAMEFUL BODIES

What God creates is resolutely *good*. The biblical writer of Genesis insists on this in near mantra-like fashion. Why then do so many people treat their own bodies as a source of shame? I do not mean that so many of us feel *guilty* for having made an occasional mistake or a social gaffe; the offer of forgiveness can restore relationship when we inevitably do something wrong. Shame, however, differs significantly from guilt. While guilt usually attaches to particular things we *do*, shame attaches to who we *are*, and often to the bodily sense each of us has of the self.

The experience of shame can erupt from a wide range of diverse encounters and relationships, yet it seems remarkably universal. Shame can sometimes function in healthy ways—curtailing antisocial behavior, for example, or in helping us to refrain from unhealthy habits. Yet it also carries the potential to diminish the sense of self and curtail flourishing relationships. The unwanted experience of being seen most often triggers that sense of shame and the urge to retreat from view. Most people first experience this in their own families where "we learn to hide, to disconnect from ourselves, where we first feel divided from others and alienated."[11] L. William Countryman would agree and describes those early experiences more simply as learning what one's family or the wider culture considers either "clean" or "dirty."[12] While shame most often turns inward, it can

11. Gershen Kaufman and Lev Raphael, *Coming Out of Shame: Transforming Gay and Lesbian Lives* (New York: Doubleday, 1996), 15–16. While this book focuses on gay and lesbian sensibilities in particular, the first chapter offers wider insights for the dynamics of shame more generally. See also Brené Brown, *Women and Shame: Reaching Out, Speaking Truths and Building Connection* (Austin, TX: 3C Press, 2004).

12. L. William Countryman, *Dirt, Greed, and Sex: Sexual Ethics in the New Testament and Their Implications for Today*, rev. ed. (Minneapolis: Fortress Press, 2007), 10.

also be directed outward and fuel cycles of domestic violence, social bias and discrimination, and even bellicose international relations.[13]

The bodily effects of shame catalogued today by psychologists and sociologists resonate well with ancient Christian notions of the "stigmata," of being marked bodily by the wounds and scars of the crucified and publicly humiliated Jesus. Social stigma draws its power from that kind of bodily humiliation marking one's sense of embodied existence with experiences of marginalization, exile, and abandonment. Shame marks our flesh no less than a brand forged on cattle hide or a tattoo inscribed on skin or metal jewelry piercing body parts. Unlike most tattoos and piercings, however, the bodily mark of shame imbues our flesh with an aura of disgust and revulsion.[14]

Drawing on all of these sources, from Biblical texts, theological traditions, and contemporary social analyses, I find it helpful to define shame as *alienation from our own bodily goodness*. When left unaddressed and allowed to fester, this alienation can spiral into an inward collapse on the self and breed ever greater isolation. "Alienated bodies" can exacerbate troubled interpersonal relationships but also wider social disintegrations, violent hostilities toward those deemed "other," social policies that stratify and divide communities, and even environmental degradations. Expanding circles of shame, in other words, often operate in scapegoat-like fashion to expel the "other" from community—or nailing that "other" to a cross outside the city gates.[15]

The extensive and pernicious effects of shame punctuate the iconic biblical story of Adam and Eve in the Garden of Eden. This ancient story deserves renewed attention, indeed repeated and sustained attention, for reasons that have made it so iconic. The story captures remarkably well both the joys and the vexations of bodily human life

---

13. Kaufman and Raphael, *Coming Out of Shame*, 16.

14. An important counter-example of course comes from the history of institutional slavery in the United States and the practice of branding African bodies, either for punishment or identification. The legacy of this practice continues in the bodily effects of white supremacy on black bodies. See Kelly Brown Douglas, *Sexuality and the Black Church: A Womanist Perspective* (Maryknoll, NY: Orbis Books, 2006), especially her analysis of the impact on Black self-esteem, 73–76.

15. The dynamics of projection and scapegoating have been articulated well in the theories of René Girard, picked up in compelling theological proposals by James Alison in *Raising Abel: The Recovery of Eschatological Imagination* (New York: The Crossroad Publishing Company, 1996).

experienced not only in ancient societies but equally by contemporary Western culture. Recall the third chapter of Genesis. There Adam and Eve eat some fruit from the tree of the knowledge of good and evil. This was, of course, the one and only thing their Creator had told them not to do. Those familiar with shame will understand what happens next in the story, which otherwise seems quite peculiar. Immediately after their transgression, Adam and Eve cover their naked bodies with fig leaves. Peculiar, because being naked would seem to have little if anything to do with their act of disobedience. Yet their very first impulse is to hide themselves from each other, cover themselves up, and distance themselves from intimacy. Their transgression thus "sets in motion an unraveling of the connected web of relationships that God had woven earlier."[16] By weaving fig leaves together as loincloths, they unraveled the fabric of intimacy.

The impulse to hide quickly recurs when they hear God strolling through the garden, "at the time of the evening breeze," as the storyteller puts it (Genesis 3:8). As the sun begins to set after a warm and humid day and the cooler winds start moving through the trees in the lush vegetation of this paradisiacal garden, the Creator takes a moment to enjoy the creation; God takes a stroll. Nothing seems particularly unusual about this endearing detail in the story. Strolling might have been a divine habit. We might presume that God looked forward to these evening strolls, that God enjoyed inviting Adam and Eve to join in, to relish the garden and their deeply intertwined relations with it. Perhaps this storyteller would have us imagine God looking forward to "spending some quality time" with God's beloved creation. But on this occasion something has gone wrong. Adam and Eve have not only hidden themselves from each other, they have also hidden themselves from God.

So God calls out to them: "Where are you?"

This verse (3:9) ranks as one of the most poignant moments in the Bible. The Creator of the heavens and the earth calls out to the creation: *Where are you?* Do Christians hear that voice as the divine lover calling out for the beloved? I suspect very few read that question quite so tenderly. Most people likely hear the voice of an angry

---

16. Carr, *The Erotic Word*, 41.

parent in God's question, demanding a confession for a mistake. At first blush this seems to be Adam's interpretation as well. He steps out from behind the trees where he had been hiding and confesses: "I was afraid," he says, "because I was naked" (3:10).

The question persists: What does nakedness have to do with this? What is so fearsome about it? Those familiar with shame know the answer, lodged in every anxiety dream about standing on a stage dressed only in one's underwear—or in nothing at all. Nakedness triggers a primal fear of exposure, of being *seen*, not at first or even primarily as having *done* something but rather for *being* something.[17]

God then notices the novel function for fig leaves these first human creatures have just devised. Upon seeing this, God asks what would otherwise be a comic question: "Who told you that you were naked?" (3:11). I imagine most people know quite well indeed whether they are clothed or not; no one needs to tell us. But God asks anyway. As Adam and Eve hide themselves from each other, and then hide themselves from the evening breeze and the setting sun, and then even more, as they hide themselves from God—a trajectory, in other words, of ever deeper alienation from each other, from their environment, and from their Source of life—God wants to know who told them to be ashamed.

Notice that God does not first ask a question about guilt and responsibility in this story, about whether the one and only forbidden act had been committed. That question comes next, but not first. This ancient storyteller begins elsewhere, not with guilt but with *shame*. Who told you to cover yourselves up like that? Who told you to hide yourselves? Who told you to be ashamed of who you are? Who told you, God asks, to be ashamed of how I created you?

Psychologists remind us that nakedness implies much more than being unclothed. Nakedness signals exposure, that moment of being seen and seeing ourselves as foolish or absurd or even repellent. Consider the ridiculous bodily postures humans sometimes adopt when we engage in acts of sexual intimacy with each other. If these moments were filmed, many would undoubtedly laugh at themselves and perhaps find themselves chagrined by their passionate loss of bodily

---

17. For more on the sense of shame as "exposure," see Kaufman and Raphael, *Coming Out of Shame*, 38.

control.[18] Even without the aid of video, the fifth-century musings of Augustine confirm this odd conjunction of chagrin and even humiliation accompanying an act for which the Creator makes us. Augustine quite remarkably supposed the procreation of children prior to the "Fall" would have occurred rationally, without bodily passion. Perhaps this would have spared the first humans from looking silly.[19]

Among the numerous interpretations of Genesis over many centuries, two of them in particular continue to fuel the assumptions about Christianity and the human condition in Western societies today. The first comes from the Apostle Paul. In his letters to the Romans and the Corinthians, Paul interprets this story from Genesis as a story of disobedience, the kind of disobedience that results in death for humanity. He offers this interpretation as part of his understanding of Jesus as the "new Adam," the progenitor of a recreated humanity. In contrast to Adam's disobedience stands the obedience of Jesus, which results in new life (Romans 5:12–14). The second strand of interpretation comes a few centuries later. Augustine expanded Paul's approach to the story by supposing that sexual intimacy not only caused but also provided the evidence of Adam's disobedience. In Augustine's view, this tainting continues to infect the whole human race, from one generation to another, passed along by means of sexual intercourse.

Filtering Genesis 3 through these two streams of Christian interpretation has made a profound impact on nearly every society where Christian faith has been proclaimed. The effects of this impact readily appear whenever Christians distrust sensuous desires or hesitate about bodily intimacy or fear bodily passion and especially when women are blamed for all this distress.[20] These effects yield

---

18. Thomas Laqueur offers an extended account of Western society's anxiety over bodily passion expressed in large measure through male control over female bodies, which also helped to ensure an "orderly" society (*Making Sex: Body and Gender from the Greeks to Freud* [Cambridge: Harvard University Press, 1990], 58–59).

19. See Elaine Pagels, *Adam, Eve, and the Serpent* (New York: Random House, 1988), 111–12.

20. For more on locating the cause of humanity's distress in sexual desire and thus the temptations of women in early Christianity, see Peter Brown, *The Body and Society*, especially chapter four, "'To Undo the Works of Women': Marcion, Tatian, and the Encratites." This mapping to gender continued with the additional layer of race in early American history; see Douglas, *Sexuality and the Black Church*, esp. 35–45.

a poisonous fruit: the human condition itself is shameful. Nearly without exception we concur with this assessment every time we find an unclothed human body scandalous. This alienation from bodily goodness carries far-reaching implications, not only in communities of faith but also throughout social interactions, cultural sensibilities, political policies, business practices, and, of course, our personal relationships. Much depends on how Christians read divine creation; thankfully, Christians may choose more than one way to read.

Every society produces a "creation story," and these stories serve a variety of purposes. Few societies keep their stories of origin relegated to a distant past. Creation stories provide instead a symbolic engagement with the present and a way to navigate the complexities of current social dynamics. We need not, in other words, blame Adam and Eve for our distrust, our fear, and our shame. We could instead, just as many ancient readers did, find ourselves in the Genesis story.[21] Critical social theories in today's postcolonial era offer invaluable assistance in doing just that, with tools and methods for noticing the effects of one culture on another and what those effects might mean for each community, including the debilitating alienations of perceived difference.[22] The term "postcolonial," however, does not mean that colonialism itself has safely dissipated into the past, no more than Genesis remains shrouded behind the veil of humanity's primordial history. Musa Dube analyzes the lingering effects of Western colonialism on the African continent as well as the continuing eruptions of neo-colonial aspirations with respect to the denigration of the land, stratifications based on race, the corrupting influences of imperial power, and contemporary appropriations of the Bible.[23] Dube's reading of the Gospel through that postcolonial lens renders the One Story with considerable urgency, and something more. Her incisive analysis of

---

21. Most early Christian theologians avoided blaming Adam and Eve for humanity's need of salvation and instead preferred to read themselves into the Genesis narrative; one notable exception to this approach is Augustine. See Bouteneff, *Beginnings*, 144–45.

22. See the introduction to Catherine Keller, Michael Nausner, and Mayra Rivera, eds., *Postcolonial Theologies: Divinity and Empire* (St. Louis: Chalice Press, 2004), "Alien/Nation, Liberation, and the Postcolonial Underground," 1–21.

23. Musa W. Dube, *Postcolonial Feminist Interpretation of the Bible* (St. Louis, MO: Chalice Press, 2000); for a concise summary of her approach, see 15–21.

contemporary social vexations bears a remarkable consonance with Adam and Eve's dilemma.

Just like Adam and Eve, human communities today yearn to know the difference between good and evil, especially in the highly complex geo-political machinations of international politics. Just like Adam and Eve, our first impulse in the face of confounding alienations is to hide, and as comfortably as we can. Just like Adam and Eve, the fear of intimacy today disrupts ever-wider circles of sociality—creating strangers from friends, "others" from neighbors, parking lots from gardens, and institutional bureaucracies from religion. And just like Adam and Eve, all of us are God's beloved creation, the ones God longs to find. Will we, like them, allow the voice of love to penetrate our shame? To do so will mean more than finding forgiveness for whatever mistakes we may have made; it will mean hearing the voice of divine desire clearly enough to bring us out of hiding and into a whole world of difficult but immensely rewarding communion.

THE EROTIC GOD

Confession is good for the soul. Is it good for our bodies as well?

Retired Archbishop Desmond Tutu has modeled for decades his deep conviction that "there is no future without forgiveness." Tutu put this conviction into practice during his tireless leadership of the movement against Apartheid in South Africa and even more in the wake of its dismantling. Given the history of violent discrimination in that country, few would have been surprised to see a posture of retribution in the process of reweaving the socio-political fabric of South Africa. Tutu insisted differently and helped to lead the Truth and Reconciliation Commission, a public forum not merely for the airing of grievances but to create a space where forgiveness and reconciliation might emerge from the legacy of divisive hostility. The Gospel changes the world, in other words, by creating communities of reconciling love.

The mixed results of that galvanizing commission suggest that forgiveness alone cannot forge world-changing reconciliation.[24] The

---

24. See Desmond Tutu's own memoir about this work, *No Future without Forgiveness* (New York: Doubleday, 1999).

history of racial violence, whether rooted in South African Apartheid or Jim Crow laws in the United States, illustrates the limits of forgiveness when dealing with bodily wounds. Denying some people access to public lunch counters, turning dogs and fire hoses on crowds of protestors, and burning crosses on lawns to terrorize a segment of one's community—all these acts demand repentance. The fullness of reconciliation demands still more. Racial discrimination and segregation arise not from what people *do* but from who they *are* as people. This applies equally to those who are considered White and those who are considered Black. Both sides of that discriminatory divide thus live with the residue of bodily shame, though certainly experienced in different ways.[25]

Similar dynamics operate on a more interpersonal plane. The unfolding clergy sex-abuse crisis that began coming into public view in the late 1990s highlights what those involved in domestic violence have known for much longer. Victims of bodily violation tend to blame themselves, not because of their mistakes but because of the subtle conviction that they deserve that violence just for who they are.[26] This ambient circle of shame extends to the perpetrators as well, though again in different ways, just as those living with various forms of substance abuse and addiction wrestle with perceptions of a flawed existence.

The reconciling love human beings seek in the midst of systemic racism, sexual abuse, domestic violence, and the pernicious ripple effects of addiction begins with repentance and forgiveness. This alone, however, cannot address the lingering hangover of shame.[27] The controversy over "conversion therapy" for lesbian and gay people highlights particularly well the profound gap between what

---

25. Marvin M. Ellison argues that any challenge to sexual or racial violence can itself produce a violent reaction as a way to avoid the guilt and shame that it carries (*Erotic Justice: A Liberating Ethic of Sexuality* [Louisville, KY: Westminster John Knox Press, 1996], 107–108).

26. An extensive collection of essays and resources on this topic was edited by Carol J. Adams and Marie Fortune, *Violence Against Women and Children: A Christian Theological Sourcebook* (New York: Continuum, 1998); see especially Jennifer L. Manlowe, "Seduced by Faith: Sexual Traumas and their Embodied Effects," 328–38.

27. See Pamela Cooper-White, *Violence Against Women and the Church's Response*, second ed. (Minneapolis: Fortress Press, 2012), especially the conclusion, "Reconciliation: Moving Beyond Individual Forgiveness to Communal Justice," 251–61.

we do and who we are, a gap that hampers loving reconciliation. Programs designed to help people leave the "homosexual lifestyle" typically stress behaviors, but not the sense of self and the desires of the self that prompt those supposedly problematic acts.[28] Divorcing human action from human being merely perpetuates the alienation from bodily goodness at the root of human distress—shame, in other words. Abundant life will blossom only when people find themselves loved for exactly who they are rather than despite who they are. Just there Christians have something startling to say about the love that searches longingly to find us. That kind of love emerges most powerfully from erotic desire, and it originates with God.

Modern Western society generally, and Christian communities in particular, exhibit a troubled relationship with desire. We can trace this vexation in part to Puritan sensibilities and the suspicion of sensuality—the suspicion of relying on bodily sensations rather than the mind or the heart for spiritual insight.[29] Our troubled relationship with desire likewise stems from the eighteenth-century European Enlightenment and its stress on rationalism at the expense of bodily engagements with the world. The effects of the sea-change in Western ideas known as the Age of Reason linger in nearly every exhortation to "be reasonable," a thinly veiled rebuttal of inserting passion in our human encounters. Passion may certainly inflect our arguments, engagements, and navigations with others, yet the modern West persists in worrying about that beguiling, driving, and at times, all-encompassing passionate desire called *Eros*, which could easily plunge society into chaos.[30]

Lurking behind these cultural and philosophical punctuation points stands the figure of Augustine whose theological writings,

---

28. For a detailed and nuanced study of these programs, see Tanya Erzen, *Straight to Jesus: Sexual and Christian Conversions in the Ex-Gay Movement* (Berkeley, CA: University of California Press, 2006).

29. Julie Spraggon offers an intriguing analysis of Puritan sensibilities in their rejection of images for worship, their "iconoclasm," which she links to the more general suspicion of sensuality (*Puritan Iconoclasm During the English Civil War* [Rochester, NY: Boydell Press, 2003]).

30. For concerns in early American history about romantic love destabilizing the institution of marriage, see Coontz, *Marriage, A History*, 15–23, and Thomas Laqueur's analysis of early modern treatments of "hysteria" related to female genitalia (*Making Sex*, chapter 5, "Discovery of the Sexes," 149–92).

many would argue, marked Western Christian history indelibly with a deep suspicion of sensual embodied existence. Reasons for that claim litter nearly every one of his texts with cautionary tales about physical bodies and the dangers of bodily desires.[31] Augustine illustrated his anxiety with the oft-quoted, autobiographical story of climbing a neighbor's fence to steal some pears. He was neither hungry nor in any other way in need of those pears, but he stole them anyway, simply because they were forbidden—*that* made them desirable.[32] Augustine told this story, in part, to portray more concretely the recalcitrant, incorrigible human will standing in desperate need of divine grace. This Augustinian flavor of Christianity, filtered through both the Enlightenment and the Puritan heritage of Anglo-American society, casts *Eros* in the role of the ultimate forbidden fruit. Augustine certainly did not invent the "forbidden-as-attractive" dynamic in human psychology; he did, however, lodge its cautions firmly within Christian spiritual practice. Even those who have never heard of Augustine can still find the forbidden alluring; even more, the enticement alone can feel shameful.[33]

No less than two-dimensional Puritans or the progenitors of European Enlightenment, Augustine deserves a bit more texture. Augustine did not, for example, consider desire itself an enemy of Christian faith. To the contrary, desire carries the potential to shift our energies toward God: "You have made us for yourself, O Lord, and our heart is restless until it rests in you."[34] The Augustinian problem resides not in desire per se, but in the unabated pursuit of desires that eventually obscure the true longing of the human heart.[35] Contemporary critics of Western consumerism might find Augustine's point useful. Unrestrained desire—whether in human sex trafficking, substance abuse, or the alarming depletion of Earth's resources for the sake of both comfort and the ability to buy more gadgets—leads

31. Augustine noted, for example, that Mary was blessed more in her discipleship than in carrying Jesus in her womb (Augustine of Hippo, *Sermon* 25 [PL 46:937–38]).

32. Augustine, *Confessions*, Book II:9–14.

33. See Brown, *The Body and Society*, chapter 19, "Sexuality and Society: Augustine," 387–427.

34. Augustine, *Confessions*, Book I:1.

35. For the importance of desire itself in Augustine's work, see Margaret Miles, *Desire and Delight: A New Reading of Augustine's Confessions* (New York: Crossroad, 1992).

only to tragedy and even planetary catastrophe.[36] As Wendy Farley has noted, capitalist societies actually capitalize on a theological insight about humanity's endless well of desire. But rather than directing that desire toward its divine source, the marketplace directs us toward what can be purchased and consumed. Farley finds it odd and alarming that the Church has so little to say about the market's controlling power over human desire, except to fret endlessly over sexual behavior.[37]

Western society may have freighted desire with vexations, and eroticism doubly so, but not irredeemably. The ancient Greeks still prove helpful with their understanding of erotic desire as the urge to extend ourselves into encounter, intimacy, and union with another. That ancient insight can help us, in other words, to snip the insidious thread between *Eros* and mere lust for self-gratification. When I see an attractive person, I may at first have an experience similar to perusing the objects in a fine-art gallery—I see a gorgeous painting and I want to possess that object and enjoy its beauty. But the fullness of *Eros* runs much deeper. Sooner or later an attractive person awakens my desire to be desired, to be found attractive just as much as I am attracted. Only then will *Eros* blossom with its divine potential—the possibility of intimate self-offering.

Susan Griffin plumbed those depths of mutual desire and imagined *Eros* creating liminal spaces where dynamic exchanges can take place across previously impermeable boundaries. Less abstractly, she invites us to notice how the apparently intractable walls that divide races and cultures today have their foundations firmly planted in a much earlier supposition—the division between spirit and matter, mind and body, and indeed the human over nature.[38] I hear echoes of Griffin's point in what Robert Frost aimed to capture in one of

---

36. Robert B. Reich would agree by arguing that democracy can provide appropriate restraint for such rampant desire, but that democracy itself is now constrained by corporate money and its influence on public policy (*Supercaptialism: The Transformation of Business, Democracy, and Everyday Life* [New York: Alfred A. Knopf, 2007], especially chapter 4, "Democracy Overwhelmed," 131–67).

37. Wendy Farley, "Beguiled by Beauty: The Reformation of Desire for Faith and Theology," in *Saving Desire: The Seduction of Christian Theology*, ed. F. LeRon Shults and Jan-Olav Henriksen (Grand Rapids, MI: The William B. Eerdmans Publishing Company, 2011), 132–34.

38. Susan Griffin, *The Eros of Everyday Life: Essays on Ecology, Gender, and Society* (New York: Doubleday, 1995), 19–20.

his classic American poems. In "Mending Wall," Frost imagined the annual repair of fences drawing neighbors together in a mutually beneficial project.[39] The image of a fence as a symbol for *shared* work evokes Griffin's notion of liminality—a boundary that invites crossing. Not merely coincidentally, Frost wrote that poem when American individualism had reached its zenith and the North Atlantic sat on the brink of World War I. Christopher Lasch noticed this too and described the exultation of isolated individuality as an arid space, drained of its relational sustenance by the worship of self-reliance.[40] To all this the ancient Greeks would offer enthusiastic agreement. Only erotic energy has the potential to dismantle the walls of isolation, those impermeable boundaries that divide, separate, and sequester—why else would *Eros* enjoy the status of a god?[41] Christian communities would do well to ponder that very question, especially when we gather for a shared meal of bread and wine.

These strands of cultural and philosophical analysis play an important role in discerning the character of human life in relation to God and what we want to say about both. The significance of erotic desire in that discernment poses a challenge for a theological tradition that would seem to take a dispassionate God as the subject of its reflection. This too derives in large measure from ancient Greek sensibilities. In a world of constant change, some Greek philosophers posited an unmoving, changeless, eternal source. Early Christian theologians seized on this presumption with dubious results, not least the attempt to subjugate whimsical passion to the service of an anchored intellect. This disjunction, however, would not survive for long in the crucible of a religious tradition built on the bodily passions of an incarnate savior.

Diarmuid O'Murchu agrees and goes even further by proposing bodily eroticism as the primary source for our theological reflection: "[T]he essence of the divine itself is characterized by sexual passion.

---

39. Robert Frost, *North of Boston* (New York: Henry Holt & Co., 1915), 3.

40. Christopher Lasch, *The Culture of Narcissism: American Life in an Age of Diminishing Expectations* (New York: W. W. Norton & Co., 1978), 9–10.

41. For some theological and ethical reflections on the retrieval of *Eros* in this way, see: Anne Bathurst Gilson, *Eros Breaking Free: Interpreting Sexual Theo-Ethics* (Cleveland, OH: The Pilgrim Press, 1995) and Carter Heyward, *Touching Our Strength: The Erotic as Power and the Love of God* (San Francisco: Harper and Row, 1989).

In the desiring of the flesh are the very desires of God. It is in the depths of our sexual ecstasy that we experience the real energy of God's creativity."[42] O'Murchu may sound bold and even excessive to modern Western Christians, yet not so much among many of the ancients. The early Christian mystic known as Pseudo-Dionysius, for example, insisted not merely on care, or compassion, or charity, or "brotherly" love as the essence of divine life, but nothing less than *Eros*. Wendy Farley would have us notice this astonishing claim percolating throughout Christian history in which mystics regularly encounter the God who has been "beguiled" by the beauty of creation and is thus eager to pour out divine goodness on all of it.[43]

Douglas Burton-Christie follows a similar trail in his analysis of medieval monastic communities and encourages us to recalibrate the typical view of monasticism as a denigration of the physical world, including its embodied passions. Rooted in a theological eschatology, medieval monks understood their *partial* withdrawal from the world as situating them at a point of intersection between this world and the next, between anticipation and fulfillment, a situation for which only the erotic language of desire can suffice. This helps to explain the near-obsession for so many in the medieval period with the biblical Song of Songs. Much like Griffin's analysis of *Eros*, Burton-Christie describes monastic consciousness as "occupying a liminal space," a space that makes the language of erotic encounter attractive to them. These monks "stand between worlds, know the kingdom to be 'already' and 'not yet,' know their beloved to be now present, now absent. . . . *Eros* in this sense expresses a longing not to leave one world for the other but to draw them together in a tender embrace."[44] That precise moment of longing, the yearning to draw together in an embrace, *that* is what Christians celebrate with "Eucharist."

Burton-Christie nonetheless worries about his own analysis. Uncritical retrievals of historical moments can betray us with a romanticized or even sanitized version of the past that more closely

---

42. O'Murchu, *The Transformation of Desire*, 104.

43. Farley, "Beguiled by Beauty," 135.

44. Burton-Christie, "Into the Body of Another," 22.

resembles nostalgia than history. Burton-Christie acknowledges, for example, how frequently Christian traditions have sublimated bodily eroticism beneath a veil of "spirituality." Disembodying *Eros* would not only horrify the Greeks but also do violence to the precarious space medieval monastics and mystics tried so assiduously to create. Attending carefully to these historical complexities highlights a challenge shared by twenty-first-century Christians and medieval monastics alike: how to embrace the bodily roots of human sensuality without reinforcing the legacy of shame that orbits around embodied existence.

Christian worship preserves an ancient resource to address that challenge: the ritual engagement with sensuous, bodily divinity at every shared meal of bread and wine. Rather than reducing encounters with God-in-Christ to this one moment, the Eucharist instead serves as a liturgical lens through which to see more clearly all the many other ecstatic, messy, evocative, and unpredictable engagements inspired by an incarnational faith, including sexual intimacy. Eucharist, in other words, can return us to our bodies.

Making that arduous trek of return will necessarily lead rather quickly through the biblical thickets of Genesis. To be sure, returning to physical embodiment by means of a text presents a rather circuitous route, yet it can prove illuminating. Desire remains so vexing in Western culture precisely because the human body itself provokes and confounds. That vexation stems equally from traditional deployments of Genesis in religious instruction and in various forms of popular culture, including the memes of online social media.[45] Even those who have never read the first three chapters of the Bible assume they know what they would find there if they did.

When Flip Wilson famously received laughs on 1970s' television by insisting that the "Devil made me do it," he reinforced the portrayal of God as primarily a rule-maker who cares mostly about whether or not we obey. Whenever politicians make "law and order" the centerpiece of a campaign, they repeat the image of human beings as natural-born transgressors inherently prone to disorderly conduct.

---

45. A simple Google search would yield many pages of images for these online memes. See also Theresa Sanders, *Approaching Eden: Adam and Eve in Popular Culture* (Lanham, MD: Rowman & Littlefield Publishers, 2009).

Whenever the news media devote more energy to the extra-marital dalliances of elected officials than their economic or social policies, human sinfulness once again resides primarily in our urges for sexual intimacy, which above all demand regulatory control. All of this distills in the assumptions so many harbor about Genesis and, by extension, the character of Christian witness to the Gospel.

Interrogating these assumptions invites a careful assessment of their origins. Do they reflect the voice of the ancient biblical writer speaking to us from so long ago or do they come instead from an early childhood reproof for being naked? Are we hearing in these cultural voices the echoes of adolescent hazing during puberty? Do we project our failed romantic encounters or perhaps an emotionally abusive marriage into our biblical interpretations? Do the wider social mechanisms of shame yank biblical texts into our cultural sensibilities? Refusing to see Adam and Eve's shame as our own leads frequently to projecting it on others, whether by casting African American men as the quintessential sexual predators or African American women as "welfare queens."[46]

The complex interweaving of Bible, theology, spirituality, and culture generates a cacophonous din of voices. Turning down the volume can help Christian communities hear that ancient story afresh. If we could ask the biblical writer to tell us the story again, we might hear about God as primarily a passionate creator, who cares mostly about taking delight in the creation and assuring that it thrives. We might hear a story about human beings naturally born for communion, for intimacy, and for love, the very image of their Creator. We might hear about the first divine gift of intimacy in bodily sexual encounter celebrated with a moment of joyous declaration: At last! This is bone of my bones and flesh of my flesh! (Genesis 2:23).

That version of the story could reorient its focus away from us and toward our Divine Source: a creative, passionate, and erotic God. The canon of Scripture, after all, begins not with human failure,

---

46. See James W. Perkinson's careful analysis of how cultural sensibilities and theological doctrines can work in concert to support white supremacy in the modern West, such as the connection between "salvation" and the prison-industrial-complex that sequesters "the black penis 'away' from the white vagina" (*White Theology: Outing Supremacy in Modernity* [New York: Palgrave Macmillan, 2004], 36).

or sexual shame and alienation, or violence and death; it does not even begin with human being at all. The Bible begins with God, the God who creates and who loves what God makes. Just as in our own passionate artistry, we can see in divine creativity the desire for self-expression and communication. Seeing this reveals still further God's own delight in God's creation, a delight that surfaces in the haunting observation God makes about the first human, who ought not to be alone (Genesis 2:18).

Haunting, because this creature is made in God's image; the creature who ought not to be alone reflects the Creator, for whom it is likewise not good to be alone. Haunting, because the divine cry in the garden—*Where are you?*—is not an accusation, but issues instead as a plea from a lover for the beloved. Haunting, because the divine gift of desire and the means for intimacy so quickly disappears, rejected by the ones to whom the gift was given.

The Bible begins with desire, the yearning for an end to loneliness, and the longing for communion. This is first and foremost God's desire and only then the hope rising up among the creatures God makes. Eugene Rogers helpfully clarifies this theological claim by stressing divine freedom. God *chose* the vulnerability of relationship, not out of any lack or necessity, but from the depths of divine desire. "God's need is God's *wish*," as Rogers puts it.[47] Virginia Ramey Mollenkott makes the same point, highlighting both divine *and* human freedom. Biblical writers, she notes, consistently portray a God who relinquishes control over the human race, choosing to woo Israel into relationship and yearning for the mutuality born from our own free choice.[48] Only then, by starting with this image of an erotic God, do the events in Genesis 3 appear truly tragic: Who told you to be ashamed? This question cuts to the heart of human distress, not because sex itself is shameful, but because shame subverts the intimacy for which God makes us and from which God seeks a loving response.

---

47. Eugene F. Rogers, "Sanctification, Homosexuality, and God's Triune Life," in *Theology and Sexuality: Classic and Contemporary Readings*, ed. Eugene F. Rogers (Malden, MA: Blackwell Publishing, 2002), 221.

48. Virginia Ramey Mollenkott, *Sensuous Spirituality: Out from Fundamentalism*, rev. ed. (Cleveland, OH: The Pilgrim Press, 2008), 61.

This reading of Genesis can inspire us to live as embodied crea-tures of an erotic God, a life of pursuing the hope of divine commu-nion. In the course of that pursuit we will regularly seek forgiveness when we make a mistake, and even more the loving intimacy of union with others. Reading that ancient story afresh can then clarify the yearning that makes us human: to be at home in our bodies with-out shame, at home with other bodies without guilt, and at home with God without fear.

Focusing our worship on the erotic God portrayed in Genesis sets us on a homeward journey that forgiveness initiates as an indis-pensable first step. That step, as L. William Countryman describes it, "gives us space to live and to learn, and it frees us from the temp-tation to credit our own goodness for too much. God forgives us because that was and is the most liberating thing God could do for us. It is the starting place for everything else."[49] As the wider world that forgiveness creates begins to feel like home, Rowan Williams suggests what can take us even farther along that path: "The whole story of creation, incarnation, and our incorporation into the fel-lowship of Christ's body tells us that God desires us."[50] Not merely tolerated, not only forgiven, but also *desired*. Desire itself offers the startling balm we need to heal bodily shame at the Eucharistic Table, that simple meal where Christians declare this about God: "In your infinite love you made us for yourself."

FINE LINEN AND CANDLES

At the end of a long week of work, Sophia happily prepares for a special weekend meal. She takes out the laundered white linen and centers it on the table, gently smoothing out the wrinkles. After retrieving two silver candleholders from the cabinet, she polishes away two small spots of tarnish. She is eager to see how the flickering light from the recently purchased beeswax candles will play off the linen and silver. The simple meal will not require much fussing in the kitchen, but she takes care to have fresh-baked bread and a bottle of

---

49. L. William Countryman, *Forgiven and Forgiving* (Harrisburg, PA: Morehouse Publishing, 1998), 18.

50. Williams, "The Body's Grace," 59.

red wine on hand. Sophia then checks the music selections one more time; rather than just incidental to enjoying a shared meal, she knows that music can set a proper tone and mood. She feels a bit weary, but also pleased. She has been looking forward to this meal all week.

Sophia could be anticipating a romantic Saturday night dinner for two in her own home. We might also imagine her as a priest in a sacristy, preparing for Sunday morning Eucharist at her local parish. Contemporary Western society has made it increasingly difficult to notice what these two tables share in common. In a fast-food culture of overworked families, fewer people today attend carefully to the details of elaborate dinner parties, except perhaps during holiday seasons. Michael Pollan cites research suggesting that among eighteen- to fifty-year old Americans, roughly one-fifth of all eating takes place in a car. A large segment of Americans, in other words, eat nearly one out of every five meals in front of an automobile dashboard.[51] In a society where it is becoming rarer for families and friends to share meals together, the spiritual significance of doing so on a Sunday morning dwindles.

The earliest Christian communities rooted their ritual approaches to Eucharist not only in the Last Supper but also in the many other meals Jesus shared with a wide array of often unlikely guests. These early Eucharistic communities appreciated rather directly the importance of viewing all the many tables around which they gathered on a daily basis through the lens of the one Table they shared on Sunday mornings. Sara Miles found that connection startling when she realized that her congregation distributed food to homeless people from the same Table on which they celebrated Eucharist. She considers her conversion to Christian faith even more startling, prompted in large measure by supposing that her love for cooking, eating, and sharing food is the same love displayed in the Eucharist.[52]

Preparing and sharing food with friends or with a romantic partner reflects erotic desire for an often overlooked reason—when I do that, I feel desirable; I hope in turn that I make others feel the same way. When shared, food carries with it a potent reminder, not only of

51. Pollan, *In Defense of Food*, 188–89.

52. Sara Miles, *Take this Bread: A Radical Conversion* (New York: Ballantine Books, 2007).

the essential sustenance each of us needs to survive, but even more of the love and affection all of us need to thrive. Thriving communities—Christian or not—will need continually to address the need to make the promise of forgiveness tangible. Yet every member of thriving communities needs still more: the assurance of being wanted. Rowan Williams takes this insight into the heart of Gospel proclamation. If the One Story declares quite remarkably that God *desires* us, then this sets an agenda for Christian ministry. "The life of the Christian community has as its rationale—if not invariably its practical reality—the task of teaching us so to order our relations that human beings may see themselves as desired, as the occasion for joy."[53]

Imagine God taking as much delight in human flesh as we are sometimes fortunate enough to do ourselves. Most of us take the skin covering our bones for granted, except perhaps when we bruise it or cut it—or perhaps when a friend grabs our hands in a moment of crisis, or our fingers intertwine with the fingers of a beloved partner. Human flesh feels remarkably soft and resilient, creased and textured, smooth and supple. Human flesh comes in a stunning array of colors for which just "black" and "white" seem terribly crude. Pink, mocha, tan, auburn, chocolate—these are just a few of the tints and tones of the flesh that can occasion joy for us, *and* for the God who made it, the One who then offers that same flesh back to us as a gift at the Table.

In a world that runs on the modest hope that human beings might merely tolerate one another in the midst of cultural obsessions over youth and celebrity, I imagine very few people today seeing themselves as "desired" or their very own flesh as "occasions for joy." I imagine something else as well. Williams' deceptively simple rationale for Christian community suggests that desire itself imbues the cosmos of God's creation with erotic energy. I imagine this as a world-changing claim.

Imagine those in the upper classes of material wealth in the United States acting as if they desired to be in relationship with those living below the poverty line. Imagine married "heterosexual" couples with children expressing their desire for including lesbian and

---

53. Williams, "The Body's Grace," 59.

gay people in their lives. Imagine white politicians putting their own careers on the line to ensure that people of color enjoy the full range of rights due to every citizen of the United States. Imagine African Americans expressing a deep desire for relationship, friendship, and intimacy with White Americans. Some of these moments may be easier to imagine than others, yet the Gospel invites all of them and many other imaginative musings around a shared Table. The Gospel invites Christians to imagine what it would mean so to "order our relations" with one another that each of us would know unquestionably that we are not merely tolerated, not only forgiven, but also *desired.* Making such imagination a reality would change the world, just as Luke apparently supposed when he described the earliest Christians "turning the world upside down" (Acts 17:6).

Christians in the United States face particular challenges in living this Eucharistic spirituality of desire. For most of U.S. history, White people have considered Black flesh by definition undesirable. The systematic sequestering of Native Americans on reservations kept "red" flesh safely out of mainstream view. The nineteenth-century war with Mexico and the twentieth-century war with Japan rendered "brown" flesh and "yellow" flesh at least suspicious, if not inherently threatening. Could *all* flesh occasion moments of joy? The challenges inherent to that question deepen whenever we assume that our lives of sexual intimacy with a chosen partner remain roped off from public scrutiny. Public cultural sensibilities actually influence the desires that lead us to those moments of ostensibly private encounter; those intimacies, in turn, inform our engagements with social, economic, and political policies.[54] Perhaps we begin more simply by imagining sexually intimate couples recognizing their love for each other as a spiritual gift for ministries of generosity. Simple perhaps, but also central to biblical portrayals of a faithful life marked by hospitality to strangers.[55]

---

54. Kelly Brown Douglas analyzes this complex interweaving of culture, politics, and religion by noting the bodily price paid for what she calls the "narrative of civility" in the Black church and its implications for sexuality and politics (*Black Bodies and the Black Church: A Blues Slant*) [New York: Palgrave Macmillan, 2012]).

55. See Amos Yong's study of biblical hospitality and its significance for today's multicultural and interreligious conversations in *Hospitality and the Other: Pentecost, Christian Practices, and the Neighbor* (Maryknoll, NY: Orbis Books, 2008), especially his treatment of Eucharist as a location for evangelism as intimate hospitality (134–37).

Desire, pain, joy, and frustration—all of these and more reside together in the complex textures of human sensuality and relationality. These complexities reside at the very heart of Christian faith and in the spiritual practice of sharing a meal with others, both friend and stranger alike. The sensuality of our relations and our worship as Christians can bear witness to the startling declaration of the Gospel: God makes God's own self vulnerable to the fickle whims and glorious triumphs of bodily human life. The Eucharist focuses Christian attention precisely there, where God offers divine life as bread and wine as bodily occasions for joy.

These ancient claims and insights invite Christians to return to our bodies as sources of spiritual insight and transformation; not the shameful bodies so many have been taught to fear but the luminous bodies of God's own erotic handiwork. One might suppose that such an embodied practice would unfold with some ease in an incarnational religious tradition, yet Christians have always struggled with it. The Christological controversies of the first four centuries turned often to the question of embodiment. Was Jesus God and only *appeared* to be human? Was Jesus fully human and only later "adopted" as God's son? These questions continue to animate Christian reflection as we ponder what in the world we do, theologically speaking, with the body of Jesus—and therefore what we do with our own.

William Temple, theologian and Archbishop of Canterbury during World War II, succinctly framed the incarnational point when he described Christianity as the most materialistic of all religions.[56] Temple sought with this provocation to affirm as a matter of Christian principle the centrality of physical realty itself, including our bodies, not as that which we must overcome for the sake of a truly spiritual life but rather to be embraced, just as God embraced it in the life, death, and resurrection of Jesus of Nazareth.[57]

Incarnational theological reflection remains a vital first step before crafting rules, regulations, and policies for sexual behavior. Debating

---

56. William Temple, *Readings in St. John's Gospel* (London: Macmillan & Company, Ltd., 1959), xx.

57. Taking the body seriously in Christian theology took an important leap forward with the work of James Nelson. See his *Embodiment: An Approach to Sexuality and Christian Theology* (Philadelphia: Augsburg Publishing House, 1978).

only what kind of sexual activity a community permits or prohibits simply absolves us from addressing our circuitous and entangled bodily navigations with others. To speak authentically of "incarnation" at all in Christian faith and practice will mean speaking concretely and particularly about our very own bodies. In this way among many others, sexual intimacy can energize and even revitalize our spiritual engagements with Eucharist; after all, sex resists abstractions. Christians might be able to speak rather vaguely about "embodiment," but very little remains theoretical when interacting as lovingly as we can with a naked human being. Bjorn Krondorfer takes this further by stressing the importance of *particular* bodies as theologically and spiritually relevant. Rather than the idealized body, the body of Greco-Roman statuary or the body of neo-Jungian archetypes, the body Krondorfer invites us to consider is resolutely "real," and therefore vulnerable: "itching, aging, flowing, hurting, loving, dying, smelling, praying . . . growing fat, getting sick."[58] In and as that kind of body, the Gospel invites us to see ourselves as desired and occasions for joy.

Eucharistic spirituality can, in turn, help to illumine the dynamics of our intimate sexual relationships. We are not the source of our own lives nor even the meaning we may wish to ascribe to life itself. We are made by another, the creative Source of life, which we can at least begin to realize better in the complexities of finding ourselves "made" in sexual intimacy. These encounters, either fleeting or lifelong, lead us "into the knowledge that our identity is being made in the relations of bodies, not by the private exercise of will or fantasy." Being formed by the loving delight of another, in other words, can teach us about "being the object of the causeless, loving delight of God."[59]

Setting a table with fine linen and candles—we might do this for a shared meal with an intimate partner and we might do this for sharing a meal of divine encounter. The differences between the two gracefully blur in the light of that hope for which God, our Creator, makes us: Divine Communion.

---

58. Bjorn Krondorfer, ed., *Men's Bodies, Men's Gods: Male Identities in a (Post-) Christian Culture* (New York: New York University Press, 1996), 15.

59. Williams, "The Body's Grace," 64–65.

2

Fall

CARNAL WISDOM AND SPIRITUAL FOLLY

But we turned against you,
and betrayed your trust;
and we turned against one another. . . .
Again and again, you called us to return.

—"*EUCHARISTIC PRAYER C*"
THE BOOK OF COMMON PRAYER

ince the first century of Christian traditions, the Church has included bread and wine among the essential elements of Eucharist. Few would imagine using graham crackers and cranberry juice instead, especially when retrieved from a vending machine in the visiting room of a state prison. Would those elements constitute a "valid" Eucharist? Would the location? Do either of those questions have anything to do with sexual intimacy?

In the 1990s, the seminary where I was teaching admitted a prison inmate as a student. He had completed an undergraduate degree by correspondence and had by then already served as a lay chaplain in the correctional system. He had also been convicted of second-degree murder. These circumstances posed first the question of *whether* he should be admitted and then *how* the school would welcome him from a distance into our community of spiritual and vocational formation. Pastoral questions likewise occurred to those of us who visited him in the prison, including whether and how to celebrate the Eucharist with him in that setting. Could it be done without an altar, without paten or chalice, without what the Church has always considered the "matter of the sacrament"—bread and wine? Could I respond to the eager desire of a prisoner for Eucharist without any of the things that usually make the Eucharist recognizable? Theologically and pastorally the answer is yes, even with graham crackers and cranberry juice.[1]

That inmate became one of my students and eventually a good friend. One of the gifts of this relationship has been an enriched understanding of the Gospel and how it responds to the abiding hope for communion, which came vividly to light in the physical structures and regulatory regimes of a prison. Gaining access to that prison's visiting room usually took more than an hour of screenings and passing through multiple checkpoints just to catch a glimpse of this socially sequestered population. Once there, three features of that visiting room always made a deep impression. The first was the size of the tables and chairs; they were designed for elementary school students. I learned the reason for this on my first visit when my knees bumped against my chest while sitting at those tables: it prevented the passing of contraband from visitor to prisoner under the table. Second, the room's design, including the elevated guard-perch, served not only to curtail the exchange of material goods but also the exchange of physical intimacy—extended embraces, kisses, and hand-holding between couples. And third, the relatively few windows sat so close to the ceiling as to prevent any view of the surrounding landscape. Even the outdoor space attached to the visiting room, while roofless, sported ten-foot walls that blocked any scenery from flooding into the concrete-block enclosure.

Life in prison, for both inmate and visitor alike, dissolves nearly every means of human intimacy, with other humans and with the world of God's creation. The dissolution of intimacy provides a powerful theological reminder about *sin*, which involves much more than simply breaking a particular rule; sin marks the tragedy of broken relationship. To be sure, most prisoners deserve incarceration for failing to abide by the law. Broken rules, however, present only a

---

1. Louis Weil provides a helpful analysis of that very moment by noting that those engaged in it "knew Christ present in their midst, and they ate and drank in memory of him as Christians have done since the Lord's resurrection" (*A Theology of Worship*, The New Church's Teaching Series [Cambridge, MA: Cowley Publications, 2002], 114).

symptom of their underlying dis-ease: the unraveling of the social fabric that weaves us together in community. Incarceration actually perpetuates that unraveling at nearly every turn. Rather than any "correctional" function, the regulatory alienation from one's own bodily goodness in that environment serves mostly to punish, and mostly by shaming.[2]

These institutional conditions and regulations made the celebration of Eucharist with graham crackers and cranberry juice one of the more illuminating moments of my priestly vocation. There, sitting at an absurdly little table in an uncomfortably small chair, the Eucharistic prayer rang with startling clarity. It did so, on the one hand, with a powerful statement of reality—"we turned against you and we turned against one another"—and even more as a declaration of hope—"again and again, you called us to return."[3] If the Gospel cannot be proclaimed and the Eucharist celebrated at that tiny prison table, then it means very little anywhere else. The essence of the Gospel beckons unabashedly among those who have broken relational trust, whose relationships lie in tatters, who are separated from physical intimacy with other human beings and even visual intimacy with the natural world of God's creation.

State prisons reproduce institutionally what the biblical writer of Genesis portrays as the result of shame, the alienation from our bodily goodness that curtails and even prevents intimacy. Christian traditions refer to this moment in Genesis 3 as "The Fall." We might more accurately and pointedly refer to it as "The Severing"—the separation from all avenues for intimate communion with other humans, with the natural world around us, and with God. Every visit I made to that prison only underscored the despair depicted in that biblical story—isolation and alienation are synonymous with violence and death. Adam and Eve's exile from Eden mapped visually what had already happened inwardly; their means for communion had withered and only the barest hope of its recovery remained. The biblical writer leaves little room for doubt about these tragic effects: one

---

2. J. Denny Weaver believes the criminal justice system itself constitutes a form of violence by perpetuating the notion that justice is achieved through punishment (*The Nonviolent Atonement*, second ed. [Grand Rapids, MI: The William B. Eerdmans Publishing Company, 2011], 8–9).

3. BCP, "Eucharistic Prayer C," 370.

of the first post-exilic stories features fratricide (Genesis 4:1–16). Sin matters both more and less than its typical presentations in institutional Christianity. Self-styled liberal or progressive communities hesitate to mention sin at all for the sake of those who have fallen prey to its institutional abuses, whether as single mothers, lesbian and gay people, or the victims of domestic violence—not to mention those languishing in prisons.[4] Churches considered more "conservative" tend to emphasize humanity's sinfulness and even utter depravity as the central motif in Christianity's theological logic, often illustrated with a list of sexual perversions—some of them punishable, and rightly so, with imprisonment.[5]

Given the prominence of sex in Christian approaches to sin—whether as an affirmation of the unqualified goodness of sex or as a warning about its inherent danger—the perception of sin itself will chart the particular path Christians take to the Eucharistic Table. What do we anticipate encountering in that shared meal of bread and wine? If the stress falls on forgiveness alone, the frustrated desire for intimacy may well remain unaddressed. Stressing our shared goodness as God's creatures, by contrast, could easily overlook the fractured intimacies so many bring with them to that Table. God indeed calls us, again and again, to return. But return to what, or where, or to whom?

The severity of Genesis 3—the *severing* of intimate relations—raises communion itself as an ensign over every celebration of the Eucharist, the singular hope of human life. Forgiveness may and often does initiate a return to communion, but this alone fails to heal The Severing. What each of us needs in addition already resides in our bodies, the graced creations of God that convey us to the Eucharistic Table. We can intuit that source of healing every time we share a delectable meal with friends and family. Sharing food in response to bodily desire displays a deep carnal wisdom that urges

---

4. Protestant Liberalism more generally since the nineteenth century has exhibited this kind of approach that stresses social transformation rather than individual forgiveness (see Robin R. Meyers, *Saving Jesus from the Church: How to Stop Worshipping Christ and Start Following Jesus* [New York: HarperCollins, 2009]).

5. Michael Mangis stops short of prioritizing sexuality in his treatment of human sinfulness but he does suggest that sexual sins "wound us more deeply" than any other because they "strike at the core" of God's image in us (*Signature Sins: Taming Our Wayward Hearts* [Downers Grove, IL: InterVarsity Press, 2008], 45).

bodily encounters with the world of God's creation; the same wisdom prompts even closer intimate relations with a beloved partner. Whether a given meal satisfies our hunger for food or a more intimate encounter fulfills our longing for sexual union matters less than the bodily desire itself that led us to those moments. Attending carefully to that bodily wisdom carries the potential to transform our interactions with each other and, more widely, with Earth itself and the food it produces on which we rely. This potential, infused with divine grace, animates the witness Christians offer in every shared meal of bread and wine. The grace of that Table enables more, however, than only animating our witness. As we gather at that Table, God makes something new from what we bring to it—enemies become friends and friends become family in a community devoted to communion itself.

Bodily desire can, of course, just as easily cause us to stumble as it can awaken hopeful practice. Few need to read the third chapter of Genesis to realize how far every human society continues to fall from carnal wisdom and the richness of bodily intimacy. We can measure that fallen distance in every rape crisis center, with every drive-by shooting in our cities, and among the wreckage of the latest environmental catastrophe. The failure and fracturing of intimacy surround us at every turn whether or not anyone has ever read the first three chapters of the Bible. Yet that ancient story can still provoke and inspire, can still shape and inform, can still name what frustrates us and still animate our hope.

Living still in the wake of The Severing—or "East of Eden," as John Steinbeck famously described it[6]—the vitality of Christian faith today will draw from the evocative power of the One Story, the deep desire and abiding hope for divine communion. I do not mean that this story will energize programs for "church growth" or that telling the story will mount successful refutations of the cultural popularity of atheism. By "vitality" I mean that the future of planetary thriving hangs on that very story, a story that describes God's own creative, redeeming, and sustaining mission to call all creatures to the Table of Divine Communion. In that great work Christians today bear a particular responsibility,

---

6. John Steinbeck, *East of Eden* (New York: The Viking Press, 1952).

first to affirm the goodness of humanity's carnal wisdom, but also to acknowledge the tragic consequences of denying that bodily goodness. Christians bear this dual responsibility in part because too many continue to demonize the fleshiness of God's creation and just as many naively valorize the glories of bodily existence.

Human life exhibits a complex intertwining of carnal wisdom and what we might call "spiritual folly." Christian witness will indeed appear spiritually foolish if we declare bodily life either unreservedly good or irredeemably corrupt. Stressing one at the expense of the other will not only seem foolish to many, it will also fail to inspire the vocation of Christian communities to live as "repairers of the breach," to evoke the prophet Isaiah (58:12), or to recall Paul's classic description, to live with faith, and hope, and most especially love (1 Corinthians 13:13). To live, that is, as witnesses to the hope for communion in the wake of The Severing, the hope of living more fully into that intimacy on which all creatures of the erotic God depend for our thriving. This shared vocation may lodge at first in our personally intimate relationships, but then extend further into our socio-political engagements, yet further still in our ecological stewardship, and thus, in the end, in our union with God. The grace required to live in this calling would also make it honest, an acknowledgement that all have "turned against one another" even as God continually beckons all to return.

God does call us to return, but there is no "going back." Those who long for restoring Eden fail to grasp the consequences of sin, or that fracturing of relationship that American philosopher of religion Josiah Royce called the "irrevocable deed."[7] Royce certainly appreciated the importance of forgiveness in mending torn relationships; he appreciated even more the impossibility of turning the clock back to that moment before the fracturing occurred. Soothing the pain of irrevocable deeds will always require more than mercy and absolution. That "more," or what Royce evoked with his image of the "Beloved Community," requires something fresh and new born from the very circumstances that originally caused the distress. Eden is thus forever

---

7. See Josiah Royce, *The Problem of Christianity*, 2 volumes. New York: The Macmillan Company, 1913; reprint, one volume edition, with an introduction by John E. Smith (Chicago: The University of Chicago Press, 1968), 143–63.

gone; but the hope of the "heavenly Jerusalem" persists. God's passionate plea to return is not a nostalgic glance backward, but a call to live forward, to renew our commitment to that Great Work of God in building the Beloved Community with, among, and in our bodily relations—an anticipation of the heavenly Jerusalem itself.

Living here and now, "East of Eden," that Great Work will mean paying renewed attention to the "breach" so many experience in their sexually intimate lives. Speaking honestly about the painful complexities of intimacy creates a credible space for speaking meaningfully of bodily wisdom. After making some observations about each of these, I want to suggest that the intertwining of the two can offer a fruitful way to approach the Eucharistic Table holistically, with painful memories intact yet also soothed by a hope refreshed.

THE TROUBLE WITH SEX

Sex comes with plenty of trouble, even in the midst of its pleasures and ecstasies. No one needs a theory of sin to see or know the trouble sex can create. The trouble ranges from comic miscommunications to violent abuse or simply the failure to connect moments of physical pleasure with hoped-for relational companionship. Few would imagine that sex comes with any trouble at all, however, if the contemporary advertising industry were the only source of data. Billboards, magazine ads, television commercials, and pop-up windows on websites all peddle sex—or rather, they use sex to peddle products. Commercial advertising would collapse without its capacity to make sex seem naturally satisfying, if not thrilling, and even the apex of human fulfillment. Sex sells, Michael Mangis notes, because "lust and greed are natural partners."[8]

Christian theology has not escaped this wildly unreasonable exultation of sexual intimacy. After many decades and even centuries of demonizing particular sexual acts and, by extension, those who commit them, modern Christian churches stood in desperate need of rehabilitating sex itself as worthy of more than just regulatory policies. Most of the gay and lesbian theological projects that emerged in the

---

8. Mangis, *Signature Sins*, 44.

latter third of the twentieth century embraced that challenge by arguing for the goodness of sex as a divine gift, a means for divine encounter and spiritual insight.[9] Several mainline Protestant denominations likewise convened task forces on human sexuality that produced statements, educational materials, and pamphlets emphasizing the inherent goodness of sexual intimacy as a theological principle.[10] These publications and committees made astonishing leaps forward, not only for lesbian and gay people but also for the whole Church. Those leaps, however, came with a price that many were unwilling to pay. Reveling in the goodness of sex strikes more than a few as a half-truth.

The credibility of Christian witness to the Gospel requires a deep level of honesty and transparency about our own bodies and bodily relations. In the wake of centuries of Christian obfuscation around sex and sexuality, clergy and theologians today need to speak openly about the twin capacities of sexual intimacy to occasion both insightful pleasure and debilitating trauma alike. The One Story inspires us not by focusing *either* on the goodness of sex *or* on sexual failings, but instead on their complex entanglements. To tell the truth theologically and spiritually in an age of celebrity glamor, teenage "sexting," and international sex trafficking, we can begin, modestly enough, by acknowledging the troubling vexations and recurring disappointments in sexual intimacy. Attending more carefully to at least four interrelated sources of sexual consternation can make theological claims about the goodness of sex sound at least more plausible if not enticingly hopeful.

Touch Deprivation

Since at least the 1970s, medical professionals have stressed the importance of human touch for infants. While all five physical senses are important, some studies suggest that only touch proves essential for life itself. Without consistent physical intimate contact, newborn babies experience what physicians call a failure to thrive; this failure can in

---

9. See Elizabeth Stuart, *Gay and Lesbian Theologies: Repetitions with Critical Difference* (Hampshire, England: Ashgate, 2003), esp. ch. 2, "Gay Is Good," 15–32.

10. See, for example, "Keeping Body and Soul Together: Sexuality, Spirituality and Social Justice" (Presbyterian Church USA, 1991), and "Sexuality: A Divine Gift—A Sacramental Approach to Human Sexuality and Family Life" (The Episcopal Church, 1987).

some cases lead to death.[11] The importance of this insight for young children has yet to extend more widely among adults, who likewise need physical touch for our well-being. Contemporary Western society has been suffering from serious touch deprivation for quite some time, and likely many of us are failing to thrive as a result. This failure has been compounded by the danger now associated more widely with "touching." The still unfolding clergy sex-abuse crisis as well as sexual improprieties in private boarding schools and universities have rendered "touching" synonymous with nearly any unwanted and inappropriate physical contact, genital or not. The quick association so many make between "touch" and "genitals" in this cultural climate speaks volumes about the challenge—and thus also the opportunity— to speak more clearly of a broader view of sexual intimacy as well as the theological and spiritual implications of that expanded perspective. Pastors, counselors, and teachers can begin seizing that opportunity by acknowledging how the depth of Western society's touch-deprivation puts even more pressure on genital sexual intimacy to meet all of our needs for physical touch. Sex cannot possibly bear that burden, which so often contributes to both its dissatisfactions and confusions.

Risk and Vulnerability

The advent of HIV and AIDS in the United States in the early 1980s generated public health campaigns promoting "safe sex." These campaigns soon modified their message by promoting more reasonably "safer" sex to acknowledge the impossibility of removing absolutely all risk of bodily infection from sexual intimacy. To restrict these messages to the risks associated with bacteria and viruses, however, overlooks an equally significant emotional challenge in making sex "safer." Desire itself always carries risk because desire makes us vulnerable. Sex is an offering of the self, even in casual encounters, and very little can protect us from the potential of looking silly or feeling unwanted. Recalling Rowan Williams' observations, bodily miscommunication can happen more quickly and with more serious

---

11. The controversial experiments on monkeys by Harry Harlow in the 1960s provided a breakthrough in the understanding of human touch for both physical and emotional health. See Deborah Blum, *Love at Goon Park: Harry Harlow and the Science of Affection* (New York: Perseus Publishing, 2002).

consequences than verbal miscommunication. "Nothing will stop sex from being tragic and comic," Williams writes. "It is above all the area of our lives where we can be rejected in our bodily entirety, where we can venture into 'exposed spontaneity' . . . and find ourselves looking foolish or repellent."[12]

Christian history bears ample witness to the risks inherent to bodily vulnerability *and* why such risks litter the trail toward divine encounter and communion. John Blevins, for example, credits risk-aversion for the frequent turn to *agape* in Christian theology rather than *Eros*. The untamable and even ambiguous character of our erotic lives, he notes, frequently resists the clarity and unanimity that the Church has so often sought to promote in sexual ethics; *agape* seems safer and easier to control. Seeking to manage the perplexities inherent to erotic desire, however, not only sidesteps the "tragic and comic" in our sexual intimacies; it also subverts the spiritual insights that often accompany those encounters. Blevins cites an ancient Christian mystic known as Pseudo-Dionysius, who made no sharp theological distinction between the love known as *agape* and the desire of *Eros*. The mystical insight, as Blevins notes, proves startling: God desires to know us just as much as we desire to know God; even more, and like so many of our human intimacies, what we will know in that divine encounter cannot be known in advance.[13]

Sexual intimacy will always come with risk; this is also true for religious and spiritual practice. God's own vulnerable self-offering at the Eucharistic Table beckons us toward that kind of relational life, not of absolute safety but of sharing the risk of approaching the unknown.

The Binary Gender System

Contemporary Western society lives with a relatively new way to categorize the human species that most people today assume stretches back to the dawn of time. This new mode of categorization neatly divides human beings into two *kinds*—male or female—rather than supposing that men and women are different *types* of human being. Thomas

12. Williams, "The Body's Grace," 62.

13. John Blevins, "Uncovering the Eros of God," *Theology and Sexuality* 13:3 (2007), 289–300.

Laqueur refers to this shift as a culturally generated "biology of incommensurability" that sought ways to argue scientifically and not merely socially for a strict separation of gender roles.[14] The implications of this binary gender system extend into nearly every arena, from social policy and economics to religious institutions and even ecology. This system, of course, makes a profound impact on our interpersonal relationships as well, informing and shaping every sexual encounter with a host of both explicit and implicit assumptions concerning power and control, dominance and passivity, aggression and acquiescence.

These socio-scientific assumptions actually structure our intimate encounters by shaping, both bodily and emotionally, the self we believe we are offering to another as well as the self we might receive from another. Our deepest and most closely held desires spring in large measure from this structural, binary system of gendered relationships, which we in turn bring with us in various ways to Eucharistic celebrations. Largely left unspoken, the dynamics at that Table can scramble the gendered character of offering and receiving, of active giving and passive reception—perhaps especially when a woman presides at that celebration. Eucharistic relations, in other words, carry the potential to loosen the categorical boxes so often placed around "male" and "female" that can, and just as often, hamper the relational intimacies we seek; our bodies mean more and carry far more mysterious insights than those boxes can define, which sexually intimate partners often intuit.[15]

Sex Is Not Like Pizza

An organizer of a conference on sexuality and spirituality introduced one of the plenary speakers by telling a joke. "Sex is like pizza," he said. "Even when it's bad, it's still pretty good." The awkward silence that followed indicated a savvy audience; they knew that the premise of the joke was not true. While mediocre pizza can still prove modestly satisfying, when sex feels bad or wrong, it can feel *really* bad, and with few, if any, redeeming qualities. Like an "open secret" in Western

---

14. Laqueur, *Making Sex,* 35.

15. See Elizabeth Stuart, "Sacramental Flesh," in *Queer Theology: Rethinking the Western Body*, ed. Gerard Loughlin (Oxford: Blackwell Publishing, 2007), 65–75.

culture, few want to admit what most of us have heard or experienced: sex frequently draws social power games into its orbit; it fuels and becomes an occasion for both physical and emotional abuse; and even when a sexual encounter proves satisfying, it rarely lives up to the cultural hype surrounding it. In the time it takes the average reader to finish reading this page, at least two women will have been physically battered in the United States, most likely by an intimate partner.[16] That shocking statistical reality also means that every Christian congregation includes a good number of sexually battered people, even though most of them will never make that personal history known. Sexual abuse of any kind will not only inflect our bodily intimacies with others but also our participation in shared patterns of worship, including the memory of bodily trauma evoked at the Eucharistic Table.[17] In addition to explicit trauma, more than a few people worry about themselves when sex does not feel pleasurable or when they seem to have little interest in it or when they wonder whether there might be something a bit more to hope for, even after an enjoyable encounter.

The January 2013 issue of *Psychology Today* ventured into many of these areas of socio-sexual analysis by featuring an extensive overview of a recent book by Alain de Botton. The magazine's editors organized their summary around the secrets and hidden desires of human sexuality.[18] The secrets include the sexual fantasies that most people resist sharing for fear that others would find them troubling, if not dangerous or even disgusting. The desires include the unusual places where people imagine having sexual intercourse or how often they think about having sex or what they might prefer to wear—and then remove or use for bodily pleasure. Given the untamable qualities of sexual desire, which can sometimes induce inappropriately risky behavior or sexual addictions, de Botton advocates for setting limits, and proposed important reasons for regulating sexual activity. He then named religion as the perfect candidate for that limit-setting, regulatory function.

---

16. See the Office on Violence Against Women in the U.S. Department of Justice: *www. ovw.usdoj.gov*.

17. See Beth R. Crisp, "Spirituality and Sexual Abuse: Issues and Dilemmas for Survivors," *Theology and Sexuality* 13:3 (2007), 301–14.

18. Alain de Botton, *How to Think More about Sex* (London: Macmillan Publishers, 2012).

Historically, religion has indeed proposed limits for human sexual activity, sometimes even successfully. Yet even when it appears positively as a limit-setting guide in the pages of an otherwise secular magazine, an unspoken gap widens between religious instruction and how people actually live—with hidden secrets and desires. Articulating behavioral rules alone will nearly always fail to address the perplexities that generated the need for regulation in the first place. Before regulatory monitoring, religion ought to stand ready to assist us in our attempts to make meaning from the bodily desires for intimacy, hidden or otherwise. To do so here and now, "East of Eden," challenges us not to return to that paradisical garden, but to seek hope from the severing of intimacy that occurred there. The biblical writer in Genesis brilliantly provided that very challenge.

SAGACIOUS SERPENTS

The "Fall" of Adam and Eve in Genesis 3 sets in motion a horrifying expansion of their alienation from bodily goodness best described as "The Severing." It begins when they cover their genitals, the most obvious source of bodily communion. This covering quickly expands as they try to hide behind a tree, to hide not only from the evening breeze of their garden paradise but also from their Creator. As this biblical chapter unfolds, Adam and Eve find themselves expelled from the garden and suddenly at odds with their environment that no longer feels "natural"—Adam must toil and sweat to produce food while Eve must groan in pain to bear any offspring (Genesis 3:16–19). These distinctions between male and female illustrate The Severing even further—mutuality collapses, not only in their interactions with each other but also in the disparate consequences each now faces as a result. Their exile from Eden, rather than an arbitrary punishment for breaking a rule, makes geographically visible the depth of their separation from each other and from the rest of God's creation—a severing initiated by bodily, sexual shame. In short, the tragedy of Genesis 3 depicts the daisy-chain effects of alienating ourselves from carnal wisdom, from the insights that reside in our bodies, precisely where the Creator planted them.

The ancient storyteller in Genesis offers a rather peculiar source for this bodily insight. The narrator does this with a dramatic shift at the beginning of the third chapter. Prior to this, the story in the first two chapters features God as the primary actor. As chapter three begins, however, the spotlight shifts to one of the Creator's creatures. Depending on the English translation of this biblical text, the creature that seizes center stage in Genesis 3 is the most "subtle" or the most "crafty" and "clever" of all the creatures in the Garden. Some later traditions would invite us to imagine this creature as the most lovely and attractive and therefore brimming with desire. The ancient Greek translation of Genesis 3:1 portrays this creature as wise, as "sagacious." This creature was a serpent.

The peculiar wisdom of this creature appears in just a few short verses in the text, yet it reveals a crucial insight into the human condition. John the Evangelist apparently agreed with that assessment by featuring this creature rather prominently in another widely familiar biblical text—the third chapter of the Gospel according to John. Both Christians and non-Christians have at least heard about that chapter with reference to being "born again" (3:7) and the classic declaration that "God so loved the world" (3:16). Between these two verses John inserts an odd biblical image. "Just as Moses lifted up the serpent in the wilderness, so must the Son of Man be lifted up" (3:14). Why would John have Jesus pair himself so closely with the image of a serpent?

John may have had the third chapter of Genesis in mind as he scripted the encounter between Jesus and Nicodemus. In that chapter, the sagacious serpent asks Eve a question: "Did God say, 'You shall not eat from any tree in the garden?'"

Oh, no, Eve responds, "we may eat of the fruit of the trees in the garden; but God said, 'You shall not eat of the fruit of the tree that is in the middle of the garden, nor shall you touch it, or you shall die.'"

The serpent then begs to differ with a response that may well describe the source of human distress ever since: "You will not die; for God knows that when you eat of it your eyes will be opened, and you will be like God, knowing good and evil."

Note that nothing in this poignant exchange paints that serpent as Satan or the "devil." That association comes much later, mostly in Christian interpretations of this passage.[19] The poignancy of this encounter resides instead in its carnality. Two embodied creatures of God confront desire—how to live and to relate with powerful urges for bodily engagement. Moving too quickly toward deception and disobedience as the interpretive keys for this story will rush past the riches of desire percolating throughout these verses. Eve herself rushed by too quickly as she blames the serpent for her transgression; nothing shuts down the process of intimacy more quickly than projecting our shame outward into blame.

But why a serpent? Why not a talking lion or a parrot or some other animal? Lurking in the background of both Genesis 3 and John 3 are ancient Mediterranean societies, like those of the Egyptians and the Canaanites, where images of serpents enjoyed multivalent meanings. At times the serpent symbolized eternity, with depictions of a snake eating its own tail as an image of the circularity of the infinite. Serpents could also symbolize healing, as the shedding of a snake's skin signified the promise of new life. These ancient societies knew just as well that snakes can be dangerous and deadly. That mix of risk and hope lingers in the old aphorism about how to soothe the effects of a hangover—just take a sip of that "hair from the dog that bit you." That which causes the disease, in other words, also provides the cure.[20]

These ancient cultural sensibilities found their way into the odd biblical story from the Book of Numbers, the one John's Jesus prompts Nicodemus to remember. There we read about the Israelites wandering through the desert and stumbling into a vast nest of poisonous snakes, the bites from which make many of them ill and more than a few of them die. Apart from this story's ancient Mediterranean context, what Moses does next seems inexplicable. He fashions a bronze image of a serpent and lifts it high upon a pole. Anyone who looks upon that image, Moses says, will be healed—and they were (Numbers 21:9). Some have suggested that this story influenced the development of the now-familiar image of a snake wrapped around a

---

19. See Miguel A. de la Torre, *Genesis*, A Theological Commentary on the Bible Series (Louisville, KY: Westminster John Knox Press, 2011), 70–71.

20. For more on the ancient appropriations of the image of a serpent and its relevance to this biblical story, see Christoph Levin, "Genesis 2–3: A Case of Inter-Biblical Interpretation," in *Genesis and Christian Theology*, ed. Nathan MacDonald, Mark W. Elliott, and Grant Macaskill (Grand Rapids, MI: The William B. Eerdmans Publishing Company, 2012), 93–98.

pole as a symbol for medicinal arts; that which causes the disease also provides the cure.

All of this lends added texture to the appearance of a serpent in Genesis 3, a creature that had long been feared as a risk to human health yet still symbolized the possibility of renewal. Here that potent mix of risk and renewal distills into temptation, a defining moment of spiritual folly in the human condition. The sagacious serpent knows exactly where humanity's weakness resides: "Eat the fruit," the serpent says, "and you will be like gods." The tragedy of this moment has less to do with breaking a rule than with acquiescing to the experience of shame, the conviction that their existence as human creatures is deeply flawed. Rejecting bodily goodness and lamenting human life as deficient, Adam and Eve quite naturally cover their nakedness to hide themselves from each other and deny how God made them. This alone is certainly regrettable, yet the depth of this story's spiritual folly appears in Adam and Eve's desire to "be like gods."[21] Displacing the one Creator God with "other gods" defines the essence of idolatry, which ancient Israel consistently associated with sexual shame, just as Paul did in his Letter to the Romans (1:18–27).

Not so surprisingly then, this ancient storyteller paints humanity's original temptation in the form of a serpent, the folk-wisdom image of finding the cure for a disease in its cause. If being human leads to deep distress—and the whole panoply of effects deriving from shameful alienation and isolation—then the cure will come from exactly the same place, from being *fully human*. Indeed, our salvation as a species may come to this: the grace to embrace our humanity shamelessly, free at last from our fear of intimacy and no longer compelled to hide ourselves from each other, from the world, and from God.[22]

Notably, John begins his gospel in exactly the same way Genesis does: "In the beginning." For John, in the beginning was the

---

21. The translation of this verse deserves its original plural form of "god," not least to indicate the character of the temptation. Neither Eve nor Adam likely imagined that they would be God, but they would instead be "like gods" (see Walter J. Houston, "Sex or Violence? Thinking Again with Genesis about Fall and Original Sin," in *Genesis and Christian Theology*, 141).

22. Margaret Barker follows a similar path by placing the serpent, "the ancient symbol of Wisdom," in the larger context of the Bible's wisdom literature, and especially for the sake of a renewed vision of environmental spirituality (*Creation: A Biblical Vision for the Environment* [London: T&T Clark, 2012], 8–9).

Word that created all there is, and this Word, in turn, became something. This divine Word did not become a book. It did not become an institution or an idea or a set of principles to live by or a hope or a dream or a vision. This creative word, John writes, became human flesh. The Word of God becomes flesh and in this flesh is the glory of God, full of "grace and truth" (1:14). This matters to John because this human one, the one talking to Nicodemus in the third chapter, this human one will be lifted up, just as Moses lifted up the serpent in the wilderness. There we see both the cause of our distress and the source of our healing: the fullness of humanity itself. Just as the ancient Israelites gazed on an image of what had bitten them for their healing, so human beings gaze on the divine image of humanity.

When Christians speak of Jesus, we speak of the incarnation of God's own desire, the divine Lover yearning for communion with the Beloved. For John, the heartbreaking question God asked in Eden—*Where are you?*—takes on flesh. God searches for us bodily here, East of Eden, awakening our hope for communion and our longing for intimacy. Christians try to speak bodily of this mystery, hoping to embrace the very source of our distress—our humanity. Irenaeus made this point in the second century. "The glory of God," he wrote, "is the human being fully alive."[23]

Carnal wisdom can rise up from humanity's spiritual folly, our foolish rejections of bodily goodness and our many attempts to become "like gods." Christian communities speak that hope as we struggle to tune the wisdom of our bodily desires to the melody of the Table. A Eucharistic theology of sexual intimacy attends carefully, in other words, to the inextricable mix of wisdom and folly in relation to our bodies and in our bodily relations with others.

PAIRING FOOD AND WINE

White wine goes best with fish and chicken; red wine with beef and pork. These particular pairings defined "orthodox" cuisine for decades. Some things just naturally belong together. These pairings

---

23. See Myra Rivera's treatment of this concept from Irenaeus, and its complexities, in *The Touch of Transcendence: A Postcolonial Theology of God* (Louisville, KY: Westminster John Knox Press, 2007), ch. 7, "The Glory of God."

made sense prior to more contemporary winemaking techniques that created different kinds of white wine ("heavier" than more traditional ones) and wildly different reds (some as "light" as the older whites). Heretical gourmands seized on these innovations to overturn the hegemony of orthodox gastronomists. In the 1980s, fine dining restaurants began including a sommelier on staff to help diners choose a wine to enhance their meals, and especially to help them overcome their resistance to previously unthinkable pairings.

Sustained theological reflection functions like a "religious sommelier" in Christian communities, sorting through apparent mismatches, disjunctions, and counter-intuitive pairings. Featuring peculiar pairs on the menu of spiritual practice may at first prove disorienting, yet also infuses Christian ideas with an oddly compelling character. Consider the ubiquitous Christian symbol of the Cross. The Gospel according to John rather incredulously renders that symbol with divine glory; the bodily wisdom lifted high upon it reveals the spiritual folly of its violent rejection (12:27–33). Paul seized on that paradoxical pairing by describing the Cross as a source of divine foolishness to confound human wisdom (1 Corinthians 1:18–20). Early Christians captured these incongruities with their depictions of the Cross as a flowering tree. Fourth-century deacon Ephrem of Edessa imagined the "carpenter's son" fashioning the cross into a bridge over which souls can flee from the region of death to the land of the living. That bridge, in turn, buds as a tree in spring, blossoming with desire:

> Since a tree had brought about the downfall of humankind, it was upon a tree that humankind crossed over to the realm of life. Bitter was the branch that had once been grafted upon that ancient tree, but sweet the young shoot that has now been grafted in, the shoot in which we are meant to recognize the Lord whom no creature can resist.[24]

Drawing our gaze backward to the infamous tree in Eden recalls yet another counter-intuitive pairing. There the storyteller in Genesis

---

24. J. Robert Wright quotes this passage for a devotional reading during the third week of Easter in *Readings for the Daily Office from the Early Church* (New York: The Church Hymnal Corporation, 1991), 197.

featured a serpent. In that one creature resides both danger and insight, both bodily wisdom and spiritual folly.

Christian liturgical traditions transform these odd conjunctions into a meal, a ritual pairing of bread and wine with the body and blood of Christ. In that meal the religious sommelier invites sustained reflection on the union of divine and human, a truly peculiar pairing that sits at the very heart of Christian faith and practice. Far more disorienting than a sturdy zinfandel next to a delicate white fish, the divine Word in human flesh incites world-changing provocations. Perhaps this claim no longer startles as it once did, or perhaps it no longer appears to have "changed everything," as Marcella Althaus-Reid and Lisa Isherwood propose. The doctrine of the Incarnation provokes hopeful incredulity, not by its inclusion in creedal statements but by its resistance to institutional sanitizing. God is found in and among humans, for "the divine is earthy, messy and partial and is to be found there in all its glory, not in splendid doctrine stripped of all humanness."[25]

Taking these incarnational provocations into transformative work can begin but not end with the familiar (and often sanitized) cadences of liturgical piety. A world hungry for communion beckons a retrieval of the scandalous character of Christianity's ancient bodily claim, especially in the midst of our often messy bodily intimacies. Like today's fine-dining sommeliers proposing curious, intriguing, and yet compelling pairings, Christian theology invites a "Eucharistic sexual practice." The implications of such a practice extend beyond the lives of intimate couples and begin to draw into that Table's orbit the range of vexations plaguing our lives here, East of Eden. Testing the reach of those implications begins broadly, with its capacity to mute a persistent misperception of Christianity as a religion of the soul with little if any interest in the body.

Christianity has always faced the risk of betraying its own incarnational claims by separating soul from body, setting spirit in opposition to flesh, and exiling earth from heaven. That risk simmered in the religious stirrings for social reform that eventually coalesced into the galvanizing movement of the nineteenth century known as the

---

25. Marcella Althaus-Reid and Lisa Isherwood, eds., "Introduction," *The Sexual Theologian: Essays on God, Sex, and Politics* (London: T&T Clark, 2004), 7.

"Social Gospel." The swift retreat of Christian faith from the public square in early modern Euro-American history alarmed a number
of clergy and theologians who had grown dismayed over rampant
poverty, inhumane working conditions generated by the industrial
revolution, and of course the institution of slavery.[26] These social gospelers worried that heavenly minded Christians would do very little
earthly good in the face of these social challenges. Left unaddressed,
these challenges would threaten the integrity of gospel proclamation,
especially in light of the alienation from bodily goodness that the
biblical writer so deftly portrays in Genesis 3. Domestic quarrels and
the schisms of the body politic alike bear the wounds of The Severing, a denial, even refusal, of the carnal wisdom with which God
endows us.

Thankfully, traces of that wisdom linger, in conversations as mundane as friendly complaints about a bad meal or the more profound
confessions among close friends about unfulfilling or even traumatic
sex. Bodily desire prompts these complaints and confessions, and
urges something more: the carnality of spiritual insight. Bodies shimmering with the desire for communion turn instinctively to either
food or sex or both. The inevitable disappointments that accompany
those moments—whether rare or frequent—sculpt the contours of
the desires we bring to the Eucharistic Table, not only as individuals
but also and especially as the *social* body of Christ.

Highlighting the social character of a shared meal presents
another incongruous pairing. This one sits uncomfortably in modern sensibilities as a theological irritant: individual autonomy and
collective culpability. More plainly, the disappointed desires we
bring to the Table urge renewed attention to an ancient claim: my
salvation depends on yours. This claim seems particularly troubling
in the United States, the most comfortable and most secure society human history has ever known. Not everyone, of course, feels
safe in North Atlantic communities. Yet the generally comfortable
circumstances of people with financial means and cultural power

---

26. For a helpful introduction to this era and its social movements, see Edwin Gaustad and
Leigh Schmidt, *The Religious History of America: The Heart of the American Story from Colo-
nial Times to Today*, rev. ed. (San Francisco: HarperSanFrancisco, 2002), ch. 11, "Cities and
Social Gospels," 231–54.

have, over time, eroded the historical urgency previous generations expressed for a truly social Gospel; the emphasis instead fell on the individual's need for forgiveness.[27] Unprecedented comfort, in other words, presents few reasons to suppose that salvation has anything to do with a critical analysis of social structures, cultural institutions, or economic systems—precisely the kind of analysis that inspired and mobilized the first few centuries of Christian faith.

The emphasis on individual responsibility, however, could not withstand the test of deeper forms of social analysis. Nestled within modernity's comfort zone, a disconcerting realization began to dawn more widely: our comfortable security was built on the backs of African slaves, indigenous peoples, and non-white immigrants and has come at the price of stripping the planet of natural resources. No one today chose to create a society like this, but nearly everyone benefits from it, every day. This raises the truly unsettling possibility that we are *collectively* culpable for what we did not *individually* choose.

To be sure, individual sins do accrue to individuals, but as Daniel Castelo argues, repeating the same sins over time can "establish and perpetuate conditions that make it difficult for those who are not the direct perpetrators of such acts to live righteously and holy in their own lives." Castelo cites systemic racism as a classic case in point.[28] Contemporary theologian Robert Neville goes further and calls this collective dilemma "blood-guilt." He chooses that image carefully and deliberately, to recall the animal sacrifices instituted in ancient Israel to atone for the people's sin (Leviticus 1–7). Neville draws our attention there to note that those sacrifices atoned for *unintentional* sins, for the guilt over the prices paid for the life then enjoyed by the community—whether or not individual members stood personally responsible.

Blood-guilt certainly troubles and confounds the dominant sensibilities of the modern West; even more, it appears childish and even primitive, as Neville readily admits. We pay a further price, however, by continuing to deny the cost of our present comfort, especially

---

27. See the introduction to Derek Nelson, *What's Wrong with Sin? Sin in Individual and Social Perspective from Schleiermacher to Theologies of Liberation* (London: T&T Clark, 2009), 1–14.

28. Daniel Castelo, *Theological Theodicy* (Eugene, OR: Cascade Books, 2012), 69.

when no shared mechanism appears to address that collective guilt. Neville frames the vexation succinctly:

> The prices of civilization have been paid, we are the beneficiaries, and we bear that cumulative blood-guilt. Late-modern culture in the nineteenth and twentieth centuries has warred with greater violence than any predecessor, perfecting mass murder and mindless destruction of culture and wealth. Enlightenment rationalism seeking only personal responsibility boggles before such behavior. Economic competition, which is supposed to increase wealth, is utterly contradicted by the martial and other kinds of violence that it has made acceptable. Dismissing sacrificial rituals as superstition, and thus lacking acceptable sacrifices as ways of coming to terms with the blood-guilt of high civilization, late modernity unwittingly legitimates more blind and unmeasured violence.[29]

Neville most certainly does not wish to reinstate animal sacrifices to assuage modern anxieties. Most Christians recognize where Neville wants to lead instead—to the blood shed on the cross by the Lamb of God, an atoning sacrifice for blood-guilt to which we have access at the Eucharistic Table. Lest anyone fail to grasp his meaning, Neville pushes us further to see at least one layer of meaning at that Table, which he quite pointedly refers to as ritualistic cannibalism.[30]

Following Neville's lead would seem to take us quite far afield from tender bodily intimacies and mutual self-offerings in Eucharist. Yet the particular path he retrieves from ancient traditions, just one among many, beckons renewed attention to the wider social fabric to which our personal intimacies contribute and from which so many ecstasies and heartaches alike derive. Bringing all of that with us to the Eucharistic Table can catalyze shared accountability for bodily alienations and for the sacrifices inherent to mutual intimacy that often go unnoticed. The panoply of social forces that alienate me from my own bodily goodness likewise construct my sense of self—a

---

29. Robert Cummings Neville, *Symbols of Jesus: A Christology of Symbolic Engagement* (Cambridge, UK: Cambridge University Press, 2001), 72–73.

30. Neville, *Symbols of Jesus*, 60–65. His observations here belong to a much longer arc of an argument that includes multiple layers of meaning for Eucharist, not all of which ought or even can be engaged at the same time.

self I seek to offer to another for the sake of mutual intimacy. Few pause to consider this daisy-chain analysis in moments of bodily intimacy with another, whether simple or sublime, yet the Eucharistic Table invites and urges that very pause.

Nineteenth-century social gospelers struggled with that "pause" though in different ways. Their vexations redoubled in the hands of mid-twentieth-century feminists who insisted that the "personal *is* the political," and later still among feminist theologians who located individual sins firmly in the social structures of alienation. Rosemary Radford Ruether, for example, foregrounds our alienations from one another as the primary locus for thinking theologically about sinfulness, what I have been calling The Severing of Genesis 3. Beginning with our alienation from one another, Ruether believes we can then see more clearly how this alienation "expresses itself in personal relations and social relations of negation of others, as well as self-negation, that are sick-making and violent."

Derek Nelson quotes that passage from Ruether's work in his extensive treatment of modernity's retreat from social constructions of sin and their gradual renewal.[31] Nelson analyzes the shift in Christian understandings of sin from broadly communal to nearly exclusively individual in the modern period, which twentieth-century liberation theologians sought to correct. He applauds those attempts while also lamenting their apparent lack of a more robust conception of human beings as essentially social and relational. That lament, unfortunately, does not appear to extend into the social fecundities and tribulations of sexual intimacy. Feminists of the 1960s may have insisted on the political character of even the most ostensibly personal relations, yet the legacy of modern individualism persists, not least in the supposition that genital sexual relations remain a solely private matter.

Marcella Althaus-Reid and Lisa Isherwhood recall attending a conference on theology and sexuality where political and economic topics surfaced regularly. Several "Third World" theologians at one point asked them why they devoted so much time to sexuality and gender in the midst of the more pressing, worldwide economic crises

---

31. Nelson, *What's Wrong with Sin*, 158.

and oppressions that destroy so many lives. The two responded with a question of their own: You're asking what love has to do with this? They meant, of course, to reclaim the traditional importance, even primacy, of love in Christian theology. They meant as well to show how love dissolves the containers that separate spirituality from justice, sexuality from capitalism, and bodily intimacy from environmental catastrophe.[32] In short, they meant to serve as provocative theological "sommeliers" in that moment, presenting apparently audacious food and wine pairings that would, precisely for their audacity, render the good news of the Gospel in bold relief—the good news, that is, of the One Story, which unites all concerns bearing on human thriving and flourishing with the hope of divine communion.

The legacy of privatized intimacies and individualized salvation persists elsewhere as well—at the Eucharistic Table. Approaching Eucharist as an occasion for individual communion with God alone leaves mostly untouched the tragic arc traced in Genesis 3. John D. Zizioulas calls this modern tendency the "psychologizing" of the Eucharist, not only restricting communion to an inner disposition but also framing it solely as a "vertical" relationship. Zizioulas, by contrast, renders the Eucharist as that moment when Christians cease to be individuals and become Church, where faith, hope, and love cease to be "mine" and become "ours." The Table thus presents the path toward God as the path toward neighbor:

> In this way, the human ceases to be an individual and becomes a person, that is to say, a reality which is not a fragment . . . Contemporary humans live every day under the weight of the opposition between the individual and the collective. Their social life is not *communio but societas*. And because there is no other choice, their violent reaction against collectivism leads to individualism and *vice versa*: for, paradoxically, the one presupposes the other.[33]

These irreducibly social effects of divine grace draw our attention back to the tragic effects of The Severing in Eden. It begins with

---

32. Althaus-Reid and Isherwood, *The Sexual Theologian*, 1–2.

33. John D. Zizioulas, *The Eucharistic Communion and the World*, 128. See also Bieler and Schottroff, *The Eucharist*, 53–56

the disruption of sexual intimacy, but then ripples outward as Adam and Eve hide themselves from their own natural environment and eventually from God. This widening arc of alienation and isolation leads not only to exile but also to violence, beginning, significantly enough, with fratricide, as Cain kills his brother Abel. As the story-teller describes it, the ground itself cries out with the blood of that slaying (Genesis 4:10). The whole arc of the tragedy in Genesis 3, and not merely a portion of it, contains the collective disappoint-ments in humanity's hope for communion. We bring all of this with us to the Table, seeking in a shared meal the divine grace we can-not find on our own. I realized this with fresh acuity by celebrating Eucharist in a prison.

The visiting room in a state prison portrays with unmistakable clarity the troubling mix of individual guilt and collective shame. Removing law-breakers from the general population certainly pro-vides for public safety in some cases, yet this alone falls far short of addressing both the societal causes and the social effects of "irrevoca-ble deeds." Prisons rarely provide an effective "correctional system" and serve mostly as centers of punishment when they remove human beings from nearly all forms of intimacy. Rather than "correcting," this system only replicates the tragic breach depicted in Genesis 3. Declaring the promise of forgiveness begins to repair that breach but leaves untouched the fullness of hope that inspired Isaiah to imagine not only repairers but also builders of cities to inhabit (Isaiah 58:12). Eucharistic practice—even with graham crackers and cranberry juice—recalls equally the memory of "turning against one another" and the hope of God's call to return.

The poignancy of that divine call suggests that human beings hope not only for something to be done *for* us, but also for some-thing that we ourselves can do, something that we can contribute to the Great Work of God's mission in the world. The hope of the Gospel, in other words, appears not only in a declaration but also in a call, a passionate plea from the divine lover to the beloved: *come home*. Where we find ourselves at "home"—in our bodies without shame, among others without guilt, and with God without fear— may well constitute the most pressing concern of the twenty-first century. The corrosive effects of The Severing continue to erode possibilities for political solidarity, communal accountability, and planetary flourishing. Evidence of that erosion fills newspapers with stories on poverty, violence, and global climate change that most now expect to read on a daily basis. Less expected and rarely reported, but equally significant evidence populates the materially prosperous, financially secure, and socially mobile classes. An age of anxiety and uncertainty offers little protection for anyone from the despair wrought by even a vague sense of "homelessness." Paul Ricouer captured such angst concisely:

> There is a secret bond between eroticism and absurdity. When nothing makes sense any longer, there remains instantaneous pleasure and its artifices. Eroticism is then a revenge not only on the insignificance of work, politics, and speech, but on the insignificance of sexuality itself.[34]

The yearning for home resides deeply in and among us all.[35] Christians name that yearning whenever we tell the One Story at the Eucharistic Table. Today, that naming and that telling alike beckon all of us to return to our bodies as a source of carnal wisdom in the midst of spiritual folly. Christians have historically referred to that homeward journey—the traveling as well as the destination—more simply as the hope of "salvation."

---

34. Quoted in O'Murchu, *The Transformation of Desire*, 106.

35. See Scott Cowdell's compelling analysis of how modern Western culture relentlessly creates "homeless hearts" in *Abiding Faith: Christianity Beyond Certainty, Anxiety, and Violence* (Cambridge, UK: James Clarke & Company, 2009), ch. 1, "Homeless Hearts: Faith and the Modern Self," 7–47.

3

Salvation

BODILY GLORY AND RELIGIOUS VIOLENCE

*In the fullness of time . . . bring us to that heavenly country
where, with all your saints, we may enter the everlasting heritage
of your sons and daughters . . .*

—*"EUCHARISTIC PRAYER B"*
THE BOOK OF COMMON PRAYER

In the mid-fourteenth century an Ottoman prince was kid-
napped by pirates along the Aegean Sea. After a pricey ransom was paid and the prince was released, Latin speakers at the time
would have described that exchange with the verb *redimere*, which
means to "buy back." From that verb we derive the English word
"redemption." If those pirates had encountered a ferocious storm at
sea but were rescued from peril, Latin commentators would likely
have used the verb *salvare* to describe both saving the ship and pre-
serving lives. That verb lies behind the English word "salvage" as
well as "salvation."

The Evangelical church of my youth used the words "redemption"
and "salvation" interchangeably, even though their root meanings
refer to rather different kinds of things. The notion of being bought
back with a pricey ransom and being rescued from peril coalesced into
a singular meaning in that Midwestern congregation (and indeed for
much of Christian history over at least the last five centuries). That
singular meaning focused on the forgiveness of sins accomplished by
the crucifixion of Jesus. I mulled over that theological claim nearly
every day, even as a teenager—or rather, *especially* as a teenager. The

onset of puberty in that pietistic tradition brought bodily changes and their attendant desires squarely into the spiritual spotlight. Merely the thought of genital sexual intimacy occasioned for many of us the need for salvation, to be redeemed from sinful desires.

I focused on that need quite particularly on the one Sunday evening per quarter when we celebrated a service of Holy Communion. On those occasions an uncharacteristically brief sermon was followed by an even shorter exposition on Paul's account of the "Lord's Supper" (1 Corinthians 11:23–26). The organist then offered quiet background music while ushers passed a silver tray laden with tiny pieces of saltine crackers down each row of pews, and after that another tray filled with tiny plastic cups of grape juice. All of us in that service ate and drank quietly and neatly, nearly surreptitiously, so that one could almost forget that any of these things were food and drink, let alone a "supper."

Each of us chewed and sipped together in that "meal," but we might as well have done so alone in a mostly private moment of spiritual reminiscence. Every word in those services of Holy Communion was spoken reverently, every gesture and shared act offered with such sanitary propriety that virtually nothing about those services evoked for me the gruesome and bloody trauma endured by the one with whom we were supposedly communing for our salvation and redemption. Even less evident were any traces of erotic energy percolating in this invitation to "commune" with another body, traumatized or not.

Regardless of the denomination or tradition, nearly every ritualized expression of Eucharist consists in highly stylized, even sanitized, gestures. That kind of "ceremonial container" is particularly important for a liturgical moment that intertwines images of torture, suffering, and death with evocations of bodily tenderness and intimacy. This Eucharistic container, however, does not offer space to "re-enact" the Last Supper—much less the Crucifixion. All the other meals Jesus shared with a wide array of guests as well as the accounts of his resurrection likewise contributed to the development of the Church's memory and hope that distilled over time into the ritual celebration of Eucharist. Paul cautioned the Christians in Corinth to attend carefully to those multivalent and ritualized meanings of table fellowship, especially since they had taken the "Lord's Supper" as an occasion for gluttonous feasting (at the expense of those who were hungry) or drunken excess (1 Corinthians 11:17–26). Rather than restricting the meaning of that shared meal, a ritual container creates space, not for historical *re-enactment* but for shared *interpretation*.[1] Elizabeth Stuart rather oddly but helpfully refers to this shared activity as "parody." She does not mean mockery or jest, but rather a "repetition with critical difference" that can make new or deeper meaning from a past event. The Eucharist itself, she explains, is:

> an extended repetition with critical difference on the Last Supper, the critical difference being that in the Eucharist the meal element is caught up in a new reality, the reality of the heavenly liturgy opening up to us through the cross and resurrection. The Last Supper itself was probably an extended repetition with critical difference of the Seder meal, the critical difference being the inauguration of a new covenant and the creation of a new community called to live out the outrageous hospitality of God.[2]

Jesus' table fellowship, his suffering, death, and resurrection—all contribute to the moment when Christians break bread and pour wine together, a moment of making visible God's own desire for Holy Communion.

Eucharist does more, however, than make meaning from historical events; ritual interpretation invites *participation*. To do this with a shared meal that provokes the memory of betrayal and bodily trauma can easily perplex as much as inspire. What then does salvation actually entail? Where and why do we seek redemption? I thought I knew how to answer those questions many years ago as I piously nibbled on a saltine and sipped some grape juice. I found the assurance of forgiveness comforting in those ritual moments, but I had yet to ponder what the assurance in that context could not fully address: the denial of bodily goodness and its multilayered, pernicious effects, including the countless moments of violent betrayal they spawn. It

---

1. Charles P. Price and Louis Weil present the many theories that have attached to the Eucharist throughout Christian history and note that each does more than merely "recollect" a past event but reads and interprets that event in a variety of ways (*Liturgy for Living* [New York: The Seabury Press, 1979], see esp. 185–91).

2. Stuart, *Gay and Lesbian Theologies*, 108.

had not occurred to me, for example, to consider what salvation might mean for the bodies of people of color living in the throes of a white supremacist society or for the bodies of women navigating the social structures of a patriarchal society or for the bodies of non-human animals in the midst of ecological degradation. I certainly did not imagine in my youth that sexual intimacy had anything to do with all these socio-economic concerns, much less the "abundant life" that John's Jesus declared he had come to offer (10:10).

Biblical texts present wide-ranging effects for discerning God's saving and redeeming work—liberated slaves, rescue from enemies, economic prosperity, physical healing, restored relationship, and even rising from the dead to name just a few. While writers of the Christian testament rooted their musings on salvation in the death and resurrection of Jesus, they did not suppose that Christian faith guarantees bodily safety. To the contrary, and as early Christians quickly discovered, living as a disciple of the one who suffered and died at the hands of the Roman Empire can put us more directly in harm's way, especially when discipleship calls us to resist the violence of imperial regimes.

We live in a violent world; humans always have. Human relationships have always been scarred by violations, both small and large. Our bodies have always been bruised by the heels of those climbing over us to reach new levels of dominance and control. First-century Palestine displayed that violence in the form of Roman occupation and imperial oppressions, and as a people struggling under the weight of economic exploitation and bodily intimidations, including frequent crucifixions to keep them terrorized and compliant. Reading the gospel texts through the lens of that imperial violence can shed considerable light on the violent disruptions of intimacy plaguing twenty-first-century life on countless fronts. The impulse to imperial domination certainly appears in strained international relations and neo-colonial machinations, but likewise much closer to home and therefore much closer to our bodies. J. Denny Weaver proposes a helpful framework for analyzing socio-religious violence by defining it broadly to mean harm or damage. Killing certainly belongs in that framework, but only as one of the more extreme forms of violence. Weaver outlines this framework with these examples:

The system of chattel slavery that existed in colonial America and the United States for two and a half centuries was most certainly violence. But the continuation of racist practices today under other names is also violence. Social practices which proscribe set roles for women and limit their opportunities are examples of violence. Social structures that impose poverty are violent.[3]

That list also needs to include the violence that extends unspeakably toward environmental collapse, which puts people of color, women, and the poor at the greatest risk of bodily harm and damage.

Christians gather at the Eucharistic Table not only with the memory of all that violence but also in the midst of it, and there we pray: "In the fullness of time bring us to that heavenly country where, with all your saints, we may enter the everlasting heritage of your sons and daughters."[4] Andrea Bieler and Luise Schottroff would include that prayer among many that inspire an "eschatological imagination." They do not mean an imaginative *escape* from all the worldly forces that dehumanize and violate, but rather an imaginative *vision* of those forces transformed. Eucharistic practice continually feeds that vision of being at home with one another free of violent oppressions, where the glory of bodily intimacy shines freely and unimpeded by the controlling forces of empire, regardless of the form those forces take.

Imagination and context belong together in this approach to Eucharist, as the salvation we seek in our desperate yearning for redemption must surely come from within the ambit of our distress and not only as a vague ensign flying beyond the limits of our sight. The "heavenly country" inspires and animates our lives with others by tapping into what we have already glimpsed, no matter how fleetingly. "We imagine the world to come, the coming of Christ, and the reign of God by analogy to something that is familiar to us, either in our actual experience or an unfulfilled yearning."[5] Eucharist invites us equally to remember honestly the context of violence bred from denying our bodily goodness and, with a honed spiritual imagination,

---

3. J. Denny Weaver, *The Nonviolent Atonement*, second ed. (Grand Rapids, MI: William B. Eerdmans Publishing Company, 2011), 8.

4. BCP, 369.

5. Bieler and Schottroff, *The Eucharist*, 26.

to crane our necks to peer over that rising tide of despair toward an expanding horizon. Eucharist invites, in other words, the experience of a fourteenth-century prince languishing in the exile of his kidnappers—the hope of ransom. It invites as well the experience of those kidnappers floundering in a storm—the possibility of salvaging these mortal ships sailing on trackless seas and bringing them home to the harbor of a distant shore, now made near at that Table.

The Eucharistic Table unites these images of salvation and redemption, but not without the risk of transposing them into still more violence. The violence memorialized at that Table, for example, plays a significant role in what many Christians adopt in the "satisfaction" theory of atonement. This theory proposes that Jesus died in the place of sinful humanity, thereby satisfying God's demand for justice. While just one among several possible approaches to atonement in Christian history, satisfaction theory has wielded a disproportionate influence not only on theology and spiritual practice, but also and therefore on socio-political dynamics in Western society for centuries. Weaver again frames these dynamics concisely and rather pointedly:

> [S]atisfaction atonement, which assumes that God's justice requires compensatory violence or punishment for evil deeds committed, can seem self-evident in the context of contemporary understandings of retributive justice in North American as well as worldwide systems of criminal justice.[6]

Securing justice with violence flags still further risks. Making torture, suffering, and death the necessary means for a greater end in a religious rite can quickly "baptize" and thus justify the sacrifices made by victims of domestic violence or the forms of torture deployed in today's "war on terror." Rita Nakashima Brock worries, for example, that the decisive turn taken toward the satisfaction theory of atonement in medieval Europe merely eroticized violence. The gospel writers surely had something else in view:

> The purpose of such writing is assuredly not to valorize victims, to reveal "true love" as submission and self-sacrifice, or to say that

---

6. Weaver, *The Nonviolent Atonement*, 3.

God requires the passive acceptance of violence. Such interpretations mistakenly answer the abusive use of power with the abnegation of power.[7]

Simply put, as Sharon Baker reminds us, the *kind* of God we believe in will inevitably shape how we live. Christians who view God as a warrior, Baker writes, "may also believe that God commissions nations and people to go to war, killing others in order to protect the innocent."[8] William T. Cavanaugh despairs over these socio-religious connections and returns our gaze to the imperial context of the final meal Jesus shared with his friends. Far from providing even tacit approval of state-sponsored terror, Cavanaugh depicts the Eucharist as a counter-cultural act, echoing Bieler and Schottroff's stress on imaginative vision:

> The Eucharist is the imagination of the body of Christ, the liturgical enactment of the redemptive power of God in the bodies of believers. To participate in the Eucharist is to live inside God's imagination. As a result, it makes possible resistance to the state's attempt to define what is real through the mechanism of torture.[9]

The State's "mechanism of torture" may seem safely distant from our North Atlantic intimacies, but Eucharist stubbornly re-presents violence whenever Christians gather to share that meal and reflect on God's saving and redeeming work. Wheat ripped from the earth and ground into grain before baking it into loaves; grapes plucked from their vines and crushed for their juice to ferment into wine— like nearly every other form of human food, we create bread and wine with acts of violence. These elements then serve to commemorate yet another violent act in the Christian memory of crucifixion. The Johannine evangelist may have struggled with all this violence as well. He

---

7. Rita Nakashima Brock, "Paradise and Desire: Deconstructing the Eros of Suffering," in *Saving Desire*, 61.

8. Sharon Baker, "The Repetition of Reconciliation: Satisfying Justice, Mercy, and Forgiveness," in *Stricken by God? Nonviolent Identification and the Victory of Christ*, ed. Brad Jersak and Michael Hardin (Grand Rapids, MI: The William B. Eerdmans Publishing Company, 2007), 222.

9. William T. Cavanaugh, "Torture and Eucharist: A Regretful Update," in George Hunsinger, ed., *Torture Is a Moral Issue: Christians, Jews, Muslims, and People of Conscience Speak Out* (Grand Rapids, MI: The William B. Eerdmans Publishing Company, 2008), 94.

chose to liken the suffering of the cross to a pregnant woman's labor pains, which pale in comparison to the glory of newborn life (John 16:21–22). Indeed, John insists on locating nothing less than divine glory in that symbol of torture (12:23). "Unless a grain of wheat falls into the earth and dies," John's Jesus says, "it remains just a single grain; but if it dies, it bears much fruit" (12:24). Christians have ever since taken that fruit from those seeds to make bread, taken that bread and broken it, and then offered it as a sign of communion. Surely Christians ought to pause whenever we do that and ponder whether religious violence can ever truly save us from imperial violence.

As we pause at the Table, ways to read and re-read that ancient meal can surface fresh, more intimate hopes for redemption. The context of betrayal and anticipatory violence of the Last Supper, for example, can easily overshadow the deep desire infusing that table fellowship. The ancient Greeks would likely agree with that assessment even though they too fell prey to endorsing violent acts of redemption. The abduction of Helen of Troy "launched a thousand ships" in ancient mythology, the attempt to buy her back at the cost of the Trojan war. The storied violence of that legend tends to eclipse the desire for intimacy that fueled it in much the same way the Cross tends to veil the tenderness of the Last Supper. Two particularly poignant moments from John's construal of that meal imply something quite remarkable about God and about God's passion in Christ to redeem us, God's own "Helen of Troy."

Unlike the other three gospel accounts, John's version of the Last Supper focuses less on the meal itself than on the provocative moment when Jesus washes the feet of his disciples (13:3–11). That bodily moment of intimate tenderness is followed by another. The disciple "whom Jesus loved" reclined on Jesus' breast during the meal, presumably sharing the kind of whispered small-talk that intimates often do.[10] These two Johannine moments portray what many couples, households, and friends experience in cherished moments of communal intimacy around a shared table. Yet a third moment in this story disrupts these expressions of intimacy with a yearning for redemption.

---

10. Regardless of the character of this relationship, what seems to matter most in these passages is the personal intimacy Jesus shared with this "beloved." For more on the speculative and provocative implications of this relationship, see Theodore Jennings, *The Man Jesus Loved: Homoerotic Narratives from the New Testament* (Cleveland, OH: The Pilgrim Press, 2003).

In the wake of tender foot washing and in the midst of intimate bodily contact, John inserts a moment of disrupted affection. Jesus declares just then that one of his companions will betray him. Peter seeks some inside information about this distressing declaration from the one leaning on Jesus' chest:

> Simon Peter therefore motioned to him [the one whom Jesus loved] to ask Jesus of whom he was speaking. So while reclining next to Jesus, he asked him, "Lord, who is it?" Jesus answered, "It is the one to whom I give this piece of bread when I have dipped it in the dish." So when he had dipped the piece of bread, he gave it to Judas son of Simon Iscariot (John 13:24–26).

Tenderness disrupted by betrayal distills in microcosm the defining predicament of the human condition so eloquently portrayed in Genesis 3—the severing of intimacy that leads to alienation and ultimately violence. John thus offers a glimpse of that for which humans yearn and simultaneously thwart. In that final meal, John portrays both the meaning of human existence and its unraveling all at once. Surely in that iconic moment we find a vivid portrayal of the human longing for redemption, for being bought back from our exile in a strange and arid land of loneliness and hostility. The longing, that is, to arrive to that "heavenly country" where the imperial mechanisms of violence no longer repress or disrupt the glorious intimacies of bodily life.

American philosopher of religion Josiah Royce excavated these ancient themes and proposed loyalty as that which finally makes us human. By "loyalty" Royce did not mean blind obedience or slavish conformity. He sought instead to discern whether anything about our moral engagements led "our practical human life homewards, even if that way proved to be the infinitely long."[11] I read Royce turning toward intimacy as the indispensable ingredient in those engagements that unify individuals in the service of a common cause. Among the many "causes" to which we might devote ourselves, a properly human, and therefore divine, cause will always

---

11. Josiah Royce, *The Philosophy of Loyalty* (New York: The Macmillan Company, 1908; repr. with a new introduction by John J. McDermott, Nashville, TN: Vanderbilt University Press, 1995), 6–7.

teach us to love or at least to hope for a universal unity in the midst of our violent fragmentations. Royce called this intimate union the "Beloved Community," where both memory and hope are shared in common—the memory of violence certainly, but also and equally, the hope for intimacy and communion.

The stress on intimate loyalty mattered to Royce as a way to explain why moments of betrayal rise to the level of the truly tragic, or what Royce called "irrevocable deeds." Irrevocable because once betrayal disrupts loyal intimacy, no one can turn the clock back as if the betrayal had never happened. Forgiveness begins to heal that rupture, but only a renewed intimacy can take a community toward the wholeness that makes us human with each other. Royce went further still and proposed that only a deeper intimacy than had existed before the betrayal suffices to qualify as the "atonement" we seek for an irrevocable deed.[12]

Detaching atonement from either memory or hope drains it of its power to inspire our imaginations and replicates the most common ploy of imperial regimes—defining reality with torture and terror. Both politically and liturgically, the honesty of remembering tragic betrayals would quickly devolve into paralyzing grief, if not for the anticipation of graceful transformation. Similarly, setting our sight on bodily glory alone risks denying the daily and planet-wide recurrence of violence that mars human existence. That galvanizing mix of memory and hope renders the Eucharistic Table with divine resistance—that is, *God's* resistance to any supposition that religious violence provides the *source* of bodily glory. That Table invites us to see violence instead as the *context* for an embodied hope—the hope for salvation, yes, and especially the hope of redemption, of being bought back from a realm of imperial domination to enjoy the "heavenly country," our divine heritage.

Can these Roycean proposals really lead "our practical human life homewards"? The earliest Christians believed so whenever they gathered to share a meal. Today's sexually intimate couples might

---

12. Karl Barth devoted one of his infamous extended "notes" in his massive *Church Dogmatics* to Judas, noting that betrayal, by definition, always originates within the bonds of community. Barth, like Royce, referred to those moments as "irrevocable deeds" (*Church Dogmatics*, vol. 2, pt. 2, ed. G. W. Bormiley and T. F. Torrance, [London: T&T Clar, 1957], 458–66).

believe so as well whenever their intimacy provides a haven from the socio-political regimes of imperial domination and control. Uniting table fellowship and haven-creating intimacy may well hasten our homeward journey, but not without an important caveat.

A "home" worthy of God's promised salvation will necessarily mean more than securing a mortgage on a single-family residence in suburban America or a finely appointed urban loft. Such spaces alone cannot make "home" from a world of patriarchal domination, white supremacy, environmental catastrophe, and all the many other instantiations, both small and large, of imperial violence. Only by tuning our varied intimacies to the melody of the Eucharistic Table will the "heavenly country" appear more vividly on our collective horizon. Only then will the hope of that shimmering country inspire the radical dismantling of the countless imperial mechanisms of control, both subtle and overt, that infiltrate and thus disrupt even the most ostensibly private moments of bodily intimacy.

Rowan Williams freely acknowledged that the panoply of human crises do not derive solely from disrupted intimacies or distorted sexual relations. He did insist, however, that those distortions present a paradigm case for human distress.[13] I would modify that claim and urge Christian communities to notice the inextricably gendered character of troubled human and planetary relations. At the very root of the imperial urge to dominate and control lies the presumed and deeply entrenched supposition of male superiority. While countless historical and contemporary examples would bolster that claim, we need not look any further than the third chapter of Genesis. There the ancient storyteller astutely identifies the source of human despair for both women and men alike—the hierarchy of gender dominance.[14]

Energizing Christian witness to the One Story today will mean facing courageously the historical legacy of gender domination and its ongoing violence. In the following observations I want to bring those gender dynamics more fully into view. Only in that light will the Table's invitation to a life of self-offering resist the imperial demand for sacrificial violence. Sexual intimacy demonstrates that profound gospel insight in every moment of tender, mutual self-giving. The

---

13. Williams, "The Body's Grace," 64.

14. See Carr, *The Erotic Word*, 42–43.

Eucharist presents the same tenderness and vulnerability, and in so doing that Table brings the "heavenly country" into view, our heritage as God's daughters and sons.

MOTHER EARTH AND FATHER GOD

After a romantic dinner for two, replete with convivial conversation and the shared intimacy of familiar flirtations, you and your partner gladly retreat to the bedroom (after a delectable dessert) for that anticipated time of deeper bodily intimacy. Regardless of how this time together unfolded, would you pause to consider whether this intimate evening had anything to do with socio-economic relations or even global climate change? Might you wonder if this shared intimacy in any way reflected the evolution of religious rites or Christian liturgical practice? Could you imagine giving thanks for even the temporary haven of safety from a generally violent world that this evening provided? I imagine most sexually intimate couples answering yes to the last question, but not to the previous two. Recalling the emergence of modern science offers a way to blend all three of those questions into a pathway toward Eucharist and for telling the One Story with renewed conviction.

Sex, no less than food, makes compelling science. Human beings have learned more about both in the last two hundred years than human beings have ever known about them in all the millennia prior to the modern period. We now know about hormones, eggs, and sperm. We know about neurological changes during sexual arousal and the release of endorphins at orgasm. We know that many of these same physiological changes happen when we eat a chocolate brownie—and why sugar now counts as poison among some nutritionists. What we have learned about sex and food has quite literally re-shaped human life, both for good and for ill, in our relationships with others and also with restaurants as well as grocery stores.

The history of science and its entanglements with culture linger behind all of these innovative insights. That history likewise reflects a deeply gendered perception of reality. Thomas Laqueur, for example, casts a spotlight on the role modern science played in controlling women's bodies, not least by analyzing the meaning and purpose of female orgasm. For many centuries men happily assumed that pregnancy required a woman's orgasmic climax; controlling a woman's bodily passion thereby controlled procreation. Even though it becomes increasingly clear in the modern period, as early as the sixteenth century, that pregnancy does not require female orgasm (something women have known from the dawn of time), philosophical and scientific texts alike continued to ignore this fundamental reality. More than a quirk in early modern biological science, this peculiar omission illustrates a broader concern in Western culture. Concisely put, modern Western progress relied on controlling women—exemplified bodily by varying perceptions of orgasm—for the sake of a well-ordered social, political, and religious system of relations. Laqueur draws those connections succinctly:

> Ancient accounts of reproductive biology, still persuasive in the early eighteenth century, linked the intimate, experiential qualities of sexual delight to the social and cosmic order. More generally, biology and human sexual experience mirrored the metaphysical reality on which, it was thought, the social order rested.[15]

The social order, of course, depends on reason, especially its vital role in taming human passion. This too belongs among the perduring features of Western society set in motion by the ancient Greeks. The supremacy of rational discourse informed Aristotle's understanding of what constitutes the ideal *polis*: the well-ordered society depends on subduing human passions with reason. I imagine most reasonable people find that approach quite reasonable indeed, yet the gendered implications of this vision prove more troubling. Western society traced its progress for centuries by supposing that masculinity correlated to the principle of rationality while femininity stood for the risks associated with passion. Just as the well-disciplined mind tames the wild fancies of the heart, so the reasonable man tames the unruly passions of women. This gender mapping seamlessly attached to the emergence of modern science as masculine rationality increasingly tamed the wild and uncontrollable forces of "*mother* nature." Rosemary Radford Ruether offers many examples of this gendered frame,

---

15. Laqueur, *Making Sex*, 11.

such as this one concerning Francis Bacon, the "father" of modern scientific method:

> Bacon's thought is pervaded by images of nature as a female to be coerced, "penetrated," conquered, and forced to "yield," the language of rape and subjugation of women, while the scientist is imaged as the epitome of masculine power over such "feminine" nature. Bacon ties the scientific revolution to the Christian myth of fall and redemption. Through the sin of Eve, "nature" fell out of "man's" control, but through scientific knowledge this fall will be reversed and "nature" restored to man's dominion, as representative of God's dominion over earth.[16]

Laqueur invites us to notice what might happen and indeed what did happen when societal assumptions shift and female orgasm no longer has much at all to do with fertility. Not surprisingly, evidence of pregnancy apart from orgasm finally comes to widespread cultural attention at the very same time that men would prefer to view women as passive and passionless. The preference to relegate women to the "domestic sphere" where they tame the unruly passions of their husbands, mostly through religion, took root precisely when women were advocating for a greater role in public life. Institutional Christianity contributed to this social evolution as well. Theological warnings about the risks inherent to sexual passion, even within marriage, marked Christian history from its earliest centuries and stamped gendered sensibilities with a religious imprimatur. These religious sensibilities likewise made an impact on ritual formation, vestiges of which remain in some contemporary Christian liturgies.

During my first Easter Vigil liturgy as an Episcopalian, I sat transfixed by the lighting of the new fire, the procession of the Paschal Candle to the baptismal font, and the flickering flame dancing over water. I was especially intrigued by the thrusting of that candle into the font three times as the priest blessed the water. Years later, a seminary professor made explicit what takes little sexual imagination to suppose about that liturgical moment. The "light of Christ"

---

16. Rosemary Radford Ruether, *Gaia and God: An Ecofeminist Theology of Earth Healing* (New York: HarperCollins, 1992), 195.

construed as the masculine principle of reason inseminates the dark chaotic waters of humanity's sinfulness, the feminine principle of both passion and receptivity; the Father God, in other words, controls Mother Earth.

What I heard in that seminary classroom reflects a centuries-long tradition of organizing religious practice along the axis of male dominance and female passivity—an organization that proved particularly useful in the human quest to subdue the otherwise uncontrollable forces of nature with the tools of modern scientific method. A bit more pointedly, Ronald E. Long explored that gendered history and concluded that nearly every religious tradition in the ancient Mediterranean world, including Christianity, serves a singular function: to support the dominance of socially superior males by imprinting such dominance with divine blessing.[17] This religious inflection of gendered relations replicated the wider view of sex itself in these ancient societies, which served mostly to secure social hierarchies of power. Those ancient cultures understood sex as "good" or proper when the sexually "active" partner enjoyed a higher social status than the "passive" or receptive partner. As one biblical scholar so succinctly explains, the ancients understood sex as eroticized inequality.[18] One might well wonder whether that ancient perspective continues to energize socio-political debates, let alone religious adoration of the Father God who thankfully subdues the passions of Mother Earth.

The Greco-Roman incarnation of empire collapsed many centuries ago, yet the legacy of imperial rule and its engendering of social relations continues. That legacy appears whenever the exercise of male privilege diminishes the lives of women, children, non-human animals, and the thriving of Earth's intertwined ecosystems. Imperial patriarchy appears with particular vibrancy whenever male privilege turns to violence as the first, the only, or the necessary means for "salvation." Not only physical violence, but any form of coercion that derives models of God based on the controlling impulses of the "male

---

17. Ronald E. Long, *Men, Homosexuality, and the God: An Exploration into the Religious Significance of Male Homosexuality in World Perspective* (Binghamton, NY: Harrington Park Press, 2004), 13.

18. Stephen D. Moore, *God's Beauty Parlor: And Other Queer Spaces in and around the Bible* (Stanford, CA: Stanford University Press, 2011), 153.

ruling class," which tend to perpetuate colonial and neo-colonial policies under the guise of assistance or aid or even "salvation."[19] All of
this and more hovers around the Eucharistic Table of communion.

Returning to the complex history of marriage in Western culture
sheds further light on these social and religious vexations; it might also
illumine a more enticing path toward the Eucharistic Table. The modern West mostly invented the aspiration (if not always the actuality) of
egalitarian marriages based on love. Prior to the modern period, marriage was meant to create and expand kinship networks by sealing alli-
ances among families and providing for a more stable social structure.
Bodily intimacy in pre-modern marriages served a similar purpose by
producing children. As Stephanie Coontz has rather provocatively proposed, focusing instead on romantic love as the reason for marriage
has gradually destabilized marriage itself as a cultural institution.[20]
Romantic love, as most people realize, tends to ebb and flow. Apart
from strong ties to kinship networks and their concomitant commitments to social cohesion, fewer reasons remain to stay married when
romance wanes. Among the collateral damages of this historical arc,
too few commentators mention the loss of deep friendship apart from
the marital bond as another thread that once wove human society into
a more cohesive fabric. As sex, love, companionship, and friendship all
coalesced into a single cultural institution called "marriage," the significance of lasting friendships outside that institution slowly withered.
Elizabeth Stuart explains why this might matter theologically:

> The formation of friendships is part of the larger project of learn-
> ing to embrace the stranger, but friendship also serves to break the
> bonds of culturally constructed kinship and the captivity of passion
> within sexual relationships. Friendship keeps the eschatological
> dream alive by breaking love out of coupledom, by breaking love
> out of the confines of sexual orientation, and sometimes by outlast-
> ing other forms of love.[21]

---

19. See Kwok Pui-Lan's analysis of Western Christianity's introduction of a male-domi-
nated symbolic order into non-Western cultures and its impact on the lives of women as well as
the environment (*Postcolonial Imagination and Feminist Theology* [Louisville, KY: Westminster
John Knox Press, 2005], esp. 153–58).

20. Coontz, *Marriage, A History,* 5

21. Stuart, *Gay and Lesbian Theologies,* 113.

In short, dominant Western practices of marriage in concert with industrial and technological revolutions have gradually detached couples from wider family systems, social networks, and even from the deep bonds with our natural planetary habitations. These effects bear an uncanny resonance with the ever-widening circle of alienation extending out from the severing of intimacy depicted in Genesis 3.

In contrast to that isolating alienation stands the image of the heavenly wedding banquet, the symbol for which John D. Zizioulas naturally finds in the Eucharist, but with an important modification. The eschatological character of that shared meal sets it apart from the ritual Passover meal with which Christian commentators usually associate it. While Zizioulas believes we must still read the Last Supper through the lens of Passover, especially the symbol it provides of God's saving work in history, that final meal looks forward and not only backward—it commemorates *and* it anticipates. The hope of the "heavenly country" sparked at the Table invites an expansive view of intimate family relations, and perhaps even the dissolution of gendered hierarchies that have so often accompanied notions of "family." Zizioulas explains:

> [W]hile the Passover meal is a *family* event, the Last Supper is an event that concerns a *group of friends* with Christ presiding. This difference indicates that with the Last Supper we move away from a sort of natural community in order to move to another kind of community—formed by a *group of friends* who love their master and each other . . . Much more than a moral or sentimental notion . . . this fundamental difference between the participants at the Passover meal and at the Last Supper reveals clearly the eschatological character of the Last Supper.[22]

Here the hope inspired by a Eucharistic imagination unfolds in the midst of imperial violence, a hope that responds to that violence with bodily intimacy. In this moment, the imperial urge to dominate and control dissipates in the most loving act imaginable—an unprotected offering of the self, both body and blood. The vulnerability of this offering bathes the Eucharistic Table with tender intimacy. It

---

22. Zizioulas, *The Eucharistic Communion and the World*, 3–4 (emphasis in the original).

does something else as well: it indicts institutional Christianity for its own history of religious violence. From crusades and inquisitions to paternalistic repressions, the Church has betrayed the One Story that the Table invites Christians to tell and to live, as Jews, Muslims, and so many others could easily attest. That same Table, however, continually draws us back, with painful memories intact as well as the desire to renew our hope. Sexually intimate couples can remind us when we do return to that Table where the hope of salvation can so readily appear—in the intimate offering of the self to another for the sake of life.

THE LITTLE DEATH

Most moviegoers remember the 1989 film *When Harry Met Sally* for the moment when Meg Ryan's character simulated sexual climax in a restaurant. The most frequently shared quote from the film came from a woman in that restaurant who witnessed the simulation. Speaking to the waiter, the woman said, "I'll have what she's having."[23]

That cinematic moment would seem rather far removed from Christian witness to the Gospel until one views the image of St. Teresa of Avila in ecstasy that sits prominently in a minor basilica in Rome, the *Santa Maria della Vittoria*. Carved in marble, that image attempts to capture a mystical moment of divine encounter that Teresa experienced as an "angel" piercing her with a spear, which resulted in both pain and inexpressible joy and longing. Teresa herself described that moment like this:

> In his hands I saw a great golden spear, and at the iron tip there appeared to be a point of fire. This he plunged into my heart several times so that it penetrated into my entrails. When he pulled it out, I felt that he took them with it, and left me utterly consumed by the great love of God. The pain was so severe that it made me utter several moans. The sweetness caused by this intense pain is so extreme that one cannot possibly wish it to cease, nor is one's soul then content with anything but God. This is not a physical, but a

---

23. Rob Reiner, dir. *When Harry Met Sally* (Beverly Hills: Castle Rock Entertainment, 1989).

spiritual pain, though the body has some share in it—even a considerable share. So gentle is this wooing that takes place between God and the soul that if anyone thinks that I am lying, I pray God, in His goodness, to grant him some experience of it.[24]

Teresa's text certainly stimulates a sexual imagination. Even more, that image carved in marble could easily have inspired Meg Ryan's performance on film. The image of a woman in bodily ecstasy may today seem unremarkable in some circles, yet seeing such an image carved in the seventeenth century and featured in a church surely stretches the modern Christian imagination. Not surprisingly, interpretations of this early modern sculpture vary. Some of the religious contemporaries of Gian Lorenzo Bernini, the sculptor, condemned the image as too overtly sexual (Teresa herself seemed to shy away from associating her experience with orgasm). Some contemporary commentators embrace what they consider an "obvious" portrayal of sexual climax in that statue. Many of these same commentators then critique the religious repression of bodily life that led Teresa to sublimate her erotic desire by framing it as solely "spiritual."[25]

Teresa's ecstasy raises a host of questions, both historical and contemporary. Can we reduce the visions of medieval mystics to merely spiritual disavowals of bodily life? Do modern Christians flip that dynamic by resisting the spiritual implications of their bodily ecstasies? What qualifies as "merely" spiritual for medieval mystics now counts as crudely physical for modern Christians. Where then, if anywhere, do spiritual exultations and bodily ecstasies meet and meld? The Eucharistic Table offers the hope of answering that question. Eucharist does this by recalling one of the most perplexing declarations of the Gospel: "Those who lose their life will find it" (Matthew 16:25). Eucharist invites, in other words, exactly what sexual intimacy does—the offering of self to another.

---

24. Teresa of Avila, *The Life of Saint Teresa of Avila by Herself*, trans. J. M. Cohen (New York: Penguin Classics, 1988), 210.

25. See Stephen Haliczer's contextual analysis of mystical ecstasies, especially in relation to the frequent suspicion of women's experience in medieval Christianity (*Between Exaltation and Infamy: Female Mystics in the Golden Age of Spain* [New York: Oxford University Press, 2002]).

A particular segment of Western literature offers a helpful description for these provocations with the "little death," or more commonly in French, *la petite mort*. This refers of course to orgasm, that sense of releasing the self by giving the self to another, or letting go of some part of the self as if "dying" for another. Biologists remind us that this experience has primarily to do with the release of the hormone oxytocin during both male and female orgasm. Oxytocin floods the bloodstream in the wake of sexual climax with sensations of pleasurable relaxation. This bodily sensation entices a woman to lie still (for the sake of conception) and lulls a man to sleep (presumably so that he will not disturb the woman as her body focuses on conceiving a child). Couples in long-term relationships of sexual intimacy know something else as well, just as Teresa of Avila did. Hormones notwithstanding, the giving of one's self to another does not reduce to physical release alone. Much like the Eucharistic Table provides a lens for viewing all the other tables where we share meals with others, so also orgasmic climax focuses a couple's attention on what that "little death" signifies for their life together. That moment can crystallize the many other moments of giving one's self to the other that transpire in even the most mundane interactions: doing laundry or washing dishes or changing a child's diaper or cooking a fabulous meal.[26]

The Eucharistic Table stands in that same moment of self-offering, of God's own *petite (grande?) mort*. The biblical writer of the letter to the Philippians preserved an ancient hymn devoted to the giving of the divine self for the sake of God's own creation; there the writer names that moment in Greek *kenosis*, or self-emptying. Paul, by contrast, portrays that moment in juridical terms, contrasting the disobedience of the First Adam, that leads to death, with the obedience—even unto death—of the Second Adam, that leads to life (1 Corinthians 15:19–26). Conspicuously absent from both of these biblical portrayals is, of course, the New Eve, not to mention the desire for intimacy. Biologists credit oxytocin for the urge to cuddle quietly with another, but intimate couples also recognize that urge

---

26. See Thomas Breidenthal, *Christian Households: The Sanctification of Nearness* (Eugene, OR: Wipf and Stock, 2004).

as an ancient hope—the hope of healing The Severing described in Genesis 3.

John provides what Paul lacks by placing the climax of his gospel quite naturally in a *garden* and depicts the announcement of new life as a woman encountering a *gardener* (John 20:11–18). Just as John evoked Genesis with the first verse of his first chapter—"in the beginning"—so here at the end he evokes that ancient text again with a garden, the primordial setting for the story of life and death and most especially of love.[27] If Paul urged us to see the Second Adam in the risen Jesus, here John urges us to see the Second Eve in Mary Magdalene. John restores Eden, where the new Adam does not return *to* dust but returns *from* dust to life and with Mary as his new Eve.

This Johannine portrayal could easily fall prey to the visions of Hollywood's movie producers who would likely propose a passionate embrace between this risen Adam and his startled Eve accompanied by the swell of orchestral music. John presents an entirely different kind of script. The history of Christian art and iconography graphically depicts that something "different" as the moment when Jesus refuses to be touched. "Do not hold on to me," Jesus says to Mary (20:17). Here, resurrection disrupts the old patterns of living "East of Eden," scrambling their ostensibly "natural" rhythms. Recalling the traditional language from Genesis, John omits any "cleaving," one to another (Genesis 2:24). In that way John does not *restore* Eden but imagines a garden transformed, where humans no longer cling to the ancient patterns of gendered domination and control. As Elizabeth Stuart reads this Johannine moment, we can scarcely grasp the new humanity that displaces those old patterns of relation; indeed, "the meaning is not to be grasped but to be given."[28]

John's untouchable Jesus signals the uncanny mystery of humanity fully alive. Mary's encounter with that mystery released her from cleaving to a male. Thomas, on the other hand, encountered it as the restoration of touchable intimacy. Gendered distinctions remain

---

27. David M. Carr finds remarkable resonances here with the garden in the Song of Songs (*The Erotic Word*, 163–67).

28. Elizabeth Stuart, "Queering Death," in Althaus-Reid and Isherwood, eds., *The Sexual Theologian*, 59.

in these accounts of resurrection but for the sake of dissolving their ultimacy.[29] In this reimagined Eden, patriarchal systems no longer coerce women to find meaning only in their relationship to men, and men no longer need to fear intimacy with other men as a source of their thriving. For Mary and Thomas this mysterious re-orientation seemed alien and even quite literally unbelievable. Beyond belief, however, intimacy appears. "Put your finger here and see my hands," Jesus says to Thomas. "Reach out your hand and put it in my side" (John 20:27). Releasing the one from coerced cleaving permits vulnerable intimacy for the other; both of them find what each of them needs.

The evangelists seem both bold and coy in these accounts of resurrection; God raises Jesus from the dead, but neither as a resuscitated corpse nor a disembodied spirit. These stories imply instead that we may not be able to recognize a fully human life—or perhaps, as Rowan Williams proposes, that we prefer the discomforts of the familiar to the disorientation of the new. The resurrection propels toward the unknown and into ever new encounters with the risen Christ "in the world of unredeemed relationships."[30]

The salvation we seek and the redemption we long for will rise up from the fullness of human life that we have not yet known. What we do know languishes in that world of "unredeemed relationships," a world scarred by violence, systemic racism, and entrenched misogyny. Within that very world, graceful glimpses appear of human abundance in God, including those moments of sexual intimacy when an Easter grace sloughs off bodily shame and its alienations to which we have been clinging for so long. In those moments we can taste the hope of a bodily home with another.

Paul insisted that our bodily homecoming requires *la petite mort*, a death he described as analogous to planting a seed in earth. The seed must die, but when it does, it yields an unexpected harvest (1 Corinthians 15:35–37). That harvest brims with an unimaginable

---

29. See Graham Ward's analysis of the differences between Mary and Thomas that displace or even dissolve the differences we might otherwise expect in relation to their genders ("There is No Sexual Difference," in *Queer Theology: Rethinking the Western Body*, ed. Gerard Loughlin [Oxford: Blackwell Publishing, 2007], 76–85).

30. Rowan Williams, *Resurrection: Interpreting the Easter Gospel*, rev. ed. (Cleveland, OH: The Pilgrim Press, 2002), 76.

intimacy, when we will know fully even as we are fully known (1 Corinthians 13:12). Paul relied frequently on metaphors from the natural world (trees, wheat, bodies), yet he also chided the Galatians for missing the uncanny and mysterious qualities of grace, which are decidedly *unnatural*. For in Christ, he writes, "there is no longer Jew or Greek, there is no longer slave or free, there is no longer male and female" (3:28).[31] These bodily markers of distinction, apparently rooted in the order of creation itself, stratified Paul's first-century society just as they do our own. But to the Galatians, Paul declares that Christ has inaugurated a new creation, an overturning of nature that exceeds our ability to grasp or imagine. The stalk of wheat quite improbably erupts from a tiny seed, an unimaginable bodily life born from bodily death.

The bodily gift of self in sexual and Eucharistic intimacy alike can reorient Christian witness to the One Story quite dramatically in Western culture. Rather than providing an escape from the untidy and often messy machinations of human life, the Gospel offers instead the hope of fully embracing the flesh that God creates and cherishes. The arc of the Jesus story, from birth and ministry through death, resurrection, and ascension, bends *toward* incarnation, not away from it. Life itself finds its homecoming in the ever greater union between flesh and spirit to which the risen Jesus points and into which the Holy Spirit leads us in ever deeper ways; that profound journey never ends, not even with death. Centuries ago, Gregory of Nyssa tried to imagine that ongoing journey beyond death in successive stages of erotic desire; as each stage finds satisfaction, a new vista of yearning opens before us.[32] The One Story thus urges Christians to bear witness, not to the gradual shedding of human existence for something more "spiritual," but precisely the opposite. As gospel writers seemed to imagine it, the gradual taking on of full human existence constitutes a spiritual practice, indeed *the* spiritual practice for disciples of the risen Christ—the one who sat at Table with friends and offered tokens of Mother Earth as the very life of God.

---

31. See Martin, "The Queer History of Galatians 3:28: No Male and Female," in *Sex and the Single Savior*, 77–90.

32. Bouteneff, *Beginnings*, 165–66.

BREAKFAST ON A BEACH

Shorelines mark a powerful boundary where land and sea meet. This nexus-point cycles through countless moments of turbulent erosion and gentle caresses. Water and wind working in concert constantly make and remake the contours of their encounter with soil and rock. Not all such encounters create a beach, but where they do, human beings have inevitably been drawn and enticed to those liminal locations—dry yet also wet; solid but shifting; navigable while also treacherous. Human beings stroll along them, launch ships from them, enjoy bonfires and picnics on them—and occasionally fall prey to their unpredictable dangers.

Thousands of millennia ago, all life on this planet began in the sea. Some of that life eventually sputtered up on a beach to reside on dry land. Many of us still return to that very spot to gaze across a glassy surface stretching toward a distant point where sky and water touch. Resolutely finite and mortal, we can stand transfixed by a seemingly endless stretch of water that inspires musings on the timeless and the eternal. We might do this with awe and amazement at times, yet also with a touch of wistfulness. Something can stir, perhaps deep within our ancient genetic code, that brings us to the brink of our origin, beckoning us to return. Humans gestate in a liquid solution that nearly matches precisely the chemical components of seawater; human blood plasma has nearly the same mineral composition as a bucket of water drawn from an ocean. So there we stand, on a beach, and quite unspeakably confront beginnings and endings.

Beaches have marked not only moments of philosophical liminality but also bodily sustenance. For countless generations, human communities have not merely played on beaches, but fished from them to provide what the human body needs to live and to thrive. We launch ourselves from the relative safety of a gently sloping shoreline into the unknown turmoil of the sea to gather a rich harvest for bodily flourishing. Doing so entails risk, but also sparks adventure. The elaborate rituals that sometimes accompany the launching of fishing fleets speak volumes about this potent moment.

The Eucharistic Table, no less than a beach, sits on a powerful shoreline boundary. Just as Earth's concerted efforts of water and wind create liminal places, so also baptism and the Holy Spirit shape that Table where we stand and face the profound mystery of our Source and our Destiny. The glories of bodily life sit displayed on that Table no less than the salty bodies of lovers playing flirtatiously in the waves crashing on a sand bar. Violence inevitably creeps into these liminal spaces, whether as rip tides and "rogue waves" or as sites for harvesting living creatures as food. Violence marks the Eucharistic Table as well, in the divine offering of the self that Christians remember as suffering and death. Religious violence and bodily glory—Christians display this provocative conjunction at every celebration of Eucharist just as humans have always done by standing on a beach.

Reading the complexities of Christian theological history through the gritty and liquid lens of a beach reveals more than most Eucharistic liturgical texts can carry, and for no fault of their crafters. Humans can barely speak what they feel with water surging around their feet as they sink into shifting sand, let alone articulate what it means to stand at a Table perched on that very edge of meaning itself. Theologians try, and often wax poetic. Even then words can fail. The great medieval theologian Thomas Aquinas certainly devoted much of his life to words. Yet apparently on the feast of St. Nicholas in 1273 while celebrating Mass, he decided to leave words behind. He received a vision at that Table that so affected him that he ended his work, leaving his massive *Summa* unfinished. Reportedly, to his secretary and friend, he said: "The end of my labors has come. All that I have written appears to be as so much straw after the things that have been revealed to me."[33]

No one knows what Aquinas saw or felt, but I find his story compelling in the same way that I love beaches. I love building sand castles and tempting the tidal surges to overwhelm them. I love taking steps into the surf, tentatively at first and then lurching into an oncoming wave with reckless abandon. I enjoy risking the safety of shore for a surge of surrender. The same could be said about the allure of sexual intimacy and the desire illuminating the Eucharistic Table; both sit on the shorelines of human life. We can never know for sure what will become of us if and when we give ourselves to

---

33. See Brian Davies, *The Thought of Thomas Aquinas* (New York: Oxford University Press, 1992), 8–9.

another. We might flounder in the crashing surf or, quite remarkably, soar on a wave's crest.

The carefully plotted patterns of Eucharistic liturgies tend to dampen the strangely alluring qualities of liminal, and therefore risky, spaces. Doctrinal declarations about the Eucharist—the importance of memory, the energy of hope, incarnational suffering, and embodied fulfillment—always describe divine encounter retrospectively, seeking to capture in ideas and words what language seems to fall short of expressing. John Zizioulas has tried to capture these allusive and alluring qualities of Christianity's central act of worship by foregrounding the evocation of the Holy Spirit at that Table. The "words of institution," for example, on which Western liturgies have so often focused ("this is my body," "this is my blood") feature relatively less prominently in Eastern rites than the unifying evocation of the Spirit.

Zizioulas focuses his attention there, on the Spirit who actually creates one from the many, not merely inspiring the hope for such communion. The fragmentation and violent divisions of humanity—signified by "the many"—find a saving balm in what Zizioulas calls "horizontal communion." At the Table, the Spirit creates from our fragmentary chaos the bonds of intimacy. This "oneness" likewise anticipates the ultimate communion beyond the historical fracturing with which we currently live, yet without abandoning the intimate bonds we glimpse at the Table.[34] This same Spirit hovered over the chaotic waters at the beginning of time to bring forth creation and now continually seeks new expressions of that erotic divine intent.[35]

The Johannine writer offers an image for the alluring liminality of the Table with his invitation to have breakfast on a beach. After the turmoil of crucifixion and the startling news of resurrection, Peter decides to go fishing and takes six other disciples with him. After a disappointing night, they catch sight of someone standing on the beach at daybreak. As their nets suddenly fill to overflowing, they finally recognize that stranger on the beach as the risen Jesus. Peter quickly puts on some clothes and jumps overboard to swim ashore. There Jesus offers him some breakfast—fish and bread, the very same menu enjoyed earlier by 5,000 people.

34. Zizioulas, *The Eucharistic Communion and the World*, 35.

35. O'Murchu, *The Transformation of Desire*, 68.

John includes a number of curious details in this short story, not least is Peter's nakedness in the boat. John also quite deliberately notes that Jesus "took the bread and gave it to them" (21:13), a Eucharistic moment standing where land and sea meet. After breakfast—as John describes it, *after sharing a meal*—Jesus asks Peter not once but three times whether Peter loves him and then urges Peter to "feed" others (21:15–17).

All the elements of a Eucharistic theology of sexual intimacy reside jumbled up in this short and provocative account of resurrection. As mystical writers often do, John scrambles linear logic and troubles tidy narratives. Moments of profound insight (resurrection) rise up precariously in ordinary time (Peter goes fishing). Quotidian rhythms feel comfortable yet remain vulnerable to surprise (a miraculous catch of fish). Shame continues to lurk around the relational edges of our lives (Peter covers his naked body) even as the Spirit propels us homeward (Peter leaps out of the boat). Expectations for pyrotechnic spiritual encounter frequently nestle in the unremarkable routines of bodily needs (breakfast). Restoration and wholeness ("do you love me?") offer forgiveness yet imply so much more ("feed my sheep").

I imagine Christian witness to the Gospel animated by that kind of mystical mash-up of bodily desire and spiritual insight. Forgiveness plays a key role in that mash-up but pales in comparison to standing naked and unashamed, redeemed from our long night of fruitless labor and fed with the reassuring dawn of love in the intimate sharing of food. I imagine Christian communities approaching the Eucharistic Table in a rush, clamoring for the promise of a new and barely recognizable humanity. I relish the image of leaping from our secure little boats and hoping at last to find ourselves at home in our own skin without shame, among our companions without guilt, and trusting in God without any fear.

Imagine all this and the "heavenly country" will appear, glimmering on the horizon of a distant shore yet made gracefully near, our heritage as God's daughters and sons.

4

Eucharist
EARTHLY FOOD AND HEAVENLY SEX

Because in the love of wife and husband,
you have given us an image
of the heavenly Jerusalem,
adorned as a bride for her bridegroom,
your Son Jesus Christ our Lord . . .

—*"PROPER PREFACE FOR MARRIAGE"*
THE BOOK OF COMMON PRAYER

*A*dorning a bride for her wedding proves expensive. For the average cost of a wedding in the United States, one could make a down payment on a fine house in a lovely neighborhood.[1] Adorning a church building for worship proves just as costly. Even in a moderately sized mainline Protestant congregation, a full set of clergy vestments and altar appointments for each season of the liturgical year—including chalice, paten, and candleholders (not to mention prayer books, hymnals, and bibles)—quickly adds up to many thousands, not hundreds of dollars.

Families justify the cost of a wedding for reasons similar to justifying the cost of adorning lovely worship spaces—the occasion demands it. Some Christians might cite the Psalmist, who encouraged his readers to "worship the Lord in holy splendor" (96:9). Most Anglicans know this biblical text from the Book of Common Prayer, which uses the King James translation: "worship the Lord in the beauty of

---

1. In 2012, families spent an average of $28,427 on a wedding; the highest average cost was in New York City, at $76,687 (*http://money.cnn.com/2013/03/10/pf/wedding-cost/index.html*).

holiness."[2] Congregations put this biblical exhortation into practice by creating liturgical spaces worthy of the splendid and glorious God they worship. To renew and deepen our collective witness to the One Story, we might attend just as carefully to the flip side of that commitment to beautiful churches. Congregations could, for example, return often to this question: Is our worship space lovely enough to deserve the presence of human beings, of God's own beloved?

Some years ago, I had the privilege of serving as an intern in a cathedral-sized Episcopal parish in a major metropolitan center in the U.S. That church offered a highly choreographed Anglo-Catholic liturgy on Sunday mornings in a building adorned with beautiful stained glass windows, gorgeous linens on the high altar, heavily brocaded vestments, and an angelic choir. All of that beauty stood in rather stark contrast to the grit, grime, and occasional violence of the urban streets directly outside. As Judas Iscariot might say about that ecclesial extravagance, could not this building be sold and the money given to the poor (John 12:5)?

As if responding to that ancient question, this particular parish also operated a women's shelter during the week, which provided food and temporary housing for battered women, some of whom were also homeless and single mothers. The relationship between the beautiful worship space and the women's shelter eluded me until I spoke with one of the women who stayed at the shelter. She attended Sunday morning liturgies and I finally asked her why. After looking around her at that soaring gothic structure, she said, "Oh, it's so pretty. All these pretty things—and they're here for me!"

Years have now passed and I am grateful for a similar experience with a friend whom I will call "Joan." After retiring from an administrative position, she redoubled her energies on hosting fabulous dinner parties with her husband. A devotee of the "slow food" movement and a gourmand in her own right, the food she offers at her table never fails to astonish and please. More than that, Joan collects fine china—obsessively. The table never looks the same from one party to the next in that hospitable home. The deep, saturated colors of the dining room and the wildly varied patterns of

---

2. BCP, 44.

the table's accoutrements, together with the fresh, organic, delectably made food, all combine for an experience of profound welcome. Each guest at that table marvels at the feeling of being wanted and desired. Each guest could easily agree with what I heard a homeless woman declare in that ornate church many years ago: "All these pretty things—and they're here for me!"

When intimate couples have sex, do they say to each other what a woman living in an urban shelter declared about Church? Do Christians feel that way when they worship at the Eucharistic Table? Living more fully into affirmative answers to both of those questions would change the world. I suspect few Christians pause to consider the world-changing potential of weaving food, sex, and Eucharist together in their spiritual practice, yet they reside at the very heart of Christian faith. For centuries, Christians have flirted with these erotic connections by imagining the Eucharistic feast as an anticipation of the heavenly wedding banquet yet to come. How many people today, whether Christian or not, think about the Church with images of a feast? Do we imagine ourselves adorned as a bride, the cause of God's own delighted desire? Why would any of this matter for the panoply of twenty-first-century challenges all of us now face? The potent nexus of weddings and dinner parties can start to suggest answers, even some surprising ones, especially for the sake of invigorating the socially transformative potential of Eucharistic practice.

Nearly every human society has developed elaborate rituals to celebrate a wedding. Most of the ritual fuss orbits around the bride— the dress, the veil, her comportment, her desirability. In some cultures, the bride's attractiveness corresponds directly to her dowry, to the material goods that will transfer from one family to another in the vows that make a marriage. Close friends of a bride celebrate with her and some of them likely long for their own turn in the ritual and material spotlight—"always a bridesmaid and never a bride" expresses much more than the longing for a husband. Surely everyone wants to feel as desirable as a bride bedecked in the garlands of intimacy and valued with an extravagant dowry. Surely everyone wants to feel as wanted as the dinner guests do in Joan and Jeffrey's home. Surely all of us want to see pretty things and believe that all those things have been laid out just for us.

These wistful yearnings give voice to the One Story of Christian faith—the deep desire and abiding hope for divine communion. That story continues to inspire whenever it persuades us that we are desired and desirable; it likewise commissions us to help others feel the same way. That story, however, never floats free from the cultural contexts in which Christians hear and tell it. The gendered character of social and personal relations that have always traced the contours of Christian witness now unfold in a global economic system that creates commodities from intimacies. Worship services, dinner parties, and celebrations of marital union all suffer today from the relentless commodification of human and planetary life. While the physical expressions and tokens of our affection matter, Wall Street now traces them with market indices and Internet companies measure them with the number of "clicks" received on an online advertisement for bridal gowns. This matrix of gendered economic forces deserves sustained Eucharistic reflection, especially in the light of the modern wedding industry and what we might call "bridal objectification."

Christian theologies of marriage have varied widely over the centuries, yet Christians have always tried to bring those theologies with them to the Eucharist. Episcopalians, for example, declare in our Eucharistic celebration of a wedding that God has given us "in the love of wife and husband" an "image of the heavenly Jerusalem, adorned as a bride for her bridegroom. . . ."[3] The "bridegroom" is Christ and we, all of us, are the "bride." What might that image have meant to the first hearers of it? More than just one thing, certainly, and very little having to do with modern Western marriage.

Early Christians viewed sexual intimacy and marriage with a great deal of suspicion, and often for good cultural and theological reasons. We might recall, for example, the many reasons why it matters that Christianity emerged from the context of Greco-Roman culture, and, more specifically, in the crucible of empire. In ancient Rome the husband/father, or *paterfamilias*, did not belong to the *domus*, or the household, but was rather in charge of it, and in exactly the same way that the Roman Emperor was not considered a citizen of the Empire but instead the Empire's Lord. (We can

---

3. BCP, 381.

trace the English word "domestic" back to the Greek word for house and the Latin word for master of the house; both contributed to our words "dominion" and "domination.")

A number of theologians in the first three centuries of Christian traditions found this familial pattern deeply problematic. In response, they tried to offer a subtle counter-cultural critique of the Roman *domus* as microcosm of the Empire and the *paterfamilias* as the local incarnation of the emperor. Early Christian writers did this with a socio-political reading of the biblical letter to the Ephesians: "Wives, be subject to your husbands as you are to the Lord" and "[h]usbands, love your wives, just as Christ loved the Church and gave himself up for her" (Ephesians 5:22, 25). This biblical text may leave much to be desired among those who strive for egalitarian marriages, but for early Christian communities this text sparked revolutionary aspirations. In contrast to the emperor who ruled over Rome and the household alike, Christians placed their trust and fealty in the *only* Lord, Jesus Christ. For many of these ancient Christian writers, *both* husband and wife were members of their own household, which functioned not as a microcosm of the empire but instead a microcosm of the Church as the Body of Christ. This "body" thrives by the giving of self, one to another and for the good of the other—both wives *and* husbands.[4]

The imperial and economic forces against which those early theologians bristled continue today and in ways that our ancient ancestors in faith could not have imagined. The average cost of even a modest middle-class wedding may startle, but even more so the gap between compensation packages for corporate executives and the salaries they pay to their employees.[5] In today's global economy, products assembled in one country are made from parts manufactured in another, and often with little if any assessment of environmental impact, not to mention regulatory oversight for fair wages or worker safety.

---

4. For an overview of early Christian approaches to marriage and family in relation to Roman imperial views, see Geoffrey S. Nathan, *The Family in Late Antiquity: The Rise of Christianity and the Endurance of Tradition* (New York: Routledge, 1999), 39–53.

5. Depending on the industry, the average CEO makes between 204 and 495 times as much as the average worker (*http://www.businessweek.com/articles/2013-05-02/disclosed-the-pay-gap-between-ceos-and-employees*).

Neo-colonial aspirations help to ensure those corporate profits with international trade agreements as formidable in today's world as imperial armies were in centuries past. These labyrinthine, globalized markets are on display every time an extravagantly adorned bride walks down an aisle to meet her groom. As they stand before the Eucharistic Table in a ritual of mutual self-giving, that Table displays something else as well: God's own passionate desire for communion.

What actually happens in Eucharistic celebrations? Are human lives "salvaged" from shipwreck, as the original meaning of the Latin verb *salvare* implies? Or are we "bought back" with a pricey ransom in a cosmic redemption scheme, as the Latin verb *redimere* implies? What if human beings at long last viewed ourselves as the "pearl of great value" (Matthew 13:46) and the "lost coin" (Luke 15:8–10) or the one sheep out of a hundred that the Shepherd cannot bear to lose (Luke 15:4–6)? Each of these economic images in Jesus' parables resists today's obsession with commodification. The pearl, the coin, the sheep—each is irreplaceable, each is unique. How might this "anti-commodity" gospel shape not only our Eucharistic spirituality but also our sexually intimate relationships? More pointedly perhaps, how might the dynamics of our sexual intimacies shape our approach to the Eucharistic Table, and what might that Table then inspire us to do concerning the juggernaut of unbridled commodification and corporate profiteering scarring our economic landscape?

These profound questions provoke a host of social and economic quandaries that our ancestors in faith could not have anticipated but to which they nonetheless provide a response. In a world of imperial power and allegiances, the Eucharist bears witness to the loyalty of love. This loyalty resides first and foremost in God's own Trinitarian life of mutual desire and fulfillment, a deeply mysterious life in which the Eucharist quite remarkably invites our own participation. The Eucharist invites and also makes such participation effectual, which we can observe and celebrate whenever we manage by some unimaginable grace to cross and dissolve the boundaries of hostility that keep human communities divided, suspicious, and anxious.

This vision of Eucharistic life readily appears in what often remains unspoken in our Christian faith communities—the passionate mutuality of sexual intimacy. Bodily desire leads human beings to seek both food and sex, an erotic impulse that likewise sets the Eucharistic Table. As the circle of intimate desire expands outward from that Table, it carries with it the potential to transform the many social and economic structures arrayed against humanity's hope for communion. Uniting bedroom and table, as it were, invites us to see ourselves more clearly, not as consumers of bodily objects but as passionate lovers who reflect God's own self-offering for the sake of life. As Craig J. N. de Paulo puts it, the Table urges each of us to "open the heart, one's *eros* so he or she may truly participate in the liturgy as a lover but also as one who is loved; and in this way, find God and even a deeper and unknown understanding of oneself."[6] This Eucharistic passion shines in the love of wife and husband, but just as brightly in the table of hospitality Joan and Jeffrey so lovingly set in their home. Both of these images and so many more quite properly and joyfully evoke the heavenly Jerusalem.

Traveling through our exile from Eden, the vision of the heavenly city will illumine our path more clearly if we consider, first, the ubiquitous drive to commodification in contemporary Western society and, second, the mysteriously strange life Christians evoke with the symbol of the Holy Trinity. Reflection on both inspires a spiritual practice we might refer to as "border crossing," of being drawn ever deeper into God's own life of divine intimacy. Still further, the hope for communion inspired by that Eucharistic practice equips us for world-changing ministries, or what Paul described as God's own mission of reconciliation that God has entrusted to us (2 Corinthians 5:18).

COMMODITY EXCHANGE

Christian communities sell things, from bibles to pastoral services and trinkets in gift shops. Do Christians sell worship? Do we sell the Body of Christ? How much would we pay for our salvation? Can absolutely anything be bought and sold, traded, bartered, or exchanged for something else? What could possibly interrupt a global market economy that depends on buying more, eating more,

---

6. Craig J. N. de Paulo, "A Mystagogical Ascent of Love: A Spiritual Reflection on the Sensuality of the Byzantine Divine Liturgy," in *Confessions of Love: The Ambiguities of Greek Eros and Latin Caritas*, ed. Craig J. N. de Paulo et al. (New York: Peter Lang, 2011), 216.

and procreating more children (to replace the consumers who grow old and die)?

Modern Western culture certainly did not invent the vexations associated with capitalistic economies, but we have fine-tuned those mechanisms that embed market dynamics in nearly every aspect of our daily lives. Since that moment many millennia ago when *homo sapiens* shifted to an agrarian way of life, human beings have created economies, both household-small and now planetary-large. Economies are patterns of ordering relationships, especially for the exchange of goods, whether services or things. Human societies eventually devised a monetary system to mediate that exchange—for this valuable thing I will give you something else, an agreed-upon symbol of value itself, which you can then use to obtain some other thing of equal value. The agreed-upon symbol is, of course, money.

"Commodities" have always played a vital role in human economies. Generally speaking, a commodity refers to whatever has market value without regard to its origin or seller. It makes no difference, for example, whether a bushel of wheat came from Iowa or Nebraska, or whether an ounce of gold changed hands five or a dozen times before it appears in a market—wheat is wheat, gold is gold, and the market will pay the same price for all of it. Therein lies the logic and economic genius of commodity markets. Could the same economic logic transform virtually anything into a commodity? That question ought to give us pause more than it usually does.

Ancient societies often treated members of one or more segments of the human race as exchangeable goods in slave auctions. This continued through the modern period, including in the antebellum society of the United States. Slave auctions did not end, however, with Abraham Lincoln's Emancipation Proclamation in 1863. Today's global economy includes a vast underground market in international sex trafficking in which one young woman (and sometimes one young man) will work just as well as any other human "product" to sell for bodily pleasure—a commodity, in other words. Internet pornography runs on a similar market logic—where the product comes from or who sells it makes little difference in a marketplace of buying and selling sexual pleasure; human bodies and even particular body parts function as commodities.

Food falls prey to the same market forces. I finally understood the obsession in financial markets with "pork belly futures" when I recalled my own love of bacon. Modern Western culture now lives with a horrifying system of factory farming in which very little about the lives of animals most people eat resembles a good life; most of them never even see the light of day. "Torture" reasonably describes the means to produce the food most Americans consume at most meals—torture, that is, to reduce individual beings to interchangeable commodities on an open market. Carol Adams noticed something else—the disturbing parallels between objectifying women's bodies and commodifying animals for food. Adams persuasively demonstrates the similarities between packaging non-human animals in supermarkets and packaging the human female body for sexual consumption.[7]

The objectifying mechanism that transforms living beings into commodities reaches far beyond supermarket shelves and online marketplaces; it infiltrates Eucharistic celebrations as well. Few Christians ensconced in late global capitalism can help but read some strands of Christian theology as a market economy, especially when considering the doctrine of the atonement. According to one popularized version of that theological claim, humanity's sinfulness stands as an offense against God's justice and thus demands a sacrifice; Jesus put himself in the place of humanity in that economic transaction. In that light, consuming the body of Christ at the Eucharistic Table risks not only perpetuating the commodification of human bodies but also God's own body as well. Still further, the bread broken at that Table comes from a chain of labor, or as Andrea Bieler and Luise Schottroff describe it, the "circle of production that is attached to this particular food."[8] The dirt ploughed, the seeds planted, the grain harvested, the dough kneaded and baked, the truck driver to deliver it, the storekeeper to shelve it—all this labor and more sits neatly on a sacred Table as religious commodities waiting to be consumed.

Christian congregations remain just as vulnerable as anyone else to these Western market forces that increasingly try to make commodities from everything, including the most intimate bodily relations.

---

7. Carol Adams, *The Sexual Politics of Meat: A Feminist-Vegetarian Critical Theory* (New York: Continuum, 1990).

8. Bieler and Schottroff, *The Eucharist*, 111.

Scott Cowdell calls this the "commercially profitable sexualization of commodities," which transforms our deepest desires into products:

> Partners and now children are reduced to consumer vehicles for individual fulfillment, as part of a lifestyle package commodified in terms of personal satisfaction and well-being. Hence alterity, mystery, and respect are overcome by the logic of commodification, with its attendant redundancy and wastage.[9]

Approaching the Eucharist as a symbol of the heavenly wedding banquet can draw us into that consumer-oriented orbit, barely escaping the economic grip of the modern wedding industry and its objectification of brides. In this case, of course, the "bride" is *us*. Has modern Western culture trained Christians to approach our own tradition as a religious commodity exchange? If so, a Eucharistic eroticism could break that cycle by urging us to exchange bodily commodification for sexual intimacy. Keith Jones portrays this possibility elegantly:

> Jesus's sacrifice is not the transaction that buys God off, but the genuine love that brings Jesus to share our predicament. Jesus offers all he is to God as a pattern of what all human life should constantly do, to offer "ourselves, our souls and bodies," as lovers do, without reserve.[10]

Perhaps another pairing of Genesis with the Gospel according to John could set us more firmly on the path that Jones so helpfully charts.

The ever-expanding circle of shame and its debilitating effects in Genesis 3 spills over into Genesis 4, where the tragedy of the Garden results in fratricide. Here that familiar trope of sibling rivalry includes another layer—the rivalry between agriculture and animal husbandry. Abel tends crops; Cain herds animals. Each of them presents the fruits of his labor as an offering to God yet inexplicably only one proves acceptable—the one offered by Abel. Cain responds

---

9. Cowdell, *Abiding Faith*, 29.

10. Keith Jones, *Adam's Dream: Human Longings and the Love of God* (London: Mowbray, 2007), 121.

with rage at this rejection, yet another consequence of shame, and in this case attached to one's life work. That rage leads him to kill his brother (Genesis 4:1–16).

Some have read this ancient story as a biblical witness to God's preference for a vegetarian diet. Others scrutinize this text for hints of Cain's unworthiness to offer anything at all, evidence for which this text provides virtually none. Miguel de la Torre sketches these hypotheses and suggests another: God's rejection of primogeniture, or the right of inheritance granted automatically to a firstborn. That theme echoes throughout biblical texts and we could read this one as a critique of social privilege.[11] Christians might also read this story through the lens of the "last supper" where Jesus offers fruits of the earth rather than animal flesh as the tokens for the New Covenant, presumably aligning himself with Abel's offering. John troubles that interpretation early on in his gospel account by describing Jesus as the "lamb of God" who takes away the sins of the world (John 1:29, 36). Perhaps John's Jesus heals that ancient rivalry in Genesis by combining the offerings of Cain and Abel into one—the "lamb" becomes bread and wine.

John troubles most of the typical readings of both Genesis and Eucharist by omitting any institution narrative at that final meal. Unlike the other three gospel accounts, John presents a moment of tenderness and intimacy as Jesus washes the disciples' feet. He then makes the point of this tenderness plain: "Love each other" (13:34). That exhortation could just as easily extend backwards to Cain and Abel as it could flash forward to today. But this does not exhaust John's Eucharistic musings, not by far. John finds another place in his gospel account to insert a Eucharistic narrative—the feeding of the five thousand in the sixth chapter. In stark contrast to the other gospel writers, John puts the Eucharist not in the context of betrayal, arrest, violence, and death, but instead in the context of feeding hungry people.[12] Notice that John's Jesus in that moment took the

---

11. de la Torre, *Genesis*, 94.

12. Scholars disagree about whether John intended this chapter as a Eucharistic narrative. Raymond E. Brown, however, was mostly convinced that John likely did, and certainly early Christian communities read it that way as well (*The Gospel According to John 1–XII*, The Anchor Bible, v. 29 [New York: Doubleday & Co., 1966], 246–250).

loaves, gave thanks, and distributed them (6:11), which clearly mirrors the last supper narratives in the other three canonical gospels.
"Gave thanks" in that verse comes from the Greek *eucharistein*, from
which we derive the word Eucharist.

Notice as well that this miraculous feeding leaves not eleven
or thirteen, but exactly twelve baskets of leftovers, just as there are
twelve tribes of Israel, just as there are twelve disciples. John thus
includes even Judas in that number. As John's Jesus says, "Gather
up the fragments . . . so that nothing may be lost" (6:12). Nothing
will be lost, not even the one who would betray him. Early Christian theologians interpreted the five loaves as the five books of the
Torah which, once they are broken open, yield the two great commandments, signified by the two fish: to love God and to love our
neighbors. Above all, John wants the Eucharist to stand for divine
abundance—the utterly gratuitous, wildly excessive, and shockingly
profligate abundance of God. Or more simply, in the words of a wise
woman living on urban streets, "Oh it's so pretty. All these pretty
things—and they're here for me!"[13]

John inserts something else in this Eucharistic account—resistance from established religious authorities. John's Jesus finds himself on the defensive in this chapter and responds by recalling the
founding story of his critics, including the miraculous gift of manna
in the wilderness. Certainly there, in an ancient desert, manna fits
the bill of a religious commodity: offered once each day, always the
same, and for the same singular purpose. Here John's Jesus offers
something to exchange for commodified religion—his own particular body: "I am the bread of life. Whoever comes to me will never
be hungry, and whoever believes in me will never be thirsty" (6:35).
We could—and Christians have—read this moment as one among
many that replaces Judaism with the superior expression of religion
in Christianity. John may well have meant to do precisely that.[14] We
could instead read John's Jesus as taking his place among a long line

---

13. William Temple believed that John scattered Eucharistic references throughout his gospel account to underscore the primacy of communion and its abundance in all aspects of Christian life and not only when gathered at the Table (*Readings in St. John's Gospel*, 95).

14. See Raymond E. Brown, *The Community of the Beloved Disciple: The Life, Love, and
Hates of an Individual Church in New Testament Times* (Mahwah, NJ: Paulist Press, 1979).

of ancient Hebrew prophets calling Israel back to covenantal intimacy, not as a matter of law (certainly not religious commodities)
but as a matter of spousal fidelity with God. At the very least, the
abundant life those prophets attached to such faithfulness likewise
animated the mission of Jesus (John 10:10).

Jesus echoes these ancient themes throughout John's account,
from the wedding story in Cana in the second chapter, to the image
of a vine and it's intertwined branches in the fifteenth. The constant
(though mostly unspoken) refrain throughout these moments rises up
like a beacon: God desires us. Lest there be any doubt, John inserts a
bold, even scandalous, invitation right after Jesus feeds five thousand
people with twelve baskets of food left over: Now, John's Jesus says,
take *me*; eat *me*; feed on *me* as bread for the world (6:52–58). This
qualifies as bold and scandalous not because it invites cannibalism;
this invitation scandalizes because of its *eroticism*.

No less than today, first-century societies frequently fixed their
attention on hunger and its twin expressions: the desire to eat and
the yearning for physical intimacy. Food and sex—these driving
urges for survival and communion, for thriving and union, punctuate
this ostensibly "mystical" account of the Gospel according to John in
nearly every chapter. These hungers and desires define us so deeply
precisely because we fear they will never find satisfaction and fulfillment. To that fear, John responds with abundance—with twelve
baskets of leftovers!

"The poor need not only bread," declared Monsignor Hilde-
brand. "The poor also need beauty."[15] To which I would add: the
poor also need to know that they themselves are beautiful and
desired. Pursuing that need makes us human with each other. Seeing ourselves and others as beautiful and desirable in a world not of
scarcity but of abundance would "turn the world upside down," just
as Luke supposed (Acts 17:6). Christians begin to grasp that world-
changing hope when we witness a wedding and imagine the "bride"
of the "heavenly Jerusalem." Rising up on that distant horizon of our
spiritual sight, the hope of the heavenly wedding feast sets an agenda
here and now in how we live with our intimate partners, our friends,

---

15. Quoted in Fox, *Original Blessing*, 209.

our neighbors, and, indeed, with planetary ecosystems. John makes this very point by presenting heavenly realities as earthly food. Could our earthly intimacies reflect heavenly hopes? How can the heavenly Jerusalem inspire human thriving beyond commodification?

Sexual intimacy has meant countless different things over the centuries. Whatever Christians believe it means today will fashion our approach to Eucharist and the posture we adopt at that Table. If sexual intimacy resists all attempts to reduce it to a product, a service, or a commodity in any way, then our Eucharistic practice will likewise inspire resistance to treating any living being as an object. Among the many ways Christians have drawn sexual intimacy into theological speech, one in particular runs throughout historical traditions as a vibrant thread, weaving together theological insight and liturgical practice: sexual intimacy can bear witness to God's own self-giving for the sake of life. Moreover, God continually makes this self-offering with no guarantee it will be received or reciprocated. Commodity markets would recoil from that notion. Uncontrollable risk? Watch the market plunge. Exposed vulnerability? Watch the spiritual insight grow.

Mutual self-giving played a significant role in the historical unfolding of Trinitarian doctrine as well as the textured character of Eucharistic piety. Yet, only rarely have the mutual exchanges of sexual intimacy resided comfortably in those theological hallmarks of Christian traditions. That lacuna presents a rich opportunity for Christians to renew and refresh our witness to the One Story. A Eucharistic theology of sexual intimacy would certainly fuel liturgical resistance to a commodity culture. Still more, it offers a vision of the "heavenly Jerusalem," a counter-cultural vision where commodified bodies enjoy the tender intimacies of communion.

THE MYSTERIOUS STRANGER

Several boys in a medieval European village encounter an intriguing traveler in their midst claiming to be an angel. This stranger turns out to be a nephew of Satan, and havoc quite understandably ensues, including witch trials, hangings, and untimely deaths. Mark Twain died before he could finish his novel *The Mysterious Stranger*, but the literary trope captured by that title predates Twain by many centuries and continued after him in a slew of American cultural media. The first installment of Peter Jackson's film adaptation of J. R. R. Tolkien's *Lord of the Rings* includes an important moment when the three Hobbit adventurers encounter a mysterious stranger in a tavern. Unsure at first of the harm he might intend, they eventually realize that he is none other than the lost king of Gondor, who accompanies and assists the Hobbits on their world-saving quest.

Luke the evangelist concludes his gospel account with two disciples of Jesus encountering a mysterious stranger as they traveled to a village called Emmaus. They found this stranger enthralling, and indeed their "hearts burned within them" as he spoke to them about ancient prophecies and present hopes. After arriving to Emmaus, they urged this stranger to spend the night with them at the inn. As they shared a meal and the stranger broke bread, the disciples recognized him as none other than the risen Jesus (Luke 24:31). In the fifth century, Leo the Great believed those disciples recognized something else as well, and quite pointedly drew our gaze yet again back to Eden:

> Their lukewarm hearts were fired by the light of faith and began to burn within them . . . And as they shared their meal with [Jesus], their eyes were opened in the breaking of bread, opened far more happily to the sight of their own glorified humanity than were the eyes of our first parents to the shame of their sin.[16]

Leo barely hints at the healing effects of intimacy for our shame even as Luke punctuates the narrative arc of his story with moments of increasing intimacy with a stranger—traveling on a road together, extending hospitality, sharing a meal. As intimacy deepens, so do the insights, which eventually propel them—"that same hour"—on an adventure of world-changing proclamation (24:33–35). That same narrative arc can illumine our sexually intimate relationships as well, which often surprise us. We can find ourselves deeply comforted by the physical touch of a hand on a shoulder, an embrace, or a moment of hand-holding when we were not expecting such tenderness. We might also find ourselves overwhelmed with the sensations

---

16. Leo the Great, Sermon 1 for the Ascension, 2–4: PL 54, 395–396.

of bodily pleasure that accompany genital contact. Orgasm describes one such moment, but only as a small portion of that experiential arc. We might find ourselves inexplicably "attached" to another, bound together in a mutual dance of bodily titillations and emotional affinities; we might actually declare in such moments, "I love you." That declaration can surprise both parties, but even more, the consequences of finding one's self in love, with love, and as love itself. Psychologists and biologists alike affirm what human beings have known for millennia—being "in love" constitutes a form of temporary insanity. We see the world differently. We see ourselves differently. The world itself, as we perceive it, changes.[17]

For some, the changed world of sexual passion slides rather naturally into the more cozy and relaxed realms of knowledge, of *knowing* someone. The ancient Hebrew verb "to know" often stood euphemistically for genital sexual intimacy, yet of course no one can really "know" another human being from a single moment of erotic passion. But how many such moments does it take and what, finally, do we really *know* about another person? Long-married couples will often muse on how they can finish each other's sentences, how they seem to sense what the other thinks before speaking, and how daily habits become familiar cadences. Still, as a clergy colleague once remarked, even after twenty-five years of marriage his wife seemed more "mysterious" to him than when they were first married—and both agreed that they enjoyed a happy and fruitful relationship.

While sexual intimacies can surprise us in both delightful and disorienting ways, attaching the word "mystery" to those surprises seems less likely as biologists explain the effects of hormones on cognitive functions and psychologists frame romantic attraction as leftovers from unmet childhood needs. Thomas Laqueur expands that list to include the advent of modern scientific method, industrial revolutions, the rise of evangelical revivals, and profound shifts in Western philosophy, all of which gradually eroded the uncanny qualities of sexual desire, detaching sexual intimacy from the metaphysics of an ordered world.[18] Trinitarian doctrine and Eucharistic piety have

---

17. See Frank Tallis, *Love Sick: Love as a Mental Illness* (New York: De Capo Press, 2005).

18. Laqueur, *Making Sex*, 11.

fallen prey to a similar fate. The symbolic and metaphorical character of both the Trinity and Eucharist—ideally meant to invite us ever deeper into the mystery of divine life and divine self-offering—flattens in a world that runs on empirical science. The earliest celebrations of Eucharist of course exhibited very little of the later intricacies of Trinitarian speculation. Yet both that original table fellowship and the doctrinal development alike emerged from what most sexually intimate couples experience in their first blush of attraction and tentative steps toward physical pleasure—the deep urge for communion.

Today, mainline Christian communities (among others) seem rather reticent to embrace an unapologetically Trinitarian faith and even more so to discuss the complexities of sexual intimacy. Discerning what they have in common presents a compelling entry point into Christian faith as not only good news, but *mysteriously* good news. "Mysterious," however, need not mean "complicated." Consider John's decision to articulate his vision of Eucharist in the context of abundance—feeding five thousand people with plenty of leftovers to spare. That image of excess shaped in subtle ways the development, centuries later, of the Christian view of God as triune. Christians celebrate a God of wild excess, as the love of each "person" of the Trinity not only unites them in eternal intimacy but also spills over from their relations into the fecundity of creation itself, the unfathomable reaches of the cosmos in which all of us dwell. Wendy Farley invites that startling Trinitarian vision like this:

> It is a divine love ceaselessly, infinitely pouring out the good, exuberantly sharing the beauty of being with all that can be. Eros is this paradoxical "zeal" of love that abandons itself in order to express itself. Self-enclosed love is not love at all . . . In the case of the divine, this self-othering of love is the act of creation.[19]

The uncontrollable, bodily passion that leads a lover to say "I love you" to the beloved likewise describes the ecstatic energies of the Trinity; those energies create all there is.[20]

---

19. Farley, "Beguiled by Beauty," 136.

20. Catherine Mowry Lacugna, *God for Us: The Trinity and Christian Life* (New York: HarperCollins, 1991), 355.

The various approaches to Trinitarian doctrine in Christian history all seek, both simply and profoundly, to affirm divine life as essentially relational. Still further, this divine relational energy cannot contain itself within a dyadic system; it exhibits instead a triadic character—the shared loved between the two qualifies as an equal third, opening up unimaginably wide horizons and spaces for relational intimacy. Dipping even briefly into these doctrinal abstractions may seem rather far removed from personal intimacies, yet Thomas Aquinas tried to convince us centuries ago to notice their gracious entanglements. Aquinas insisted that theology by definition relies on an "analogy of being" between God and God's creatures. We can speak about God at all, in other words, because of the divine image in which we are made. Our relationships, no matter how imperfectly, thus retain an imprint of God's own relational life; "divine life is therefore also *our* life."[21]

Needless to say, few sexually intimate couples pause in the midst of their passionate embraces to reflect on their participation in Trinitarian emanations. Moreover, sexually intimate encounters always run the risk of commodification, of turning a human subject into an object for personal gratification, not to mention the risk of "shared narcissism." Erotic energy remains vulnerable to the restriction of one's focus solely on another and creating a kind of closed circuit that shuts out the wider world of social relations. Eucharistic piety can fall prey to the same risks.

No less than the intricacies of Trinitarian doctrine and Eucharistic participation, human sexual relations exhibit their own complexities. Reflecting on how all of these interrelate offers an opportunity to enter more deeply into the mystery of each. As Sarah Coakley has tried to show, prayerful attention to Scripture can enhance *both* our sustained contemplation of God *and* our sexually intimate relations as they touch on the same hope for communion. Coakley does this by turning to Paul's letter to the Romans and to his "proto-Trinitarian" description of the Spirit "sighing" within us when we pray in the name of Christ (Romans 8:12–27). These sighs, or "groans too deep for words," Coakley reads as a profound participation in the life of

---

21. Lacugna, *God for Us*, 1.

the Triune God; they can likewise and in the same fashion inform our most intimate bodily encounters. Coakley proposes along that path that we "turn Freud on his head. Instead of thinking of 'God' language as really being about sex (Freud's reductive ploy), we need to understand sex as really about God, and about the deep desire that we feel for God."[22] This, Coakley believes, lurks behind Paul's evocative descriptions of prayer in his letter to the Romans.

Coakley also quickly reminds us that many Christian traditions retain some profound anxiety about where this analogy might lead. Augustine, for example, briefly entertained the image of the "lover, the beloved, and the love that binds them" as a way to speak of God's Trinitarian life. Eventually, however, he abandons that image for fear of its overtly carnal implications. Coakley pointedly cites Augustine himself in his treatise on the Trinity: "Let us tread the flesh underfoot and mount up to the soul." The peculiar irony of trampling flesh in a tradition constructed on incarnation may have escaped Augustine's notice, but it need not derail our own soulful ascents. Coakley agrees and turns to a particularly insightful portion from the work of the French feminist, Luce Irigaray. Coakley summarizes the insight like this:

> Sexual love at its best is not "egological," not even a "duality in closeness," but a shared transcendence of two selves toward the other, within a "shared space, a shared breath. In this relation . . . we are at least three . . . you, me, and our creation of that ecstasy of ourself in us (*de nous en nous*)." As each goes out to the other in mutual abandonment and attentiveness, so it becomes clear that a third is at play—the irreducibility of "shared transcendence."[23]

Tracing that "shared transcendence" from the bedroom to the Table poses fewer challenges than we might imagine. Here Augustine lends a better, though no less provocative proposal when he insists that we ourselves are the bread on the Eucharistic Table. In his classic *The City of God*, Augustine tried to make clear that Christian priests do not offer sacrifices to the martyrs, as if they were gods. "Indeed,

---

22. Sarah Coakley, "Living into the Mystery of the Trinity: Trinity, Prayer, and Sexuality," *Anglican Theological Review* 80:2 (1998), 230.

23. Coakley, "Living into the Mystery of the Trinity," 231.

the [Eucharistic] sacrifice itself is the Body of Christ, which is not offered to [the martyrs], *because they themselves are that body.*"[24] Here Augustine echoes Paul's declaration to the Corinthians: "Now you are the body of Christ and individually members of it" (1 Corinthians 12:27). The "shared transcendence" of sexually intimate couples thus mirrors the "shared transcendence" of Christians gathered at the Eucharistic Table. There we do not "consume" each other as commodities, but find instead the graceful invitation to participate intimately with each other in Christ—or rather *as* Christ—while the Spirit sweeps our bodily lives into the very life of God.[25]

In the end, that Table returns us to the beginning, to Genesis, where the biblical writer made a claim that has posed a riddle ever since: "God created humankind in his image, in the image of God he created them; male and female he created them" (1:27). In what precisely does that image consist? Both Jews and Christians have ventured a variety of answers over the centuries ranging from rationality to creativity as the *imago Dei,* or the image of God in human life. A Eucharistic theology of sexual intimacy offers another location for musing on that question: erotic embodiment. The One Story encourages that musing as our abiding hope for communion reflects God's own deep desire for the same thing, eternally expressed in the mutual relations of the Trinity. In this way the Eucharist invites an insight that I imagine neither Paul nor Augustine ever contemplated, even if they provoked it. In the sexually intimate moment of mutual abandonment, a moment of giving of one's self to another in a shared transcendence, we reflect, no matter how well or poorly, the strangely alluring and mysteriously Trinitarian life of God, the God in whose image we are made.

BORDER CROSSINGS

Borders and boundaries mark our lives daily at nearly every step— the threshold of my front door, the fence that separates my backyard from my neighbor's, the crosswalk at an intersection, and many less

---

24. *City of God* 22, 10: CCSL 48, 828 (emphasis added).

25. Eugene F. Rogers teases out these Trinitarian implications in various ways in *Sexuality and the Christian Body* (Oxford: Blackwell Publishing, 1999), esp. Part III, "The Way of the Body into the Triune God," 193–275.

tangible ones as well, whether encountered as different languages or cultural practices. More than seven centuries ago, Dante depicted one of the more dramatic boundaries in the Christian imagination, the one separating purgatory from paradise. Elizabeth Stuart begins her 2003 book on gay and lesbian theologies with that very border, enshrined in *The Divine Comedy*. That may seem an odd choice until we recall who, in Dante's imagination, occupied the upper cornice of purgatory, that upper-most level closest to paradise. There Dante placed all those who had committed the sin known as *luxuria*, or the inordinate and self-indulgent love of others. On that potent border Dante placed both those whom we today would call "heterosexuals" as well as "homosexuals"—the gender of one's partner mattered less to Dante than how their love for another human eclipsed their love for God. Dante did not wish to condemn love itself; indeed love brought those guilty of *luxuria* to the very brink of heaven. This is precisely Stuart's point.

The debate today over marriage equality for lesbian and gay couples, both within and outside Christian circles, illustrates the urgency of Stuart's theological retrievals from the fourteenth century. As she invites us to see, the more ancient notion that love can take us to the final border between purgatory and paradise has been replaced by the claim that some forms of love can get us there faster and better:

> The idea that all love has its origins and its *telos* (end and fulfillment) in God has been replaced in much contemporary Church teaching on sexuality with the implicit or explicit teaching that all love has its *telos* in heterosexual marriage and, for some, the bringing of new life into the world from it.[26]

More simply, if not provocatively, the exultation of marriage and family in modern Western culture comes perilously close to idolatry. Paul seemed to make the same point in the much debated and controversial line of reasoning he adopted in the first chapter of his letter to the Romans. There Paul relies on the same theological logic Dante expressed centuries later: loving another human rather, or more, than God creates an idol.

---

26. Stuart, *Gay and Lesbian Theologies*, 3.

Yet another border appears in the midst of these ecclesial arguments over sexuality. Those typically considered "conservative" in
these debates insist on restricting the definition of marriage to the
union of one man and one woman. Those on the other side of the
argument insist just as vigorously that the union of two men or of two
women equally qualifies as marriage. The border between these two
positions has been softening in some quarters, yet where it remains
its foundations are reinforced by what Stuart calls the "tedium of
repetition."[27] Stuart then astutely draws our attention to what these
two camps nonetheless have in common—an underlying presumption that marriage fulfills human life. This presumption stands dramatically at odds with the theological claim that propelled so much
of Christian history forward—only union with God fulfills human
life. Retrieving that fundamental Christian insight could inspire and
empower a profound "border crossing" in many of today's churches,
and not merely for an end to our bitter ecclesiastical arguments. The
crossing might at long last lead those in both camps to find themselves happily together on that final cornice of purgatory and ready
at last to cross over into paradise, the "heavenly Jerusalem."

Dante's imaginative vision shifts our gaze toward the ultimate
border with which Christians of all types have always struggled,
the border between life and death or between this world and the
next. Modern Western Christians who identify as "liberal" or "progressive" properly worry that attending so carefully to that ultimate
border tends to denigrate the life we live on this side of it. Focusing our attention entirely here, on the other hand, risks losing the
insight Stuart retrieved from Dante concerning our final hope, as
more "conservative" Christians would insist. Rather than imagining
a border crossing in which we leave one world behind in favor of
another, we might instead follow the lead of monastic commentators
on the Song of Songs. By situating themselves precisely, though precariously, on that potent border, those monks sought to bring both
worlds together in a tender embrace. Teetering on that edge, poised
to fall into the arms of the Beloved, medieval monastics and mystics
and all the countless others inebriated with divine love beckon us to

---

27. Stuart, *Gay and Lesbian Theologies*, 3.

join them. There we find the hopeful moment for which Christian theology seeks to give an account, as the writer of the first letter of Peter urged (3:15), even as Paul reminds us that the hope itself remains unseen (Romans 8:24–25).

The challenge of accounting for an unseen hope offers at least one way for deeply divided churches to find common theological ground on which to stand, or perhaps better, on which to teeter together in anticipation. Exploring together a Eucharistic theology of sexual intimacy belongs in any such account, and it puts us in good company, not only with those border-perching medieval monks but also all those others breathlessly circling the upper cornice of purgatory, their unseen hope at last coming into view.

Josiah Royce depicted shared theological reflection as a journey toward what he called the "Homeland of the Spirit." Traveling there requires an arduous process of *interpretation*, a process Royce imagined as, appropriately enough, crossing a border. More specifically, Royce conceived this work as similar to a traveler crossing an international border. This hypothetical traveler arrives with gold coins and bank notes of her own country, neither of which carry legal tender in the foreign country. The traveler must then exchange the coin of her own realm for the appropriate legal tender of the new one. This process of exchange consists neither in the presentation of cash-values nor in the offering of credit-values; it demands instead a process of *interpreting* the cash-values of one country with reference to the cash-values of another. For Royce, this process of interpretation necessarily involves change and growth, or what Christian traditions have called conversion. As Royce explains it, as we cross over into a new realm of experience, we discover that our "bank notes" no longer carry the same kind of value we have grown to expect.[28] By interpreting this difference, we engage in a process of mutual transformation of the sort familiar to sexually intimate couples, the very same process Christians can expect to find at the Eucharistic Table. Both sexual intimacy and Eucharistic practice invite profound border crossings and thus the willingness to surrender previous beliefs, presuppositions, ideas, and worldviews in

---

28. Royce, *The Problem of Christianity*, 285.

our intimate encounters with the "other"—a partner, a household, a community, God.

Centuries before Royce, Augustine imagined a similar journey, with the traveling tempo set by the beat of a "restless heart" that would never finally rest apart from God.[29] We might, in that light, think of the Eucharistic Table as something like a roadside rest stop where we pause for the sustenance we need as we travel. This image alone, however, does not account for the many border crossings that confront us along the way. Residents of California appreciate that accounting challenge both culturally and politically whenever they encounter the border shared by Mexico and the United States. Along the Pacific coast at the San Diego/Tijuana border sits a place called, rather ironically, Friendship Park. Ironic because there, on an otherwise beautiful ocean shoreline, stands a tall fence stretching out into the sea, an international border. The U.S. Border Patrol struggles constantly to maintain this fence, as the pounding surf and salty breezes continually erode its foundations.

As Christians watch the erosion wrought by wind and water of a highly charged border, we might ponder how baptism and Eucharist do precisely the same thing. Liturgical scholars point to the "performative" character of ritual speech acts—those acts actually do what they say. More plainly, something *happens* in our sacramental celebrations. What transpires at the Eucharistic Table may elude us at times (perhaps often), yet Christians have always prayerfully trusted that something does happen. Over time, and much like the effects of ocean breezes and crashing surf on a fence, Eucharistic practice carries us over a border and ever farther into the life of God—and with many more people accompanying us than we might have imagined.

John the evangelist wastes no time in crossing borders—and dissolving them in the process. The first chapter of the Johannine gospel presents no less than the dissolution of a cosmic border, the one between infinite God and finite humanity. The Word of God— "very God of very God," as the Nicene Creed declares[30]—became

---

29. Augustine, *Confessions*, Book I:1.
30. BCP, 327.

flesh and dwelt among us, full of grace and truth (1:14). This should surely startle us. Most would be hard pressed to imagine a more intimate moment than "becoming one" with another. Recall the biblical writer in Genesis who believed that in the union of a man and a woman they become "one flesh" (2:24). Did the first hearers of this first chapter of John recall that ancient text from Genesis? Origen certainly heard it that way in the second century.[31] Do we? Do we find this startling?

John devotes a significant portion of his gospel account to what many call the "Farewell Discourse," which Jesus delivers after sharing a final meal with his friends (John 14–17). The syntax and grammar of these chapters proves challenging, as anyone knows who has tried to read them aloud. These linguistic complexities contribute in part to John's reputation as a mystic, as in this passage from the Farewell Discourse when John's Jesus prays for his disciples:

> "I ask not only on behalf of these, but also on behalf of those who will believe in me through their word, that they may all be one. As you, Father, are in me and I am in you, may they also be in us, so that the world may believe that you have sent me. The glory that you have given me I have given them, so that they may be one, as we are one, I in them and you in me, that they may become completely one, so that the world may know that you have sent me and have loved them even as you have loved me." (John 17:20–23)

Here John leads into the conclusion of his gospel account by returning to where he began, with a startling vision of not only crossing but dissolving the border between all things human and divine. Just as Jesus and God the Creator are one, so also the disciples are one, with each other and in Jesus and thus in God. A mystical vision to be sure, but not in the way mysticism has been popularized in the modern West, as a renunciation of, or departure from the "physical" for the sake of the purely "spiritual." John insists on rooting his visionary text in bodily, organic images, including the classic depiction from the fifteenth chapter drawn from the art of vintners. "I am the vine," John's Jesus says, "and you are the

---

31. Bouteneff, *Beginnings*, 114.

branches." The fruit of these branches is nothing less than love, fermenting and delighting like wine when the disciples abide in Jesus just as Jesus abides in them.

Reading Johannine fruitfulness and imagining its delectable sweetness sets our spiritual sight toward a garden, perhaps even a paradisiacal one. Yet here again John does not "restore" Eden but sees it transformed. As John dissolves the border between human and divine, he offers healing for the primal impulse in Eden to "become like gods," an impulse bred from shame. John sees no reason to rebuke humanity's original overreach in the garden. To the contrary and quite remarkably, he invites us to reach even further. To become "like gods" aims too low for the Johannine evangelist; nothing short of *union* with God will suffice, a union imagined as the closest possible intimacy, like branches intertwined with their vine. Rather than shame, this Johannine vision of union turns instead on desire and delight, or the "light of the world" as John declares (1:5), and thus the very opposite of the shadowy life of shame.

John does not merely tell this vision, he shows it. He does so in what precedes the Farewell Discourse as Jesus tenderly washes the feet of his disciples (John 13:1–1). Even more striking, John shows this vision of intimate union in a moment of public scandal. John sets the stage for both the Last Supper and the Farewell Discourse with Jesus and at least one of the disciples visiting a household in Bethany, just outside of Jerusalem. Jesus knows this place well, a household of intimates into which Jesus had been welcomed before, the household of his dear friend Lazarus and his two sisters, Martha and Mary. On the eve of sharing a final meal with his friends and just as he apparently did every time in this intimate household, Jesus shares a meal. This time, though, Mary does something quite unthinkable—she interrupts the meal by anointing Jesus' feet with costly perfume and wiping his feet with her hair (John 12:1–8).

In most contemporary Christian circles, this story has achieved the status of heart-warming tenderness; for first-century sensibilities by contrast, John "outed" Jesus with an account worthy of scandalous tabloid gossip. A woman simply does not do to a man what Mary did to Jesus unless they are married. Even among married couples what Mary did belongs somewhere far removed from public view.[32] Nonetheless, the "house was filled with the fragrance of the perfume." Everyone there knew exactly what was happening, including that other disciple who accompanied Jesus to Bethany—Judas Iscariot.

Judas recognized the scandal immediately, but diverted everyone's attention by asking about money. "Why was this perfume not sold for three hundred denarii and the money given to the poor?" That question from Judas stands today, not as a challenge to draft better budgets for our churches or to keep the cost of a wedding lower than the down payment on a mortgage, important as those considerations might otherwise be. That question from Judas instead stands as a perduring theological and spiritual provocation. How audacious, how scandalous do Christian communities dare to appear in proclaiming the Gospel of the divine Word made flesh? What do Christian communities wish to say about God in the light of the intimacies we share with one another far removed from the public spotlight? Where else could Christians possibly talk about these things except at the Table of a shared meal, that Table where God offers God's own self as Mary did to Jesus—and Jesus then did to his disciples? Are Christian worship spaces beautiful enough to welcome God's own beloved creatures? Do we fill these spaces with the inviting perfume of intimacy?

Questions such as these mark profound borders for contemporary Christians—boundaries between propriety and scandal, between public and private, between male and female. They mark as well the border Christians have for too long hesitated to cross, much less dissolve—the border between human sexual intimacy and divine self-offering. No less than the first-century world of Mediterranean cultures, the world today longs for a vision of the "heavenly Jerusalem," a city where borders dissolve and everyone feels wanted, desired, and at home—bodily, socially, and spiritually. That vision resides at the heart of a Eucharistic theology of sexual intimacy, a theological vision that adorns everyone as a beautiful bride brimming with anticipation for Divine Communion.

---

32. David M. Carr notes many parallels between this story and the Song of Songs, including the lover wiping the beloved's feet with her hair (7:6) (*The Erotic Word*, 163).

Covenants for the Beloved Community

*Let the grace of this Holy Communion
make us one body, one spirit in Christ,
that we may worthily serve the world
in his name.*

"Eucharistic Prayer C"
The Book of Common Prayer

*T*he canonical gospels turn frequently to moments of physical intimacy. A short list begins with these: Jesus touches dead bodies (Matthew 9:25); he places his fingers in a deaf man's ears (Mark 7:33); he spits in the dirt and rubs mud on a blind man's eyes (John 9:6); he tells parables of bodily embrace and weddings (Luke 15:20; Matthew 9:15); he allows a woman to kiss his feet, bathe them with her tears, and wipe them with her hair (Luke 7:38); and he enjoys the proximity of a dear companion leaning against his chest (John 13:23). More subtle but no less significant, Matthew and Luke place the birth of Jesus in Bethlehem, a city whose name means "house of bread." Luke takes this a step further and places the newborn Jesus in a manger, a feeding trough for animals. The gospel accounts from Matthew, Mark, and Luke all lead to a final meal where the one born in the House of Bread and in a manger offers his own body as bread and his blood as wine for a new covenant.

Among the four canonical evangelists, John especially favors bodily images as metaphors for a mystical journey into God, yet he never leaves bodily intimacy behind as he charts that path—not even in his stories of resurrection.[1] Indeed, John seems even more concerned with bodily communion than the other three. John's Jesus not only tells parables about weddings, but actually attends one in a village called Cana (2:1–11). John's Jesus not only teaches about love, but actually participates in a loving household (11:1–44). John's Jesus not only urges a life of tender compassion, but actually washes his disciples' feet (13:1–11). As he does in the other gospel accounts, John's Jesus miraculously feeds multitudes, but then goes a step further to declare that he himself is the "bread of life" (6:48). In John's account, the risen Jesus not only appears after death, but cooks breakfast on a beach (21:1–14) and even invites Thomas to insert his hand in Jesus' wounded side (20:27).[2]

John's Jesus left no doubt about the kind of life divine intimacy yields. "I am the vine," John's Jesus declares to his disciples, "you are the branches. Those who abide in me and I in them bear much fruit, because apart from me you can do nothing" (15:5). Just as branches draw life from the vine to bear fruit, so also a life of intimacy with God will produce a rich harvest, for us and for everyone we encounter. Many sexually intimate couples at least intuit something similar in their lives of passion and care; bodily intimacy bears fruit, and not only or even mostly by producing children.

The canonical evangelists took their place in a long line of biblical writers who understood bodily intimacy as carrying the potential for covenantal responsibility—the potential, that is, to bear fruit. They likewise understood the intimacy of covenantal relationships in resolutely bodily terms. Rather than the verb "to make," ancient Israelites described the initiation of a covenant with the verb "to cut." Abraham realized this, both mystically and quite personally. After leaving his homeland to travel to an unknown country, Abraham despaired over having no heirs. God then told him to collect a variety of animals, cut them in two, and lay the halves side-by-side. In a dream Abraham saw a firepot and torch pass through

---

1. See L. William Countryman's analysis of John and the mystical path he charts in *The Mystical Way in the Fourth Gospel: Crossing Over into God*, rev. ed. (Harrisburg, PA: Trinity Press International, 1995).

2. See the evocative interpretation of this moment by Molly Haws, "'Put Your Finger Here:' Resurrection and Construction of the Body," *Theology and Sexuality* 13:2 (2007), 181–94.

those halved animals, which the biblical writer then interprets: "On that day the Lord made a covenant" with Abraham (Genesis 15:18). The verb translated in that verse as "made" is actually "cut," reflecting the gravity of covenantal relationship in ancient Mediterranean societies—the fate of those animals is the same fate awaiting those who break the covenant. Abraham later understood personally—and painfully—the significance of cutting a covenant when he himself was circumcised. That bodily practice recalls for me the bygone days when early adolescent boys cut their fingers to seal a compact with each other as "blood brothers." (I did that with two of my eleven-year-old friends many years ago and then quickly ran to my mother for a bandage.)

Centuries after Abraham, Timothy bore the same pain when Paul circumcised him before allowing him to join Paul on his missionary journeys (Acts 16:3). This appears to contradict Paul's passionate plea in his letter to the Galatians to avoid making any such bodily marking a sign of spiritual belonging. Paul even cited the example of Titus, for whom Paul forbad circumcision (Galatians 2:3–5). The difference between these stories (other than physical pain) has less to do with the ritual act itself than the covenantal purpose it would serve in each case. On missionary journeys, an uncircumcised Timothy might provoke scandal in Jewish communities where Paul wished to preach. The Galatian community's insistence on circumcision would, by contrast, subvert the gospel message of grace alone that Paul had worked so assiduously to plant. In both cases, the practices of covenantal intimacy depended on the particular needs of a given community. As Paul declared to the Christians in Corinth, "To the Jews I became as a Jew, in order to win Jews" (1 Corinthians 9:20).

These Pauline postures likely strike modern readers as duplicitous if not incoherent. Reading these perplexing moments through the lens of the One Story suggests an alternative. Communities always tell that story with their own cultural accents and express it with their own ritualized traditions. Ancient Israelites lived in decidedly different ways than first-century Christians, yet the abiding hope for communion animated the covenantal life of each. The same God who initiated the Abrahamic and Mosaic covenants cut yet another in the death and resurrection of Jesus. We might suppose then that the One Story led Paul to set aside consistency in ritual practice for the sake of something more important: drawing as many as possible into the orbit of the divine desire for communion.

Contemporary Western culture lives with a decidedly different kind of legacy, one marked by contractual obligation. The ethical and political paradigms generated by the European Enlightenment in roughly the eighteenth century have trained Western societies to prioritize the protection of individual interests; contracts subject to adjudication in courts of law eventually emerged as the primary means to secure those interests. The significance of contractual obligation stretches farther back than the modern West, yet this contractual framework now circumscribes nearly every aspect of North Atlantic societies, from political philosophy to social policy and civil marriage—not to mention religion.[3]

The litigious character of American society, illustrated by courtrooms staggering under a backlog of civil lawsuits, inflects the dynamics of Christian community as well. The blurring of civil and religious marriage provides a case in point, which is on display whenever an ordained minister signs a marriage license during a wedding. That rather commonplace moment in today's wedding ceremonies reinforces contractual priorities at the expense of the rich biblical witness to bodily union as the heart of covenantal relationship. Sexually intimate partners need little theological prompting to appreciate those differences and the often necessary, though unfortunate, risks of reducing intimate relationships to contracts. Formerly married couples can testify to the pain and turmoil of traversing the labyrinthine pathways of divorce law in American courts, which leaves few traces along that path of the hope for communion that first inspired their intimacy.

The often sterile procedures of adjudicating a breached contract stand in stark contrast to the bodily and bloody character of biblical covenants. Intimate couples know but rarely speak what Christians consistently (and perhaps unwittingly) proclaim at every Eucharistic liturgy: covenants are messy because they involve bodies and blood.

---

3. For background on the role covenants and contracts have played in the evolution of American culture, from the Puritans to today, see Rosemary Radford Ruether, *Gaia and God: An Ecofeminist Theology of Earth Healing* (New York: HarperCollins, 1992), esp. ch. 8, "Healing the World: The Covenantal Tradition."

Thankfully, contemporary Western families no longer display bloody bed linens to prove the consummation of a marriage in the wider community. Yet traces of that practice remain in the old aphorism about the enduring strength of familial bonds: blood is thicker than water. At the Eucharistic Table, Christians dare to suppose something further: baptismal water is actually thicker than biological family blood.[4] That Table creates "blood kin" as we not only receive the Body of Christ in that meal but also *become* that Body, which Paul boldly declared in his letters to the Romans and the Corinthians. That Pauline boldness renders the Table as a profound pattern for all of our various bodily (and sometimes bloody) intimacies—as creatures made in the divine image, as communities bound to planetary thriving, as households committed to mutual affection and sustenance, and as couples whose shared life distills all these moments into a poignant image of mutual self-giving.

The Table invites all these bodily intimacies, yet discerning the commitments that may or may not attend our intimate relationships proves challenging. Contracts, for example, even long-term contractual agreements, need not include bodily intimacy at all, though they certainly might on occasion; my contractual agreement with my bank has little to do with intimate bodily interactions. By the same token, nothing about bodily intimacy per se demands permanence. Plenty of intimate encounters last relatively briefly yet still carry profound effects, which Luke's Jesus illustrated with his parable of the Good Samaritan (10:30–37). The Samaritan in that story chose to help a stranger in extreme distress by binding that stranger's wounds, transporting him to a local inn, and paying for his lodging—an arc of literally life-saving intimacy, even if that stranger never again met the Samaritan face-to-face.

To be sure, Christians have good reasons to treat casual sexual encounters with caution, especially (though not only) when those encounters involve genital intercourse. Bodily intimacy always carries risk, both physical and emotional and therefore also spiritual. Regardless of its temporal duration, sexual intimacy is an offering of self with no guarantee that it will be understood, well received, or

---

4. See Jana Marguerite Bennett, *Water Is Thicker than Blood: An Augustinian Theology of Marriage and Singleness* (Oxford: Oxford University Press, 2008).

safeguarded against exploitation and abuse. Regulating desire, however, can never fully mitigate its inherent vulnerabilities or control its outcomes. Circumscribing genital intimacy within a lifelong commitment likewise provides no assurance of mutual self-giving in love, to which the alarming rate of domestic violence among married couples bears painful witness.

The dizzying complexities and confusing ambiguities dotting today's sexual landscape demand more from Christian churches than abstinence-before-marriage programs for our teenagers or actively denying how many couples live together before marriage—or who decide never to formalize their commitment in public. After all, no one can know in advance where a chance encounter or a fleeting moment of intimacy might lead—strangers thrown together during a crisis, an unexpected embrace after a business conference, meeting a friend of a friend at a party, an unanticipated breakfast on a beach (John 21:1–19).

Surprised by intimacy apart from its carefully plotted chronologies, we can sometimes stumble into life-changing insights. Sara Miles recalls that very thing when she wandered on a whim into a church service. Having never been baptized in a decidedly unreligious if not anti-Christian household, she unexpectedly found herself caught up in the odd rhythms of the liturgy and quite literally stumbled into receiving Eucharist:

> I still can't explain my first communion. It made no sense. I was in tears and physically unbalanced: I felt as if I had just stepped off a curb or been knocked over, painlessly, from behind. The disconnect between what I thought was happening—I was eating a piece of bread; what I heard someone else say was happening—the piece of bread was the "body" of "Christ," a patently untrue or at best metaphorical statement; and what I *knew* was happening—God, named "Christ" or "Jesus," was real, and in my mouth—utterly short-circuited my ability to do anything but cry.[5]

That moment of unexpected and virtually inexplicable intimacy eventually blossomed into an equally unexpected life of Christian

---

5. Miles, *Take this Bread*, 58–59.

conversion and communal commitment. Miles followed a circuitous path into Christian faith that many others would recognize in their own lives of unexpected, even haphazard sexual intimacy. When such a path yields not only life-changing insights but also shared commitment, the Eucharistic Table beckons renewed reflection on the dynamics of covenantal relationship.

The language of contractual obligation sets the terms and conditions for a relationship, and usually for those who want to limit their exposure to liability or to delineate the consequences of broken promises. Covenantal relationship, on the other hand, more often marks a *response* to bodily intimacy rather than defining its precondition.[6] Sexually intimate couples know what this means long before reading it in a book on theology. Bodily intimacy—genital or not—can sometimes generate a desire for particular forms of commitment. These commitments may, in turn, develop into covenantal relationship marked by shared promises. Something quite remarkable happens in this process for which the language of contractual obligation fails to provide an adequate account. Rather than restricting relational energies, covenantal vows *expand* them. Covenantal relationships create space for intimacy to send down roots, grow, and bear fruit as they afford covenantal partners the kind of security that breeds generosity and hospitality. That expanding circle of a covenant's fruitfulness played a much larger role in pre-modern forms of marriage, which were usually directed toward the thriving of a community rather than the narrower circle of obligation defined by today's civil marriage contracts.[7]

Christians celebrate this capacious quality of covenantal life whenever we gather for Eucharist. At that Table we recall our baptismal promises as a *response* to the bodily intimacy God offers to us in Christ. As the Johannine writer reminds us, "We love because God

---

6. See Adrian Thatcher's careful analysis of the differences between contracts and covenants in Christian history and especially the role played by sexual intimacy prior to sealing the covenantal relationship of marriage (*Marriage after Modernity: Christian Marriage in Postmodern Times* [Washington Square, NY: New York University Press, 1999], 120–31).

7. See Coontz, *Marriage, A History*, 110–16. Adrian Thatcher raises appropriate notes of caution in retrieving historical precedents for covenantal relationship uncritically, especially if they perpetuate transferring power to the male head of a household alone (*Marriage after Modernity*, 87–88).

first loved us" (1 John 4:19). The language of contractual obligation, by contrast, falls far short of the response Christians wish to make to that divine love. Episcopalians, for example, pray after receiving Eucharistic elements that we may be "one body, one spirit in Christ," not for our own sake alone but for the sake of serving the world in the name of Christ.[8] Covenants mold bodily intimacy with promises, certainly with regard to the intimate partners themselves, but they also create space for reshaping the world around them with the fruits of their intimate commitment.

The language of contractual obligation fails as adequate speech for Christian faith for another reason as well. For Christians, covenantal relationship at the Eucharistic Table and in the shared passion of intimate couples responds to a singular call: Give yourself to find yourself. This is the counter-intuitive logic of the Gospel exhortation to "take up one's cross" and to "lose one's life" for the sake of Christ (Luke 9:23–24). Counter-intuitive, certainly, but also frequently abused and misapplied as an exhortation to self-abnegation, especially in the lives of women and even more particularly for mothers. Christina Grenholm outlines the implications of that troubling exhortation in the historical idealization of motherhood in Christian traditions, including the expectation that mothers will sublimate their own erotic desire to the good of their children and for the sake of creating a safe haven for their husbands at home. Grenholm concludes her analysis with a call to retrieve the mutuality of desire and therefore vulnerability in a shared vocation of human flourishing.[9] *Mutual* self-giving provides the theological key to unlock the spiritual potential in such covenantal relationship, for which the Eucharistic Table can stand as the emblem in Christian communities. At that Table, divine self-offering seeks above all the fruits of a faithful desire.

Josiah Royce understood God's Beloved Community to share both memory and hope in common. That shared intimacy leads to shared commitment, what Royce called loyalty in its broadest sense. The intimate commitment of Christians likewise exhibits that expansive view, beginning with the whole of creation, our intimate reliance

---

8. BCP, 372.

9. Christina Grenholm, "Mothers Just Don't Do It," in *Saving Desire*.

on Earth and its many creatures. The covenantal promises of creation, in turn, shape covenantal communities, tribal kinships that are lived daily in diverse households with their many commitments to mutual self-giving. On this expansive landscape of bodily intimacies and promises, Christians can speak more meaningfully about the bodily union of couples. The accents and cadences of that theologically meaningful speech derive from the Eucharistic Table, where God promises to fulfill the divine desire for communion in Christ.

COVENANTAL CREATION

After forty days and forty nights of diluvial rain, Noah once again stands on dry land. At that moment he gives thanks to God with an animal sacrifice. God responds by making a covenant with the whole creation: "I will never again curse the ground because of humankind, for the inclination of the human heart is evil from youth; nor will I ever again destroy every living creature as I have done. As long as the earth endures, seedtime and harvest, cold and heat, summer and winter, day and night, shall not cease" (Genesis 8:20–21).

Was this a *baptismal* covenant? The Christian writer in the First Letter of Peter thought so, or rather, that the flood endured by Noah, his family, and Earth's representative non-human animals "prefigured" the saving waters of baptism (3:20–21). I do not mean to wonder, however, whether this was a baptismal covenant for *Noah* but whether it was for *God*. To be sure, Noah passed through the waters and then offered animal flesh on an altar, not unlike what Christians do in baptism and Eucharist. But Peter's baptismal interpretation of this story extended only to the humans. "A few," Peter writes, "that is, eight persons, were saved through water" (1 Peter 3:20). The writer of Genesis harbored a wider vision that included saving more than only humans. That writer did something else as well. He placed the emphasis of this story entirely elsewhere, on the divine vow never again to destroy; Noah makes no promises at all.

Notably in that eighth chapter of Genesis, God does not mention humanity specifically as part of the divine vow never again to "curse the ground" or destroy Earth; humans apparently enjoy the collateral benefits of God's compassion toward everything else just as Earth itself had suffered in the flood because of humanity's wickedness. Only in the next chapter does God draw humanity explicitly into this divine covenant with creation (Genesis 9:8–17). This biblical writer, in other words, would likely wish to quibble with traditional readings of the first two chapters of Genesis that designate humanity as the "crown of creation." Being set apart as the only creatures made in the divine image may have less to do with increased privileges than with greater responsibilities. Walter J. Houston extrapolates from that important caveat to address today's global crises: "[T]he integrity of the whole of creation is dependent on us because we have the power to destroy it, and will do so unless we learn how to discipline our use of power."[10]

Ancient Jewish readings of Genesis 2 take humanity's deep intertwining with the rest of creation a step further. There, God observes one thing that is "not good" with the creation—the human creature God just made seems so mournfully alone. The first attempt at a divine solution to this loneliness appears both startling and endearing: God creates a host of animals and presents them to the human to see if any of them might make a suitable companion (2:18–20). Presumably that first human could have chosen any one of those animals that God presented like a parade of desire.[11] Rather than choosing just one of these creatures, however, the human gives names to each of them. Naming a creature is itself an act of intimacy, as any parent of a newborn child knows, as well as anyone who names a nonhuman animal companion. Intimacy, in other words, infused God's creation well before the solitary human found a perfectly suitable companion. Today's ecological crises demand at least the intimacy of naming, but still more: the kind of bodily intimacy that generates covenantal relationship.

Ecological anxieties have been escalating since at least the 1960s, and while a variety of social movements for ensuring a thriving planet have enjoyed significant milestones over the last fifty years, the worldwide human family clearly still has some difficult and profound

---

10. Houston, "Sex or Violence," 149.

11. Steven Greenberg recounts this very possibility and the consternation it often provoked in the history of this text's interpretation (*Wrestling with God and Men: Homosexuality in the Jewish Tradition* [Madison, WI: University of Wisconsin Press, 2004], 50–51).

decisions to make. Activists in the past framed their work with political advocacy, legislative initiatives, and regulatory control. Each of these made a contribution in its own way, yet none of them, either alone or in combination, will respond effectively to the challenges we now face. Margaret Barker agrees, noting especially the array of competing priorities, both cultural and economic, that keep politicians focused only on short-term solutions. Barker further believes that only by returning to a biblical vision of humanity's rootedness in creation will Christians understand the urgency of the task we face and find the theological resources we need to address it.[12]

James William Gibson called that vision "enchantment," or rather a *re*-enchantment with the world of nature, which he argues holds the key to save us from environmental disaster. Gibson cites Max Weber to make his point and to provide the lynchpin image. Weber worried that Protestant Christianity had installed within modern Western culture the notion of God as entirely detached from the wider world of nature and concerned only with humans; the wider natural world, in other words, serves only as a stage on which the divine-human drama plays out. This view, according to Weber, would eventually render the natural world merely a resource for sustaining capitalist development. Even though Weber was a man of science, he rather strikingly lamented Western society's intellectualization and especially its "disenchantment of the world."[13]

Planetary life depends on whether human beings will understand environmentalism as deeply spiritual work. This work would entail an arduous assessment of Western society's perceived detachment from the non-human world around us, especially as modernity has trained most people to think of nature in mechanistic terms. This spiritual practice now requires a "quest for a new kinship with nature," as Gibson describes it. To the "re-enchantment" he proposes, I would add to that quest the need for intimacy with the "other-than-human." I mean especially the kind of bodily intimacy that prompts covenantal promises and relationship.

---

12. Barker, *Creation*, 4.

13. James William Gibson, *A Reenchanted World: The Quest for a New Kinship with Nature* (New York: Henry Holt and Company, 2009), 16.

"Enchantment" of course evokes the wonderful energy and dis-orienting qualities of falling in love. Sexually intimate human couples know well the effects of that kind of enchantment. We lapse into reverie at the most unpredictable moments, day-dreaming about that intimate partner even when work demands our full attention. We might find ourselves wondering almost inordinately about a partner's welfare or what that partner just happens to be doing at any given moment. This emotional rush of enchantment leads frequently if not inevitably to care. For some, it leads to more explicit commitments and even more to covenantal relationship. Precisely this kind of enchantment animates the One Story—God's own deep desire for communion with God's creatures. God finds us enchanting, in other words, and commits to the thriving and flourishing of all, human and otherwise.

Bringing our sexually enchanting relationships to the Eucharistic Table does seem rather far removed from the panoply of concerns associated with global climate change. Yet that Table might still inspire a deep commitment to Earth's other-than-human animals as well as the planetary ecosystems on which they rely, especially as we offer at that Table elements from Earth as signs of divine intimacy. Rowan Williams would encourage us to pause at that Table and consider what we want our bodily lives to communicate in that moment of offering.[14] Our bodies and not only our words communicate constantly, whether we realize it or not, in how we interact with each other, the food we eat, the cars we drive, the things we recycle. What, then, do we wish to communicate with our embodied lives on this planet? Surely intimacy can launch us toward an answer to that question—the intimacy of necessity (our absolute reliance on Earth for our survival), but even more the intimacy of enchantment.

Enchanting intimacy can likewise begin by writing a book, like this one. Authors frequently lament the solitary and often lonely act of writing. The process of writing this book, however, has been anything but a lonely endeavor. As I type these very words, my Australian shepherd dog Tyler sits next to me. I know that at any moment he will nudge my hands off my laptop computer, lick my fingers, and stare at me. I will know exactly what that means: the time has come

---

14. Williams, "The Body's Grace," 61.

for our afternoon walk in the regional park. Returning the gaze of a different species certainly qualifies as enchanting (and sometimes unnerving). It also qualifies as a moment of intimacy. That interspecies gulf will never be fully bridged, of course. But neither will the unimaginable gulf between the infinite God and finite humans. At the Eucharistic Table, God has created at least one way to bridge that gulf with an equally unimaginable intimacy. As God offers God's own self to us, the Creator would urge us to offer our own lively commitments to the creatures with whom we share this planet.

COVENANTAL COMMUNITIES

Imagine what would happen to global markets if there were no skilled translators to negotiate the terms of trade between French-speaking companies and Chinese entrepreneurs. Imagine crafting the North American Free Trade Agreement (NAFTA) without bilingual negotiators. Imagine worldwide currency exchanges without anyone to translate the meaning of one nation's monetary system to another. Ancient societies could imagine the results just as well as we can, and the challenges contributed to the Tower of Babel story in Genesis (11:1–9).

Most commentators read that story with human hubris as the interpretive key to its meaning—human beings tried to build a tower that reached into heaven. That impulse resembles what the sagacious serpent tempted Eve to consider by eating the forbidden fruit— humans would become like gods. The disruption of human community by fragmenting human speech into countless languages thus serves as divine punishment for human pride. It could just as easily bear witness to the economic frustrations borne by confounded human speech, frustrations that demonstrate the tragic severing of intimacy portrayed earlier, in the third chapter of Genesis.

Economies run on intimate exchanges, even in their most abstract terms. Individuals, families, households, tribes, communities, nations—all of these function with intimate interactions for the sake of prosperity and posterity. Economics is a matter of life and death, quite literally, and devising a shared language helps to quell the panic that can ensue from miscommunication. For good reason, then, commentators have noted Luke's apparent "reversal" of Babel

in his Pentecost story (Acts 2:1–13), when the divisions of different languages dissolve into a common language of Gospel. Less frequently noted, this Pentecostal reversal carries profound economic
significance in the next few chapters, where Luke makes those life-
and-death consequences plain.

Luke describes a remarkable social reordering among the earliest
Christians, with traditional household economies integrated into a
larger economic community where "no one claimed private ownership of any possession, but everything they owned was held in common" (Acts 4:32). This micro-economic system served a number of
purposes, not least for the care of those beloved members of the community who could not care for themselves (6:1–6); this system also
exhibited a covenantal character, as the truly strange story of Ananias
and Sapphira graphically illustrates. For this economic experiment in
communal intimacy to work, all the members contributed all of their
property and they laid this "at the apostles' feet" (Acts 4:37). Ananias,
however, decided to keep some of his own property for himself. When
he lied about this decision in the community, Luke wrote, Ananias fell
over dead (5:5). His wife, Sapphira, not knowing what happened, later
told the same lie to the community and met the same fate (5:10).

More than one thing likely troubles contemporary readers of this
story from Luke's Acts of the Apostles, not least of which is the dissolution of nearly every line between "public" and "private" in this
early Christian community, and perhaps even more, the notion that
private intimacies have anything to do with a public economic good.
For modern readers, the economic decisions made by a husband and
wife in their own household properly remains their own business, not
subject to whatever the wider community thinks or should even know
about it. Audre Lorde objected to that division and laments its "horror." Erotic energy fuels not only intimate relations with other people,
but also intimate relations with our work and wider communities. The
"principal horror" of any system that defines the "good" in terms of
profit or ownership rather than human need, she writes, is how it robs
our work of its erotic value—the value of what I would call shared,
covenantal intimacy born from the erotic desire for communion.[15]

---

15. Audre Lorde, "Uses of the Erotic: The Erotic as Power," in *Sister Outsider: Essays and
Speeches* (Freedom, CA: Crossing Press, 1984), 53–59.

Sorting through the complexities of today's globalized economy can of course quickly prove daunting. This challenge intensifies during a time of what Kathryn Tanner calls "economic dead ends," when there seems to be no other way to organize and manage the systems of exchange in which all of us live.[16] Christians gathered at the Eucharistic Table might well offer compelling alternatives to those "dead ends." After all, no one on his or her own or even as a nuclear family can address the challenges posed by multi-national market forces. Practicing a Eucharistic intimacy, however, can spark the kind of creativity that no one person could manufacture alone. Only the kind of shared commitment prompted by that Table of intimacy can generate the imaginative proposals all of us need for a sustainable future. Doing this work together as a faith community, Luke's provocative descriptions of early Christians might help us imagine a world where mortgaged walls dissolve those barriers that divvy up neighborhoods into individual consumer units and tease out transformative possibilities for a much wider network of relation—of "covenantal communities," perhaps. Ancient biblical texts will surely not provide blueprints for that creative work, but they can inspire our imaginations. Luke's storytelling in Acts makes a good place to begin.[17]

Whatever else we wish to make of that odd biblical story of Ananias and Sapphira, it can urge faith communities today to resist any attempt to abstract our sexual intimacies from the vast economic systems and social hierarchies in which those intimacies unfold. Even the word "intimacy" can easily mask the troubling history of the public institution of marriage, which the state has frequently exploited to maintain racial segregation, gender conformity, and healthy profit margins for multi-national corporations.[18] Only the covenantal commitments born from those intimacies, which we bring with us to the

---

16. Kathryn Tanner, *Economy of Grace* (Minneapolis, MN: Fortress Press, 2005), 33.

17. Herman E. Daly and John B. Cobb, Jr. offer a detailed road map for analysis and reflection, as well as practical strategies on all of these issues and more, including the need to move from individualism to "person-in-community" and from cosmopolitanism to "communities of communities" (*For the Common Good: Redirecting the Economy toward Community, the Environment, and a Sustainable Future*, second ed. [Boston: Beacon Press, 1994]).

18. See Marvin M. Ellison, *Same-Sex Marriage? A Christian Ethical Analysis* (Cleveland, OH: The Pilgrim Press, 2004),102–106. For an analysis of the construction of racial categories in relation to marriage, see Peggy Pascoe, *What Comes Naturally: Miscegenation Law and the Making of Race in America* (Oxford: Oxford University Press, 2009).

Eucharistic Table, can offer a broader vision of the Gospel's reach into otherwise intractable economic, political, and ecological dilemmas. Institutional Christianity has already pioneered a path toward that vision in our history of organizing households of many different types into something called a "congregation." Making these "aggregations of households" more explicitly covenantal in character might illumine a sustainable way forward for the thriving of all, especially when households themselves emerge from the experience of sharing Eucharistic intimacy.

COVENANTAL HOUSEHOLDS

Who was that one disciple in particular whom Jesus loved? Most commentators have assumed that this beloved was John the Evangelist, who provides the only gospel account of this particular relationship, and who does so with rather veiled, if not coy, references to this anonymous companion. Rarely do these commentators entertain another and perhaps obvious candidate in John's gospel: the one in whose house Jesus frequently stayed and where he enjoyed significant meals; the one over whom Jesus wept at the news of his death and who Jesus then insisted on bringing back to life to enjoy yet another significant meal with that disciple's sisters. That one was Lazarus.[19]

What kind of intimacy did Jesus enjoy with this Bethany householder and his two sisters? In what ways did his intimacy with Lazarus differ from the intimacy he enjoyed with the disciple who leaned against Jesus' breast at the last supper? Or perhaps that intimate disciple at the meal was actually Lazarus. John's account leaves all of these questions unanswered, and thankfully so. Human societies tend to prefer more precise definitions for relationship patterns, and modern Western society especially so. The ambiguities in John's text open up a much wider horizon for reflecting on the theological and spiritual significance of multiple forms of intimacy, including those that coalesce into "households."

---

19. One of the few commentators who wonder about Lazarus (among other gospel characters) is Theodore W. Jennings, Jr. in *The Man Jesus Loved: Homoerotic Narratives from the New Testament* (Cleveland, OH: The Pilgrim Press, 2003), 51–52.

The synoptic gospels (Matthew, Mark, and Luke) all make reference to a significant reordering of first-century household patterns in the ministry and teaching of Jesus. When told that his mother and siblings were waiting to see him, Jesus apparently dismissed the absolutist claims of those biological bonds. "Who is my mother, and who are my brothers?" Pointing to his disciples, he then declared, "Here are my mother and my brothers! For whoever does the will of my Father in heaven is my brother and sister and mother" (Matthew 12:47–50). John takes that radical teaching and makes it more incarnate. He does this by referring more than once to the household of intimacy Jesus enjoyed with Lazarus, Martha, and Mary in Bethany.

John grants a peek through the living room window, as it were, into the life of this first-century household, which certainly offers much on which to reflect theologically concerning intimacy and commitment. More than this, John opens a window on the complex interactions among households, religious institutions, and the State. The tidy lines modern Western society tends to draw between those entities were virtually non-existent in the ancient Greco-Roman world, including Israelite culture. Recall how the organization of the empire intertwined with the organization of the *domus*, the household. Just as the emperor ruled rather than belonged to the empire, so also the householder—the husband/father—reigned over the household economy. Disrupting these household patterns posed a threat to the wider patterns of imperial rule.

Early Christian theologians attempted precisely that kind of disruption, theologically subtle as it may have been. "Subtle" to us perhaps, many centuries later, but Rome's imperial regime sought fiercely to quell it, with violent persecution if necessary.[20] Christianity's perceived threat changed dramatically following the so-called Edict of Milan in 311 during the reign of Constantine. As that moment officially "tolerated" Christianity in the empire (even if it did not immediately elevate it to the level of "official" imperial religion), Christian theologians felt less compelled to critique the State under whose patronage they now enjoyed new freedoms.

---

20. See Elaine Pagels, *Adam, Eve, and the Serpent* (New York: Random House, 1988), esp. ch. 2, "Christians Against the Roman Order."

The first few centuries of Christian traditions surely stand as a cautionary tale about the price Christians pay to secure political tolerance if not favor. Those centuries can caution us about something else as well. No matter the form it takes, the State will always insist on having a controlling interest in the shape of household intimacies, even in societies that continue to believe such locations remain securely protected in a "private" realm. The structure of the State, after all, simply reflects the aggregate dynamics of its many households, and thus the various intimacies that constitute them—witness the complex forms created by the Internal Revenue Service as just one example among many. Not only political structures, of course, but also religious institutions likewise share a stake in household patterns of intimacy.

John's peek into the intimacies of a first-century Bethany household offers a hint at the wider socio-political implications of household intimacy, not least by noting something quite peculiar. By raising Lazarus from the dead, Jesus threatened the safety of the whole household. Peculiar, because most Christians likely read the Lazarus story as an instance of God's victory over death—how could this possibly pose any risk? The risk Jesus took flared into danger in two respects: the spectacle of life from death threatened the authority of established religious leaders and it drew even wider public attention to this particular household of intimates. John collapses these socio-political dynamics into a single verse: "So from that day on [the religious leaders] planned to put [Jesus] to death" (11:53).

John provides yet another hint for considering the wider social and political ramifications of intimate households and their covenantal relationships. As Jesus died at the hands of Roman imperial power, he does something quite remarkable, given his extreme suffering—he creates a household. As Jesus neared his final breath, he sees his beloved disciple and his own mother standing at the foot of the cross. In that moment he binds them together and from these two he creates a family. "Woman," he says, "here is your son." To his disciple he says, "Here is your mother." And from that hour, John writes, the disciple took Mary into his own home (19:26–27). Most commentators assume that the "beloved" disciple in this poignant moment was John himself. I like to imagine it was Lazarus.

Where else would Jesus commit the care of his dear mother but to the household of intimates that he himself had enjoyed?

COVENANTAL COUPLES

What did Adam and Eve know of "marital" fidelity and how did they learn it? More pointedly, what did Abraham know about it when Sarah persuaded him to sire a child with their slave Hagar? What about King David? We might not want to ask Bathsheba about that, but we might find a more fruitful answer if we asked Jonathan. We might find a similarly insightful response in the story of Ruth and Naomi. Mixing together these biblical stories of marriage with biblical images of deep friendship surfaces the profound mystery of human attachments and their relationship to God.

The meaning of marriage has always seemed both obvious and elusive, not least in religious communities. What precisely bonds a couple together? How do they express that bond in their communities and how ought communities respond when that bond falters? Where do we locate evidence of divine life in the simultaneously messy and ecstatic lives of couples living in vowed covenantal relationships? All of these questions prompt yet another: What finally does *fidelity* actually entail? As I have been suggesting, these questions for couples belong on a broader theological landscape where we can reflect on covenantal relationship itself and the many types of commitment generated by bodily intimacy. On that landscape, the question of faithfulness frequently appears as more perplexing than we might imagine.

No one of course is born knowing what fidelity means; each of us has to learn what faithfulness looks like and how to live into its expectations and fulfillments. When bodily intimacy between two people generates the desire for commitment, that couple will need support in remaining true to their promises. They also need something more and prior to that support: help in discerning the rich textures and consequences of living *faithfully*. An extended *family of faith*—a congregation—provides precisely that discernment and support, at least ideally.

The divorce rate in the United States (still hovering around fifty percent) and the marriage equality movement for gay and lesbian

couples continue to pose ethical quandaries, yet also rich theological opportunities to explore the contours of intimate fidelities. The
Eucharistic Table stands ready to prompt that kind of reflection,
especially when congregations sort through the many ways institutional Christianity has melded with Western culture, which often
blind all of us to a host of socio-religious assumptions with which we
live on a nearly daily basis.

Consider the complex evolution of marriage in Western society, and the appearance of something quite novel, beginning roughly
in Renaissance-era Europe. The emphasis on the contractual and legal
aspects of marriage, especially those concerning the inheritance of property, started to mesh with notions of romantic love. Combining these
elements into a single cultural institution called "marriage" quickly tied
fidelity to sex, for both economic and emotional reasons and not just
the former. More crudely put, early modern Western culture began
to circumscribe the meaning of marital fidelity to genital exclusivity.

Bodily propriety may seem an obvious feature of marriage, but
its social significance in contemporary society would startle most
pre-modern communities. They would be startled, for example, by
the amount of energy spent by marriage and family therapists to convince their clients that one's spouse need not supply the entire range
of one's emotional and relational needs.[21] Married couples can enjoy
a wide array of rich and meaningful friendships, social networks, and
even collegial intimacies without putting marital fidelity at risk. To
suppose that married couples need convincing to participate fully in
these expansive social networks speaks volumes about the societal
shifts in our understandings of marriage—and fidelity.

What therapists often leave unspoken bears on religious communities generally and Christian congregations in particular. Western society has inherited and perpetuates an approach to faithfulness
as relational "containment"; fidelity refers to what one *cannot* do
in a contractual agreement. No one needs to say explicitly what

---

21. John Gottman provides just one among many such resources that laud the importance
of friendships outside the marital relationship as one of the keys to fruitful marriages (*The
Seven Principles for Making Marriage Work: A Practical Guide from the Country's Foremost
Relationship Expert* [New York: Crown Publishing, 1999]). See, for example, his note concerning adultery, which most often results from the desire for friendship more than or even rather
than sex (16).

"infidelity" means in today's marriages—genital sexual intimacy occurred with someone other than one's spouse. When adultery refers only to the violation of genital exclusivity, even the most emotionally arid relationship can retain its status as a "marriage" as long as one's genitals are not shared with anyone but one's legal spouse.

Christian traditions offer a much broader view of fidelity and its effects. Biblical texts and contemporary pre-marital counseling programs imply such an expansive view when they invite us to consider marital fidelity as a reflection of God's own faithfulness. The allegorical treatment of God's relationship with Israel as one of marriage and the galvanizing portrayal of the Church as the "bride of Christ" are just two examples. Needless to say, these biblical images portray something more about divine faithfulness than genital propriety. Exploring the depths of divine intimacy and faithfulness presents a wider spiritual horizon for living into the profound gifts of fidelity among covenantal couples. Rather than focusing only on what covenantal partners must not do, the Church can bear witness even more to what covenantal faithfulness makes possible in our lives, or what we might call the "fruits of fidelity."

Both biblically and theologically, faithfulness means much more than abiding by rules and regulations. Ancient Hebrew prophets measured faithfulness by the quality of communal relations it creates, which led them to denounce the "adulterous" practices of Israel. Idolatry certainly qualified as "adultery" for those prophets, but even more so its effects: the covenantal people no longer cared for orphans and widows, they no longer showed hospitality to strangers, they refused to tend the land responsibly, and they perpetuated economic injustice for the poor. Faithfulness, by contrast, will yield an abundant harvest of care, generosity, and justice. Gospel writers portray Jesus encouraging the same approach among his listeners at nearly every turn. Rather than worrying only about proper ritual observance, Jesus focused his spiritual attention on the kind of life such observance ought to create. Matthew's Jesus proposed a way to discern that life: "A good tree cannot bear bad fruit, nor can a bad tree bear good fruit . . . You will know them," Jesus says "by their fruits" (7:18, 20).

Contracts end with broken rules; covenants flourish as intimacy bears fruit. This theological approach to intimate commitments would at the very least offer a soothing balm for married couples who worry about their marriage when the giddy and ecstatic qualities of romance start to ebb. Marriages end, of course, for many reasons, but Christian communities can offer a far richer metric for covenantal relationships than what one usually finds in tabloid accounts of celebrity weddings: does your sexual intimacy create emotional space and a shared capacity for ministries of generous hospitality? That question applies to Christian couples *because* it applies to all other forms of intimate commitment that populate our congregations today. The fruits of fidelity expand beyond, but also in concert with covenantal couples whenever fidelity inspires care for local ecosystems, hometowns, dearest friends, or a faith community. Paul recommended this kind of analysis when he discerned the presence of the Holy Spirit in the fruits that presence yields: "love, joy, peace, patience, kindness, generosity, faithfulness, gentleness, and self-control" (Galatians 5:22–23).

This biblically and theologically capacious approach to fidelity does not obviate responsibility or obligation; to the contrary, it actually makes the contractual aspects of human relations seem but a shadow of the rich covenantal fruitfulness that awaits those whom God calls into particular forms of committed intimacy. Responding to that call tells the One Story anew each time, whether in our commitments to ecosystem solidarity or building communities of economic justice or forming households of gracious welcome. Sexual intimacy takes all of these many forms and each exhibits a variety of qualities, including the covenantal commitments that grow from them.

Liturgical traditions invite Christians to interpret and assess all of our many intimate commitments through the lens of the baptismal covenant, which extends well beyond an individual's relationship with Christ. By water and the Holy Spirit, God unites Christians to the wider social reality described as the many members of Christ's body and further still, and because of this, to God's wider mission in the world. The fruits of our baptismal fidelity, in turn, bear witness to the One Story at the heart of God's own Trinitarian life of creative, redemptive, and sustaining grace—the very grace that binds couples together in covenantal union.

Matthew, Mark, and Luke make the galvanizing announcement of the Kingdom of God central to the Gospel, and with it, the need to repent (Mark 1:15). John shapes that proclamation into an image of beloved community, like branches intertwined with its vine (15:1–4). John never mentions repentance, but he does write about sin, mostly by assuring his readers of forgiveness (1:29). The importance of covenantal faithfulness has always accompanied Christian witness to this good news of God's grace. The type of covenants animating God's Beloved Community have varied over time, often depending on the many diverse cultural contexts that have shaped Gospel proclamation.

Baptism and Eucharist run throughout Christian history as the most visible testaments to the Church's sacramental life of covenantal grace. Participating in these divine mysteries makes Christians Christian as they inspire the One Story of God's own deep desire for communion. These mysteries likewise come with risk, not only the risk of vulnerability that attends every intimate relationship, but also the risk of relying on rule-keeping to evaluate one's covenantal life in God—and perhaps especially *someone else's* life in God. Rules and regulations actually reveal very little about the quality of a relationship. Those who never stray from the letter of the law might still miss its spirit, especially in relationships of intimate commitment. As Adam blamed Eve and Eve blamed the serpent (Genesis 3:12–13), the tragedy of lost intimacy retreats behind the anxiety over disobedience.

The temptation to transpose covenantal faithfulness into regulatory regimes or mechanisms for moral scrupulosity infects every Christian community, even those that stress an absolute reliance on divine grace. The perennial obsession over "earning one's keep" and its twin note of caution—"there is no free lunch"—has fueled the Protestant work ethic for centuries, and rather ironically. Sixteenth-century reformers shook the foundations of medieval Christianity with their insistence on salvation through grace alone, yet the churches born from that watershed moment have in turn exhibited a deep preoccupation with law, mostly to quell the anxiety that accompanies the energies of desire.[22] The 1979 Book of Common Prayer, for example, revitalized a "baptismal ecclesiology" in part by

---

22. See Jan-Olav Henriksen's analysis of these complex dynamics between law and desire in "Desire: Gift and Giving," in *Saving Desire*.

articulating the covenantal responsibilities that accompany the rite of incorporation into Christ's body.[23] These baptismal promises have provided a helpful framework for Episcopalians to articulate the practical pathways of Gospel living in the world. Along that path, however, the promises themselves can eventually overshadow the graceful and intimate union that inspired them.

Gospel writers worried about that risk, as did Paul. The Christians in Galatia could hardly miss it in Paul's stinging rebuke of their reliance on law rather than grace (Galatians 3:1–5). Mark's Jesus sidled up to the same point, though more gently, if not obliquely, when he reminded his listeners that the Sabbath was made for humanity and not humanity for the Sabbath (2:27). Just as most of Israel's ancient prophets had done, Jesus called his people back to the purpose of covenantal relationship with God and the fruits that such a relationship can yield. Most married couples know this about their own relationships, at least in theory. The obligations and responsibilities of marriage do not exist for their own sake but for the fruitfulness of a couple's bodily intimacy.

The fathomless mysteries of divine grace and intimacy illumine the expansive space of covenantal relationship, not least by blunting the sharp edges of obligation in a litigious society accustomed to contractual rigor. The Book of Common Prayer suggests as much with a profound declaration: "The bond which God establishes in Baptism is indissoluble."[24] The implications of that theological claim ought to startle more than it usually does in a society trained at every level to expect consequences for broken rules. The Prayer Book's baptismal covenant thus contains no language whatsoever about contractual breach. God's own desire for communion remains unblemished and undiminished by our inevitable human failures to embody the One Story in how we live. Our failures actually serve to remind us of the graceful intimacy that inspired baptismal faithfulness in the first place. As Paul tried to reassure the Romans, where sin increases, grace abounds all the more (5:20). Paul certainly did not mean to encourage laxity, much less a libertine approach to Christian life, but

---

23. BCP, 304–5.
24. BCP, 298.

rather the perpetual promise of its renewal. That life of fellowship, breaking bread, resisting evil, proclaiming Good News, loving neighbors, striving for justice and peace, and respecting the dignity of every human being[25]—these are the *fruits* of covenantal relationship, not its *precondition*. Baptism creates space for a gracious Eucharistic intimacy to grow in ever-expanding circles of care and devotion, step-by-faltering-step.

For these reasons among others, a *Eucharistic* and not only a baptismal theology belongs at the very heart of Christian reflection on sexual intimacy. Institutional Christianity has too frequently lost that spiritual focus by making the quality of one's life a condition for enjoying the status of the "desirable beloved" at the Table. No one stands at that Table for having earned a place there—save only for having been born as God's own cherished creation. Christian liturgical traditions still retain traces of that amazing grace, but not nearly enough.

Inscrutable mysteries and formidable borders alike have characterized many, if not most, Christian liturgical rites for celebrating Eucharist. Ritual gestures can foreground the profound mystery of God's gracious self-giving in Christ even as institutional regulations erect barriers to those deemed unworthy to taste the gift of God's own life. Yet there the Table continues to stand in our midst, whether starkly in austere simplicity or ornately in brocaded splendor, bearing witness to the audacity of the One Story—the deep desire and abiding hope for divine communion. The vitality of Christian witness today relies more than ever on telling that story—boldly, courageously, and audaciously.

The traditional pattern of Eucharistic celebration now lends a particularly counter-cultural character to Gospel witness. I mean especially the pattern of presenting only a taste of bread and sip of wine in something called a "meal." Today that pattern confounds how Western society trains all of us to live as avid consumers in a world brimming with commodities. Endless consumption defines the meaning of life itself in late global capitalism in ways that would likely make Augustine multiply his warnings about the unfettered pursuit of desire. As Western culture throws itself into the frenzy of consuming,

---

25. These summarize the vows of the Baptismal Covenant (BCP, 304–5).

desire itself actually withers. Pursuing more and more "stuff" anes-
thetizes hunger until we hardly know what we really want.

Consider the quintessential day of food consumption in the
United States late in November—Thanksgiving. On that day many
people stagger away from the table of feasting as nearly every bodily
system shuts down to focus on just one task—digestion. The last thing
on anyone's mind at that moment is desire, except perhaps for sleep.
That moment encapsulates well a consumerist culture, which runs
not on desire but on constant digestion. We shop, buy, eat, consume,
and digest as much as possible in a vain attempt to touch the deeper
longing that most of us have now forgotten. In a culture literally hell-
bent on digestion, sharing the simplest of meals can reawaken our
memory of desire.

At the heart of Christian liturgical practice sits that meal we likewise call "Thanksgiving," but little about that rite resembles the late-
November feast of food. By receiving only a bite of bread and a taste
of wine and calling that moment a "feast," the Church invites a profound recalibration of gratitude. Even as the word *eucharist* means
"thanksgiving," that rite depends on desire, not digestion. Christians
celebrate Eucharist with the hope of reawakening our desire and
sharpening our hunger, not just for more bread and more wine, but
our hunger for an end to loneliness and violence, an end to hostility
and alienation; our hunger for an end to poverty and homelessness;
our hunger for a flourishing planet of social and economic justice;
our hunger for a re-enchantment with the wideness of God's world
and all its many creatures. We give thanks at that Table for the as-yet-
unimaginable city where we find a tree planted by the river of life, a
tree whose fruit leads not to shame but to healing (Revelation 22:2).
The Eucharistic "feast" sharpens our hunger for all this and thus for
the Communion none of us has yet enjoyed in its fullness even as
many have nonetheless glimpsed it in the mutual self-offerings of
sexual intimacy.

Eucharist can quicken the desire that dwells deeply in every
human heart, the desire for that communion we cannot now fully
imagine but of which we have precious and priceless hints—the bud-
ding flower in spring after a long winter, the wag of a happy dog's
tail on a trail in a regional park, the touch of a dear friend when

we thought we were all alone, the collective energy of a community sacrificially devoted to justice, the shared meal of a household full of children, the soft voice of a beloved in the hush of evening. These are precious moments, yet never the last word, never the consummation, never the final chapter; they are always the preface to an unfolding story that God calls us to keep telling and, especially, to keep living.

I decided to write this book, in part, as a response to that divine call. As I have found my own life deeply enriched by reflecting carefully on what I have been calling the One Story in these pages, I also lament how few have heard it or have seen it lived among them. We could perhaps blame the manifold failures of institutional Christianity to lend a credible voice to that story, but that alone falls short of an explanation. Human faults and foibles—as present in the Church as much as anywhere else—actually play a vital role in the One Story; our behavior can never diminish God's desire for communion, nor the divine commitment to fulfill its hopes. The One Story does not require flawless telling by perfect communities but rather honest telling by audacious communities. The world will care less about how Christians stammer in our telling and stumble in our living if we bear witness to a divine voice that enthralls and entices rather than cajoles and condemns. The world has already heard enough about the divine rule-maker and eagerly waits to hear about the Passionate Lover.

Imagine Christians bearing witness to the voice of Divine Love. Imagine the transformation in your own life if Christian faith spoke more directly to your deepest desires for communion. Imagine the voice of God speaking to you like this:

Arise, my love, my fair one,
    and come away;
for now the winter is past,
    the rain is over and gone.
The flowers appear on the earth;
    the time of singing has come,
and the voice of the turtle-dove
    is heard in our land.[26]

---

26. Song of Songs 2:10–12.

Imagine Christian congregations organizing all of their worship, business practices, and pastoral care around that passionate voice, doing everything possible to ensure that you and everyone else feels unmistakably wanted and desired—that you know yourself as *desirable*. Imagine returning week-by-week to a place where you can catch an invaluable glimpse of being at home in your own body without any trace of shame, at home among others without any shade of guilt, and at home with God who made you without any vestige of fear.

Imagine passing through the whole arc of your life and being fed continually at a table set with bread and wine—a table where all of your fumbling and fortuitous attempts at bodily intimacy with others are welcomed as graceful signs of your heart's desire. Imagine a lifetime of coming to that Table and hearing, time and time again, that your own yearnings for intimacy have crafted the menu for the banquet that has been "prepared from the foundation of the world." Imagine coming to the end of your mortal existence when you are laid lovingly in Earth by the community who cherished you. Imagine at that moment realizing with considerable astonishment that the arc of your life has only just begun, a moment when you hear once again the voice of the One who made you:

> Arise, my love, my fair one,
>   and come away. . . .
> Let me see your face,
>   let me hear your voice;
> for your voice is sweet,
>   and your face is lovely.[27]

Imagine that—in the face of your beloved animal companion, your dearest friend, your cherished lover, your family of faith. Imagine that and you will, by some amazing grace, perch on the brink of Divine Communion.

---

27. Song of Songs 2:13b, 14b.

Reading Biblical Sexuality for Mission and Ministry

For by water and the Holy Spirit
you have made us a new people in Jesus Christ our Lord,
to show forth your glory in all the world.

—PROPER PREFACE, "OF GOD THE HOLY SPIRIT"
THE BOOK OF COMMON PRAYER

God joins Christians together as members of Christ's body for the sake of love—to show us divine love, to enable us to love one another, and to invite us to love God in return. Christians manifest this life of love in communities of forgiveness and reconciliation, with liturgies of worship and praise, and as a people devoted to ministries of generosity and service. Episcopalians express this shared life of love in various ways viewed always through the lens of a shared meal. At the Eucharistic Table we declare that baptism commissions us to show forth God's glory in all the world.[1] God's glory of course shines in countless ways, refracted through particular communities and cultures, shimmering in all sorts of intimate relationships, among the wildly diverse ecosystems of this planet, and from the unfathomable reach of innumerable stars and galaxies. How then do Christians show forth that glory?

The second-century theologian Irenaeus proposed that the "glory of God is the human being fully alive." I have tried to suggest in this book how sexual intimacy contributes to that gloriously abundant life, which Christians likewise celebrate at the Eucharistic Table. Sexual intimacy and Eucharistic celebrations share at least one

---

1. BCP, 378.

profound feature in common, what I have called in these pages the One Story—the deep desire and abiding hope for divine communion. As Christians seek to live into that story more fully, we will always do so in kaleidoscopic fashion, with intersecting and overlapping intimacies, relationships, and commitments. We offer all of that as Eucharistic communities trusting and praying that we will, no matter how imperfectly, show forth the glory of God.

Both historically and today Christians have also believed that some forms of sexual intimacy are more appropriate than others, and further, that some sexual practices actually subvert God's purposes for spiritual thriving. Curiously in some respects, those beliefs have varied over the centuries and have not always aligned particularly well with biblical perspectives. Prior to the sixteenth-century Protestant Reformation, for example, the Church considered marriage inferior to the celibacy of vowed religious life. That position seems consonant with the views of Jesus and Paul in the Christian Testament, but not with most of the texts of the Hebrew Bible. Today's Western standards for sexual propriety likewise resist tidy mapping to biblical sensibilities. Biblical writers generally permit early adolescent marriage, polygamy, concubinage, and sex with slaves; they also forbid sex during menstruation, masturbation, exogamy (marrying outside of one's own tribe), and nudity (even in one's own home). Most Christians today would disagree with each of those biblical perspectives.

Walter Wink catalogued those mismatches in greater detail and concluded that the Bible presents something like a patchwork quilt of cultural mores and religious regulations that confound nearly every attempt to synthesize them into a single biblical sexual ethic. He did this to highlight the difficulties in arguing biblically about lesbian and gay relationships. Rather than seeking a systematic sexual ethic from the Bible, Wink proposed instead to read human sexuality through the biblical lens of Jesus' love ethic.[2] I would extrapolate from his approach and propose that Christians read all biblical texts through the lens of the One Story—God's own mission to draw all creatures to the Table of Divine Communion.

---

2. Walter Wink, "Homosexuality and the Bible," in *Homosexuality and Christian Faith: Questions of Conscience for the Churches*, ed. Walter Wink (Minneapolis, MN: Augsburg Fortress Press, 1999).

Biblical sexual ethics have played only a minor role in this book, not because they are unimportant but because they have too often distracted Christian communities from the kind of theological and spiritual reflection that sexual intimacy and Eucharistic celebrations invite. I turn more explicitly to those biblical questions here for those who find the theological invitations of this book compelling, yet still worry that biblical writers condemned the sexual intimacies of lesbian, gay, bisexual, and transgender (LGBT) people. The approach I want to invite involves reading the Bible both responsibly and faithfully for the sake of enriching Christian mission and ministry.

These quandaries over the Bible are not, of course, new. Biblical texts have played a significant role in both religious and civic life for hundreds of years, and often with precious little agreement over how to interpret them. In the nineteenth and twentieth centuries alone, the Bible frequently took center stage in public debates over the institution of slavery, the role of women, economic reform, civil rights, and eventually human sexuality. The tools of historical scholarship can help us read these texts responsibly, to clarify the differences in cultural contexts between ancient societies and our own, for example, and appreciate the challenges in translating biblical languages. Anyone can read biblical texts responsibly by following the best practices developed by biblical scholars on these and many other interpretive challenges. Reading the Bible faithfully, however, demands more. Faithful readings transpire in a community of interpreters seeking prayerfully the meaning God would have them make from those texts for their communities and for their witness to the Gospel.

Comprehensive scholarly treatments of the most troubling biblical texts regarding lesbian and gay relationships have been available for many years. Rather than only repeating those arguments, I want to invite Christian faith communities to think differently about that debate itself, and thus also about the Bible. This invitation unfolds first with some brief observations about reading the Bible responsibly and then, second, with some illustrations of reading the Bible faithfully. These two approaches to reading biblical texts need not stand in opposition; to the contrary, uniting them will help to ensure a thriving Christian witness to the One Story, and in so doing, show forth God's glory in the world.

READING THE BIBLE RESPONSIBLY

Most Christians realize that biblical texts come from ancient cultural contexts far removed from contemporary, North Atlantic societies. Modern science draws those distinctions vividly, but they appear in other ways as well, including the configurations of marriage and family life, cultural mores, and economic systems, to name a few. How then do we read these ancient texts responsibly, respecting the original cultural sensibilities that shaped them and resisting the temptation to insert our own cultural perspectives into those texts? Eighteenth- and nineteenth-century biblical scholars crafted tools for that kind of reading that we now group together in a toolbox called "historical-critical method." This method relies on *historical* investigation, to appreciate the original contexts in which those texts were written, and on *criticism*, or the careful analysis of the literary genre, rhetorical form, linguistic style, and source materials of each text. Reading responsibly, for example, would distinguish between the poetry of the Song of Songs and the chronologies of 1 and 2 Kings, or between the thick metaphors of apocalyptic prophets and the letters of Paul.

Historical-critical tools have shaped my approach to the biblical texts in this book, even when they are mostly invisible. Those tools have persuaded me to rely on three broad convictions. First, Biblical texts never speak for themselves; they always require interpretation. Indeed, texts do not speak at all, as Dale Martin reminds us. But people do speak, and people of faith often speak with biblical texts. How we speak with biblical texts derives in large measure from our various cultural contexts and social histories.[3] We can never fully rid ourselves of those cultural filters in our reading, but we can endeavor to make them more visible in our interpretations. This is especially important in today's multicultural global village where unexamined cultural assumptions in one context can lead to troubling interpretations in another. Or more severely, as Musa Dube recounts, where Western culture is viewed as the only suitable lens through which to read biblical texts.[4]

---

3. See Martin, "The Myth of Textual Agency," in *Sex and the Single Savior*, 1–16.

4. Musa W. Dube, *Postcolonial Feminist Interpretation of the Bible* (St. Louis, MO: Chalice Press, 2000), 13.

Second, translating ancient languages and cultural idioms into contemporary linguistic usage is itself an act of interpretation. Many words and concepts in both ancient Hebrew and Greek have no direct equivalents in modern languages, and translators often disagree about how to render difficult words and phrases.[5] Ancient Hebrew, for example, has no direct equivalent for the modern English word "wife." Translators must then assume a marital relationship in the biblical text when the generic word for woman appears in conjunction with a man. The challenge of translation readily appears whenever American advertising agencies attempt—and sometimes fail—to translate a corporate slogan or brand name into international settings. (The Gerber baby food company discovered this, to their dismay, when they realized that the French verb *gerber* means "to vomit.")

And third, excerpting small sections or even a single verse from a particular biblical book can damage the integrity of that book as a whole. Everyone does this from time to time, just as I have in this book. We do this with many other texts as well. A lawyer, for example, will sometimes build a legal argument based on just one article of the United States Constitution or even an isolated phrase. The argument may appear sound but always deserves further scrutiny with respect to the Constitution as a whole. Making biblical arguments likewise remains subject to shared inquiry to help ensure that interpreters take responsibility for how and why they quote a particular passage. The purpose in citing a particular passage, furthermore, will likely and frequently does vary depending on the context of a particular community of interpretation.[6] Rather than just a single meaning for a given text, this approach to shared interpretation yields a rich tapestry of meanings over time, as the long history of Christian readings of the Bible so often illustrates.[7]

---

5. Among the many sources for the challenges in translating ancient languages as well as interpreting across cultural contexts, see the collection of essays edited by Joel B. Green, *Hearing the New Testament: Strategies for Interpretation*, second ed. (Grand Rapids, MI: The William B. Eerdmans Publishing Company, 2010).

6. See Martin, "Community-Shaped Scripture," in *Sex and the Single Savior*, 149–60.

7. John L. Thornton offers compelling examples of the insights we can glean from how Christians read the Bible in the past in *Reading the Bible with the Dead: What You Can Learn from the History of Exegesis that You Can't Learn from Exegesis Alone* (Grand Rapids, MI: The William B. Eerdmans Publishing Company, 2007).

These convictions take on further texture and even urgency whenever faith communities cite biblical passages concerning human sexuality and gender. Additional frames of reference can help Christians read those particular biblical texts responsibly. We should note, for example, that the word "homosexual" was invented in the nineteenth century and appears nowhere in the original Hebrew or Greek versions of the Bible. German sexologists coined that term to describe their view of a particular "sexual orientation" or identity that they believed was evident among some human beings. This concept would have been completely foreign to biblical writers, and even many "homosexuals" today reject that term because of its historical associations with pathologizing same-sex attraction.

Equally if not more important, appropriate sexual relations in ancient Mediterranean societies had very little to do with gender and much more to do with the social status and power of one's sexual partner. Socially acceptable sexual relations were mostly understood as involving a socially dominant partner with a socially submissive partner. Men were by definition socially dominant while others were considered socially submissive: women, slaves (of either gender), lower economic classes (of either gender), and youth (of either gender). The modern notion of "peer marriage" or a union of equals would have been entirely unknown in ancient Mediterranean cultures.[8] In addition, contemporary scientific and biological understandings of sexuality, procreation, and gender were mostly unknown in the ancient world. Both sociologists and biologists today present a much broader view of what constitutes gender in relation to sex, which has as much or even more to do with brain chemistry than external genitalia.[9]

All of these convictions and tools shed considerable light on the passages most often cited to exclude gay and lesbian relationships from Christian communities. Biblical writers actually devoted very little

---

8. Stephen D. Moore describes this ancient worldview a bit more severely by noting that absolute inequality was intrinsic to both good worship and good sex. In that context, sex is basically "eroticized inequality" (*God's Beauty Parlor and Other Queer Spaces in and Around the Bible* [Stanford: Stanford University Press, 2001]), 153.

9. See Christine Gudorf, "A New Moral Discourse on Sexuality," in *Human Sexuality and the Catholic Tradition*, ed. Kieran Scott and Harold Daly Horell (New York: Roman and Littlefield Publishers, 2007), 51–69; and Joan Roughgarden, *Evolution's Rainbow: Diversity, Gender, and Sexuality in Nature and People* (Berkeley, CA: University of California Press, 2004), 5–6.

energy and attention to same-sex desire and relationships. Only five passages in the Bible are most often quoted and appear to have any direct relation to this topic: Genesis 19:1–13; Leviticus 18:22, 20:13; Romans 1:26–27; 1 Corinthians 6:9–10; and 1 Timothy 1:8–11. Two other passages are sometimes mentioned as well: the first two chapters of Genesis and Jude 6–7. Not only these particular texts, but also the whole Bible deserves both responsible and faithful reading. Christians do this, I would propose, not to articulate a timeless interpretation of a biblical passage but to nurture Christian witness to the good news of the Gospel in each new generation and cultural context. It was for that reason, after all, that the Church sought faithfully to discern which texts ought to be included in the canon of Scripture.

READING THE BIBLE FAITHFULLY

Anyone can undertake a responsible reading of biblical texts by using the tools of historical-critical method. The results of those readings can be assessed and adjudicated with some rigor by the standards set by established biblical scholars. Reading the Bible faithfully demands more from us, and the results are more difficult to assess. Faithful readings aim to further the spiritual vitality and thriving of religious communities, which quantitative measurements rarely capture. Faithful readings require the twin commitment to prayerful discernment and communal interpretation of this collection of texts held sacred by those who read them. Christian communities treat the Bible as sacred for many reasons, not least because they trust those texts will yield spiritual insights for situations and questions that the biblical writers themselves may not nor could have anticipated. Mining insights for contemporary contexts from ancient texts thus relies on prayer, trusting that the Spirit will guide us further into truth, as John's Jesus promised (John 14:26). Those texts are considered sacred for another reason as well. The Church chose some texts and not others for the biblical canon, in part to assist the Church in its God-given mission. Discerning and articulating that mission with others remains crucial for reading the Bible faithfully today.

Every biblical text deserves both responsible and faithful reading, yet today the ecclesial controversies over sexuality and gender continually draw the Church's attention to a small set of biblical texts that perpetuate deep divisions, hostilities, and even violence in the lives of gay, lesbian, bisexual, and increasingly transgender people. A great deal of biblical scholarship has offered ways to read those texts responsibly, but few have suggested ways to read those same texts faithfully. Here I want to offer a way to unite responsible and faithful readings as part of our baptismal commission to show forth God's glory. Episcopalians can do this by reading the Bible through the lens of the Baptismal Covenant in the 1979 Book of Common Prayer. The rationale for this approach reflects the method for theological reflection lived in Anglican communities for centuries. Anglicans have always relied first and foremost on the Bible for theological insights, but never in isolation from historical traditions understood in the light of human reason and experience.[10] In what follows I will illustrate this method with just a few of the texts that have been frequently cited to exclude lesbian and gay people from the promise of divine communion, and especially in relation to three of the promises made in the Baptismal Covenant.[11]

"Continue in the Apostles' Teaching and Fellowship"
(LEVITICUS 18:22 AND ROMANS 1:26–27)

Religious communities by definition set themselves apart from other communities around them in what they believe and how they live. A host of reasons inform those distinctive practices, not least the desire to participate in God's own mission in the world. We might recall that the original meaning of the word "religion" combines the Latin *relegere*—to "re-read"—as well as *religare*, to "bind fast," just as ligaments bind bones together. The former suggests a process of passing on a tradition while the latter evokes the vital necessity for keeping a skeleton from falling apart into an amorphous heap. Ancient Israel and early Christian communities exhibited this religious commitment to distinctive beliefs and styles of living in different ways, yet they

---

10. See Urban T. Holmes, III, *What Is Anglicanism?* (Wilton, CT: Morehouse-Barlow, 1982), esp. ch. 2, "The Bible," 17–24. See also my own attempt to describe this Anglican approach to theology in *Dancing with God: Anglican Christianity and the Practice of Hope* (Harrisburg, PA: Morehouse Publishing, 2005), esp. ch. 1, "Waltzing the Two-Step: A Hopeful Theological Method," 21–40.

11. BCP, 304–5.

shared several features of that commitment in common. Both Mosaic law and apostolic teaching, for example, relied on a strict aversion to idolatry. Significantly, particular sexual practices often accompanied religious traditions of the ancient Mediterranean world that biblical writers understood as idolatrous.

Consider the broad socio-religious context of ancient Israel when reading Leviticus 18:22 and its analogue, 20:13. Those verses would appear to prohibit male "homosexuality," yet they also belong to an extensive array of dietary restrictions, commandments, and ritual practices often referred to as the "Levitical holiness code." Two features of ancient Israelite society can provide important assistance in interpreting these difficult passages: the process of constructing a religious identity for Israel distinct from its surrounding cultures, and the strict gender hierarchy of the ancient Mediterranean world.[12]

Leviticus 18:22 condemns sex between men; more particularly, it prohibits treating a man like a woman. The Hebrew word used for this condemnation, translated as "abomination," appears most often with reference to the cultic practices associated with the worship of foreign gods. Similar condemnations of child sacrifice and bestiality in this same chapter strengthen the connection to idolatrous rituals.[13] An "abomination," then, could refer to any practice taken from Israel's surrounding cultures and which diluted or distorted Israel's unique religious and cultural identity.[14]

Equally important, the patriarchal ordering of that ancient society relied on male privilege. Sexual practices reflected this gendered ordering as men assumed an active role and women a passive one, which perpetuated the dominance of men in all other spheres of

---

12. Insights from Jewish commentators and scholars on these and other important aspects of biblical interpretation deserve renewed attention in Christian communities. See for example: Steven Greenberg, *Wrestling with God and Men: Homosexuality in Jewish Tradition* (Madison, WI: University of Wisconsin Press, 2005); and Daniel Boyarin, *Carnal Israel: Reading Sex in Talmudic Culture* (Berkeley, CA: University of California Press, 1995).

13. See Martti Nissinen, *Homoeroticism in the Biblical World: A Historical Perspective* (Minneapolis, MN: Fortress Press, 1998), 37–56.

14. Some scholars contest these connections between the Holiness Code and "pagan" cultic practices. Saul Olyan, for example, finds those connections weak, and stresses instead notions of "boundary violations" and concerns over the land's "purity" in male sexual acts that "feminize" a male sexual partner ("'And with a Male You Shall Not Lie the Lying Down of a Woman': On the Meaning and Significance of Leviticus 18:22 and 20:13," *Journal of the History of Sexuality*, 5 [1994], 179–206).

cultural and religious life and reinforced the treatment of women as property.[15] More bluntly, sex in the ancient world was always understood with reference to penetration: one partner penetrates (the socially dominant one) and the other is penetrated (the socially inferior one). This hierarchy defined sex as a relation of social power; sex between socially equal males would undermine that power dynamic and disrupt patriarchal dominance.[16]

If these brief observations qualify as a responsible reading of Leviticus, how can they inform faithful readings in today's Christian communities? Scripture continues to bear witness to the primacy of covenantal relationship with the one true God of Israel, whom Christians proclaim in the life, death, and resurrection of Jesus Christ. In that light, rather than shaping our lives and households based on ancient cultural patterns, each new generation faces the challenge to discern how our covenantal relationship with God shapes all of our relationships. The Apostle Paul seemed particularly concerned about that very challenge.

Paul held a number of opinions about human sexuality that may seem a bit peculiar to the modern reader. He recommended to the Christians in Corinth, for example, that the work of Christian ministry is best done by remaining unmarried (1 Corinthians 7:25–32). But for gay and lesbian people, the first chapter of his letter to the Romans (especially 1:26–27) has played a particularly troubling role. Several important issues arise when interpreting this Pauline passage, including the difficulties in knowing what Paul meant by "unnatural" in those verses, to whom he was addressing these concerns, and the rhetorical purpose of his letter overall.[17] It is particularly important to place Paul's description of sexual behavior in that first chapter in direct relation to his condemnation of idolatry. For Paul, the consequence (not the cause) of worshiping false gods is a distorted understanding of sexuality, its purpose and goal (1:22–23).

---

15. These social hierarchies appeared not only in the treatment of women but also of children, as well as the practice of concubinage and slave-holding in ancient Mediterranean households. See Carol L. Meyers, "Everyday Life: Women in the Period of the Hebrew Bible," in *The Women's Bible Commentary*, ed. Carol A. Newsom and Sharon H. Ringe, expanded ed. (Louisville, KY: Westminster/John Knox, 1998), 250–59.

16. Jack Rogers, *Jesus, the Bible, and Homosexuality: Explode the Myths, Heal the Church*, revised ed. (Louisville, KY: Westminster John Knox Press, 2009), 68–69.

17. See Countryman, *Dirt, Greed, and Sex*, 119–23. See also Martin, "Heterosexism and the Interpretation of Romans 1:18–32," in *Sex and the Single Savior*, 51–64.

The Greco-Roman world of the first century exhibited many different kinds of sexual relationships and practices (just as the world does today). We cannot know for sure which kinds of sexual behavior Paul had in mind in this passage, though he is clearly troubled by them. Since Paul was writing to Christians in Rome, some have suggested that he was concerned with the religious cults devoted to fertility gods and goddesses. These cultic rituals may have included self-castration, drunken orgies, and having sex with young temple prostitutes (both male and female).[18] Christians quite properly condemn all those behaviors as violations of the human body, which Paul identified as the very temple of the Holy Spirit (1 Corinthians 3:16–17). Those alleged cultic practices, however, have nothing to do with Christians today who also identify as lesbian, gay, bisexual, or transgender—modern identifications about which Paul would have had little if any experience or knowledge.[19]

Some commentators have also noted the rather unusual phrase Paul uses to describe those sexual practices in Romans (*para phusin* in Greek, which could mean "against nature" or "contrary to nature").[20] That same phrase appears again in this same letter, but there he uses it to refer to *God*. In chapter 11, Paul describes Gentiles as belonging to a "wild olive tree." God lops them off that tree and, "contrary to nature," grafts them on to the one true tree of Israel (11:24). This startling claim can at least give us pause today in trying to decipher what "natural" really means, both for us and for God.[21]

---

18. For the controversy over ancient fertility cults and the alleged sexual practices associated with them, see Robert A. Oden, Jr., *The Bible without Theology: The Theological Tradition and Alternatives to It* (San Francisco: Harper and Row, 1987), ch. 5, "Religious Identity and the Sacred Prostitution Accusation," 131–53. For more on the Greco-Roman cultural background of the New Testament and the sensibilities of first-century Palestinian Judaism, see Robin Scroggs, *The New Testament and Homosexuality: Contextual Background for a Contemporary Debate* (Philadelphia: Fortress Press, 1983).

19. See Nissinen, *Homoeroticism in the Biblical World*, 103–13.

20. See William Stacy Johnson, *A Time to Embrace: Same-Gender Relationships in Religion, Law, and Politics* (Grand Rapids, MI: The William B. Eerdmans Publishing Company, 2006), 98–99.

21. See Eugene F. Rogers on this odd phrase and its implications for salvation: "Sanctification, Homosexuality, and God's Triune Life," in *Theology and Sexuality: Classic and Contemporary Readings*, ed. Eugene F. Rogers (Oxford: Blackwell Publishing, 2002), 225–30. See also Tobias Haller's approach to this and many of the other biblical passages considered here in *Reasonable and Holy: Engaging Same-Sexuality* (New York: Seabury Books, 2009), esp. 167–74.

These potentially responsible readings of Paul provoke further questions about how to read him faithfully, especially in concert with Leviticus. Paul's broader insight about idolatry provides that link, and can compel the Church to continual discernment and assessment of our common life. In a world where sexual intimacy seems subject only to regulatory control, Paul would urge us to see our sexual lives as deeply intertwined with our worship of God. How we "do" sex and how we "do" worship are flip sides of the very same spiritual coin, a Pauline argument that has contributed to my own approach in this book for developing a Eucharistic theology of sexual intimacy.

The primacy of our covenantal relationship with God in Christ can shed even further light on Paul's recommendation to remain unmarried. Single people can play an important role in bearing witness to the good news of the Gospel in a number of ways, including by reminding all of us that human sexual relationships of any kind are not the final purpose or goal of human life. Only union with God in Christ fulfills human life and the whole of creation, as the rest of Paul's letter to the Romans makes clear (8:18–25). At their best, human relationships can only point us toward our final fulfillment. People who make an intentional decision to remain unmarried offer important signposts on that spiritual journey to which all of us are called and in which nothing, including marriage, should supplant our devotion to God and to God's household, the Church. That conviction properly belongs to the "apostles' teaching and fellowship" that Christians adopt in our witness to the One Story and which we renew at the Eucharistic Table of communion.

"Seek and Serve Christ in All Persons"
(GENESIS 19)

Religious communities do set themselves apart from the wider society even as many of them likewise aspire to adopt an expansive if not universal posture of compassion toward all. The insistence on extending hospitality toward strangers is the most frequent expression of that aspiration. Many biblical texts in both the Hebrew Bible and the Christian Testament point to hospitality as the primary expression of covenantal faithfulness, which should be understood well beyond its relegation in Western society to proper manners.[22] The ancient story of Sodom and Gomorrah's destruction in Genesis 19 illustrates that spiritual priority rather dramatically, but has more often been interpreted and appropriated to condemn "homosexuality." Popular interpretations of this passage rely less on the biblical story itself than on the cultural reception of this story over many centuries of European history. The term "sodomy," for example, does not appear in the Bible, and what it has come to mean (including within North Atlantic jurisprudence) has little to do with the biblical text itself.[23]

The story turns on whether certain visitors to Sodom will be received graciously and hospitably by the city's inhabitants or exploited and even raped. The sin of Sodom's citizens thus refers explicitly to the codes of hospitality in the ancient near east rather than to same-gender sexual relations.[24] Other biblical writers who referred to Sodom never highlighted sexuality or even mentioned it at all. Ezekiel, for example, made the sin of "sodomy" uncomfortably clear: "This was the guilt of your sister Sodom: she and her daughters had pride, excess of food, and prosperous ease, but did not aid the poor and needy" (16:49). Ezekiel's description represents the approach most often taken by writers in the Hebrew Bible, who usually associate the sin of Sodom with violence or injustice.[25] In the Christian Testament, Jude 7 refers to this story in Genesis as well, yet that verse does not describe "sexual immorality" with any precision (it could refer to rape, for example), and the "unnatural lust" of Sodom's inhabitants could also refer to the fact that the strangers sent to Sodom were actually angels (see Genesis 6:4).

---

22. See Exodus 22:21, Leviticus 19:34, Deuteronomy 24:19–21, Malachi 3:5, and Hebrews 13:2, among many others. For an overview and analysis of the centrality of hospitality in the Bible and in early Christianity, see Amos Yong, *Hospitality and the Other: Pentecost, Christian Practices, and the Neighbor* (Maryknoll, NY: Orbis Books, 2008).

23. See: Jay Emerson Johnson, "Sodomy and Gendered Love: Reading Genesis 19 in the Anglican Communion," in *The Oxford Handbook of the Reception History of the Bible*, ed. Michael Lieb, Emma Mason, and Jonathan Roberts (Oxford: Oxford University Press, 2010), 415–34; and Michael Carden, *Sodomy: A History of a Christian Biblical Myth* (London: Equinox Publishing, 2009).

24. The definition of "sodomy" varied rather widely throughout Christian history and coalesced exclusively around particular sexual acts only in the eleventh century; see Mark D. Jordan, *The Invention of Sodomy in Christian Theology* (Chicago: The University of Chicago Press, 1997).

25. See Daniel Helminiak, *What the Bible Really Says about Homosexuality*, rev. ed. (Tajique, NM: Alamo Square Press, 2000), 47–49.

Jesus likewise evoked the story of Sodom, not for the purpose of sexual ethics but in the context of sending out his disciples to do the work of ministry. Those who did not receive his disciples, he said, would suffer a fate worse than the citizens of Sodom (Matthew 10:15). Luke's Jesus makes the same point. Those who do not receive God's emissaries risk destruction (10:8–12). Gospel writers expanded on these themes in various ways, including Matthew's exhortation to see Christ in others, especially the hungry, the thirsty, the naked, the strangers, those who are sick, and those in prison (25:31–46).

As early as the 1950s, biblical scholars attempted to place Genesis 19 in this original cultural context and to revive an interpretive approach to that story that resonated better with how other biblical writers read that story.[26] Biblical writers themselves, in other words, would have us apply Genesis 19 to *all* people rather than only to some, and the lesson for all of us is the primacy of hospitality, or the love of neighbor, as Jesus himself commanded. This reading of Sodom's destruction qualifies as both responsible and faithful whenever it inspires us to seek Christ in everyone we meet and to extend Eucharistic hospitality to everyone—without exception.

"Respect the Dignity of Every Human Person"
(GENESIS 1–2)

The distinctiveness of a religious community can sometimes subvert its most admirable aspirations. Adopting a particular religious identity and way of life can inadvertently, and on occasion purposefully, render those outside the community as inferior. Christians fall prey to this temptation whenever we suppose that baptism creates a tiered structure of divine favor, or more severely, that baptism neatly divides humanity between the saved and the damned. Christians can resist that temptation by returning to the creation accounts in Genesis and reading them through the lens of the new creation inaugurated by God in Christ.

---

26. One of the earliest examples of this approach was Derrick Sherwin Bailey, *Homosexuality and the Western Christian Tradition* (London: Longmans, Green, 1955).

Biblical scholars have noted for some time that the first two chapters of Genesis present more than one account of creation. Each likely came from a distinct source, which a later editor then stitched together in the final text. Appreciating the differences between these two versions helps to ensure a responsible reading, but also a deeply faithful one. The wondrous creativity of the God we worship, for example, cannot be captured in a single account or from just one perspective. Uniting responsible and faithful readings of Genesis also invites renewed scrutiny of two interrelated convictions that appear frequently in today's debates over sexuality: first, "gender complementarity" describes God's creation of human beings as male and female; and second, only the procreation of children within monogamous marriage can express that complementarity adequately. The extensive biblical scholarship available on these passages—in both Jewish and Christians traditions—nuances those two convictions in some important ways.

The first of the two accounts of humanity's creation (Genesis 1:26–27) assigns distinct gender differentiation to humanity as a whole not to individuals, just as both male and female alike apply to God, in whose image humanity is made.[27] Similarly, the command to "be fruitful and multiply" (1:28) applies to the human species rather than individuals. This matters for those who remain single or for whatever other reasons choose not to have children, not least Jesus and Paul; this verse would otherwise equate childlessness with sinfulness.[28] Moreover, the generative aspects of loving and faithful commitment can be seen in many different ways and not only in bearing and raising children. As Paul Marshall notes, "Certainly those of us heterosexuals now beyond our child-bearing years would hope not to be as good as dead as far as our contribution to the community is concerned. . . ."[29]

The second account in Genesis provides specific reference to the creation of distinct individuals (2:7–22), and, for the first time,

---

27. See Steven Greenberg's analysis of how these first two chapters of Genesis have been interpreted in various ways in *Wrestling with God and Men: Homosexuality in the Jewish Tradition* (Madison, WI: University of Wisconsin Press, 2004), and on the question of gender in both creation accounts, esp. ch. 1, "The Birth of Gender and Desire," 41–59.

28. Johnson, *A Time to Embrace*, 115–16.

29. Paul Marshall, *Same-Sex Unions: Stories and Rites* (New York: Church Publishing, 2004), 38–39.

something that is *not* good in God's creation. "It is not good," God declares, "for the human being to be alone" (2:18).[30] Here the story turns on the importance of companionship and not, as in the first account, on the procreation of children. Significantly, the companion God provides for the solitary human is not defined by "otherness" but by suitable similarity. In this passage, "there is no emphasis . . . on 'difference' or 'complementarity' at all—in fact, just the opposite. When Adam sees Eve, he does not celebrate her otherness but her sameness: what strikes him is that she is 'bone of my bones, flesh of my flesh.'" Reducing this story to the fitness of particular anatomical parts, as some have done, misses the poignancy of this story: "God sees the plight of this first human being and steps in and does whatever it takes to provide him with a life-giving, life-sustaining companion."[31] Moreover, neither of these two chapters in Genesis refers explicitly to marriage. The purpose of these creation accounts, rather, is to affirm God as the creator of all things and "the priority of human companionship."[32]

Reading Genesis 1 and 2 responsibly and faithfully can assist Christian witness to the goodness of God's creation and perhaps especially to the glory of God that resides in every human being. Respecting that God-given dignity in all persons made in the divine image remains vital, not least for the sake of embracing the full humanity of women. The unqualified dignity with which the biblical writer treated both men and women in these accounts of their creation stands out as quite remarkable in the patriarchal culture that produced them. Ancient Mediterranean societies generally considered women to be human, but decidedly deficient versions and thus properly subservient to men.[33] Dale Martin relates this ancient view of the inferiority of women—as "deficient men"—to the difficulties in translating, let alone interpreting, two Greek words in the New Testament that have also been cited regarding "homosexuality." Some English versions translate those words—which appear in

---

30. For the significance of this translation of the verse, see Johnson, *A Time to Embrace*, 114–15, 117.

31. Johnson, *A Time to Embrace*, 120.

32. Johnson, *A Time to Embrace*, 112.

33. Johnson, *A Time to Embrace*, 275, n. 16.

1 Corinthians 6:9 and 1 Timothy 1:10—as "sodomite" or "homosexual." The meaning of the Greek in both cases, however, remains obscure and elusive. Martin believes it likely that these words referred to cultural practices involving sexual exploitation (perhaps including rape) and also effeminate behavior, which for men in that society triggered both alarm and disgust.[34]

Writers of the Christian Testament would urge yet a further step in reading Genesis faithfully. Both John and Paul invite us to read creation not by looking backward, to origins, but by looking forward, toward consummation. John begins his gospel account with the incarnation of the divine Word through whom all things were made and concludes that account in a garden, with Eden transformed by resurrection. Paul makes the same point more explicitly. All those who are in Christ, he declares, are a new creation (2 Corinthians 5:17).

Living into that promise and anticipating its fulfillment, Paul encouraged the Christians in Galatia to understand their baptism into Christ's death and resurrection as erasing the social and cultural hierarchies with which they were most familiar: "There is no longer Jew or Greek, there is no longer slave or free, there is no longer male and female; for all of you are one in Christ Jesus" (Galatians 3:28).[35] Paul's bold conviction can renew and inspire Christian witness to the One Story. Just as nothing in heaven or on earth can separate us from the love of God in Christ (Romans 8:38–39), so nothing can prevent the fulfillment of God's own desire for communion, the abiding hope that draws us to the Eucharistic Table.

Christians will of course continue to wrestle with difficult biblical passages on all sorts of topics. The struggle itself indicates a lively religious tradition in which we seek prayerfully to discern how God would have us live. Paul described a central feature of that discernment in the thirteenth chapter of his first letter to the Corinthians, sometimes called the "love chapter." Intimate couples frequently choose this biblical passage for their weddings, yet Paul wrote it to describe the character of Christian community more broadly.

---

34. Dale B. Martin, *"Arsenokoites and Malakos: Meanings and Consequences,"* in *Biblical Ethics and Homosexuality: Listening to Scripture*, ed. Robert L. Brawley (Louisville, KY: Westminster John Knox Press, 1996).

35. See Martin, "The Queer History of Galatians 3:28," in *Sex and the Single Savior*, 77–90.

The Christians in Corinth apparently struggled with the diversity of their community, which had at times divided into a number of factions. Paul reminded them that the one body of Christ consists in many members who exhibit a variety of spiritual gifts—such as teaching, healing, prophesying, and interpreting. Even those who seem to be the weakest members of the community, Paul writes, are actually indispensable (1 Corinthians 12:22). He encouraged the Corinthians to strive for these diverse gifts from the Spirit, yet he also urged them to follow what he called "a still more excellent way" (12:31). That way is love. Apart from love, all the other spiritual gifts accomplish very little indeed. Paul offered his elegy to love and its defining features—patience, kindness, never boastful, arrogant, or resentful—for a conflicted community. Love mattered there and then, just as it does now given the finite limits of human understanding. "For we know only in part," Paul argued (13:9), and "we see in a mirror, dimly" (13:12). Until that day when we will know fully even as we are fully known, we live by faith, hope, and love. The greatest of these three, Paul writes, is love (13:13).

The Johannine writer urged the same primacy of love in the midst of our unknowing. We do know that love has made us children of God; what we will become, however, has yet to be revealed (1 John 3:2). In our desire to know more fully—to know God, to know ourselves, and to know each other—we will inevitably make mistakes, both small and large. Even some of our most deeply held convictions may prove in the end to have been wrong. Even so, the abiding hope of communion does not depend on perfect knowledge, but instead on the perfection of love (1 John 4:12).

If, as John insisted, love enables us to approach the day of judgment itself with boldness (1 John 4:17), then we need not fear approaching the Eucharistic Table with our faults and foibles, including the many disagreements we still harbor over biblical interpretation. Indeed, gathering at that Table even when, and especially when we disagree with each other can bear further witness to the profound grace of the One Story—and in so doing we show forth God's glory in the world.